Culture in School Learning

Culture in School Learning

Revealing the Deep Meaning

Second Edition

Etta R. Hollins

Routledge
Taylor & Francis Group

NEW YORK AND LONDON

First published 1996
by Lawrence Earlbaum Associates, Inc., Publishers

Second edition 2008
by Routledge
270 Madison Ave, New York, NY 10016

Simultaneously published in the UK
by Routledge
2 Park Square, Milton Park, Abingdon, Oxon OX14 4RN

Routledge is an imprint of the Taylor & Francis Group, an informa business

© 1996, 2008 Etta R. Hollins

Typeset in Minion by
RefineCatch Limited, Bungay, Suffolk
Printed by Sheridan Books, Inc.

Library of Congress Cataloging-in-Publication Data
Hollins, Etta R., 1942–
    Culture in school learning : revealing the deep meaning / Etta R. Hollins.—2nd ed.
      p. cm.
    Includes bibliographical references and indexes.
    ISBN–13: 978–0–8058–4108–4 (pbk. : alk. paper)
    ISBN–10: 0–8058–4108–3 (pbk. : alk. paper)
    ISBN–13: 978–0–203–92943–8 (e-book)
    ISBN–10: 0–203–92943–8 (e-book)
    1. Educational anthropology—United States.   2. Multicultural education—United States.
I. Title.
    LB45.H59 2008
    302.43—dc22   2007038243

British Library Cataloguing in Publication Data
A catalogue record for this book is available from the British Library

ISBN10: 0–8058–4108–3 (pbk)
ISBN10: 0–203–92943–8 (ebk)

ISBN13: 978–08058–4108–4 (pbk)
ISBN13: 978–0–203–92943–8 (ebk)

In loving memory of

Mandie Cosoden Ford, Celie Winston Bridgewater,
Fannie Norvell Stevenson, Armenta Beatrice Stevenson,
Beatrice Florene Stevenson, Ivy Stevenson Sweatt,
Ethel Henley Reed, Myrtice Dixon, Charles Milton Robinson,
and Ivery Wilbon.

Contents

Foreword

HERBERT KOHL

The central thesis of this book, that an understanding of the cultural dimensions of learning is essential for effective teaching, must become a key component of educational programs throughout the country. Etta Hollins not only convincingly argues the case for this, but shows us how to build programs in teacher education institutions and schools that respect and utilize the cultural strengths of learners. The book takes the reader on a step-by-step voyage through the dimensions of culture that pervade how we teach, what we teach, and how students learn. It enables prospective and practicing teachers to examine their own cultural roots and those of their students. It opens doors for teachers to understand how to remake the curriculum and shape their learning environments to facilitate the respectful communication across cultures that can lead to complex learning.

One of the most important aspects of this book is that it rejects, once and for all, any hint of blaming the student for the failures of the system. It proceeds on the assumptions that students can learn complex skills in diverse cultural and intellectual settings, and that reflective teachers can learn how to adapt their work to the character of the classes they teach without any loss of standards or lowering of expectations.

I believe that the ideas, techniques, and strategies described in this book can go far toward providing teachers with the strengths they need to teach in complex cultural settings where they have to know both their own cultural habits and modes and that of their students. Although the demands Etta Hollins suggests we have to make on ourselves require considerable self-examination and honesty, I believe that we owe no less to our students. The bonus is that through such a cultural reconstruction of the schools we can rediscover the meaning of pluralistic democracy and perhaps see a way to a more just future for all of our students and for ourselves as well.

Preface

This book presents a process for developing a perspective of teaching that embraces the centrality of culture in school learning. In this process, classroom teachers strive to construct an operational definition of culture that reveals its deep meaning in cognition and learning. The six-part process presented in this book includes objectifying culture, personalizing culture, inquiring about students' cultures and communities, applying knowledge about culture to teaching, formulating theory linking culture and school learning, and transforming professional practice to better meet the needs of students from different cultural and experiential backgrounds. All aspects of the process are interrelated and interdependent.

Objectifying Culture

It is important for classroom teachers to construct an operational definition of culture that makes explicit its centrality and systemic nature in the realities of human existence. This includes interpretative and explanatory functions that form culturally framed perceptions of the world. The definition of culture should include its function in human survival, societal arrangements, and in human development that is intellectual, psychological, social, and spiritual. The definition of culture should reveal the interconnectedness of its identifiable aspects and describe its dynamic quality in responding to fundamental changes in life conditions and circumstances. The approach to objectifying culture found in Chapter 2 facilitates constructing a working definition of culture.

The process of constructing a working definition of culture is not intended as a simple task or to be completed easily. It is a dynamic process. Early definitions of culture may be transformed as you examine culture across different regions of the United States, your own culture, and that of your students. New insights may be acquired in the process of rethinking classroom instruction and reframing curriculum for students from different cultural and experiential backgrounds.

Personalizing Culture

Personalizing culture, as presented in Chapter 3, refers to a process of deep introspection that reveals the centrality of culture in your own life. This includes acquiring an understanding of the lifelong influence of early socialization, making explicit your own personal and group identity, identifying personally held perceptions of the world that are culturally framed, and describing participation in culturally sanctioned practices and values.

Culture is such an integral part of human existence that it becomes an invisible script that directs our personal lives. This invisible script can encapsulate and blind us to the factors that make us simultaneously unique from and similar to those from other cultures. Encapsulation can lead us to view the world as an extension of self. We may view those who are culturally different as aberrant, quaint, or exotic. Teachers who hold such views are likely to base classroom practices on their own culture and encourage students to conform to their perceptions and values. These teachers may be more successful with students with whom they share a common cultural and experiential background than with those whose culture and experiences are different.

Personalizing culture is an important part of teacher education because it holds potential for decreasing cultural encapsulation by bringing subconscious aspects of culture to the conscious level for examination. You can become aware of factors that distinguish your culture from that of your students while maintaining a positive regard for both. This awareness can contribute to improving cross-cultural communication and facilitate teaching and learning.

Examples of heuristics that can be employed to help you personalize culture are (a) the use of the history and origin of a particular family surname and a study of the way of life of those to whom it is ascribed (Hollins, 1990) and (b) the use of Helms' (1990/1995) stages of racial identity to examine the impact of "race" on personal perceptions and social relationships. The careful examination of a particular line in your own family heritage reveals the continuities and discontinuities of cultural transmission while illuminating the centrality of culture in shaping your own life. Studying Helms' statuses of racial identity encourages deep analysis and introspection into the influence, transmission, and maintenance of specific perceptions and values. Both of these heuristics support personalizing culture and constructing an increasingly complex operational definition.

Learning about Students' Cultures

An approach to learning about students' cultures and experiential backgrounds in a way that informs classroom practices involves reflective-interpretive inquiry (RIQ) as covered in Chapter 4. RIQ relies on ethnographic techniques for data gathering and analysis. This is a process of systematic inquiry and analysis that will help you compile and examine information that supports understanding the relationship among culture, cognition, and school learning.

Applying Knowledge about Culture to Teaching

In Chapters 5 and 6, you apply your emerging definition of culture and data gathered using the RIQ approach in reframing curriculum content and designing learning experiences for students.

Reframing the Curriculum – Among the purposes served by the school curriculum are the transmission of culturally valued knowledge and the perpetuation of cultural values and practices. In the United States this means that most public schools continue to present a curriculum that serves the purpose of maintaining and perpetuating Euro-American culture. At this point you recognize that such a curriculum is inherently more meaningful to Euro-American students than to those who identify themselves with other ethnic and cultural groups. This creates dissonance in school learning for some groups of students. Some students will be able to tolerate this dissonance and do well; others will fail. You need to learn to reframe the curriculum to minimize dissonance that interferes with learning.

Making the curriculum simultaneously particularistic and inclusive can decrease dissonance. That is, the curriculum can be designed to address the needs of particular cultures while addressing the common needs of all groups within the society. You can use the insights you have acquired in the study of specific cultural groups to identify ways to reframe the curriculum to meet the particularistic needs of your students.

The inclusive aspect of the school curriculum promotes the understandings and knowledge that support national unity, improving the quality of life for all human beings, and for maintaining and improving the condition of the natural environment. You will be able to identify parts of the existing curriculum that are inclusive and those that need to be adjusted.

Redesigning Instruction – Classroom instruction is rarely discussed as a contributing factor in the disproportionately high rate of school failure found among some ethnic minority and low-income students. The fact that there are exemplary schools and individual classroom teachers who foster uncharacteristically high academic outcomes for these youngsters seems to have little influence on attributions of blame proposed by many educators and researchers. Most explanations for school failure blame factors beyond the control of educators. Two positive exceptions are the theory of contextual interaction (Cortes, 1986) and the theory of cultural mismatch (Au, 1980; Au & Mason, 1981; Hollins, 1982). You need to become familiar with these theories as part of the process of constructing a working definition of culture and to facilitate the formulation of a theory that will guide the planning of instruction for students from different cultural and ethnic group backgrounds. You need to critically examine these theories and the research studies that support them in an effort to determine their usefulness in guiding your own planning for productive instruction in a culturally diverse classroom. In the process of critically examining these theories, you will need to determine which questions have been answered, which have not, and what additional information might be helpful.

Formulating Theory

You need to begin formulating theory that will explain the relationship among culture, cognition, and school learning. The primary goal of such theorizing is to explain the conditions and practices that generate productive instruction in culturally diverse classroom settings. You can begin by examining research studies and making connections or by doing critiques of several existing theories. The principle of cultural mediation in instruction is presented in Chapter 7 as an example to analyze. Based on the principle of cultural mediation, classroom instruction can be divided into three categories that include culturally mediated instruction, cultural accommodation, and cultural immersion. In culturally mediated instruction, the teacher and students share the same culture that is also the medium for curriculum and instruction. In cultural accommodation the teacher and students may not share the same culture; however, selected aspects of the students' culture are deliberately employed to facilitate school learning. In cultural immersion, the teacher and students may be from different cultures and the culture serving as the medium for school learning is different from that of the students. In cultural immersion the relationship between culture and school learning is not addressed.

Transforming Professional Practice

As a beginning teacher, you will need to allow yourself time to become acclimated to the professional community. This means making time for reflection and inquiry into your own classroom practices and your participation in the larger professional community. The final chapter in this book is focused on developing plans for professional growth and ways to contribute to improving the community of professional practice.

In Chapter 8, teacher development is presented as a continuous process. The types of experiences that enhance professional growth and enable you to contribute to improving the community of professional practice include studying your own practice, studying expert practice, participating in teacher study groups and university sponsored courses and seminars, attending professional conferences, and actively sharing your knowledge with colleagues.

How to Use this Book

This book is primarily designed for preservice teachers, although many inservice teachers and graduate students may find it equally useful. Thus, attempts have been made to keep the material readable, the examples as complete as possible, and the references limited to those most directly related to the topics discussed. This book may provide important insights and direction for research and scholarly work. However, it has not been specifically written for scholars.

This book may be used as a text or supplementary text in specific courses in multicultural education, social foundations of education, principles of education, and introduction to teaching. In courses that focus on the centrality of culture in school learning, this book may be used as a basic text supplemented by the material on the critical reading list. It may be used as a supplementary text in traditional courses in multicultural education that address issues of diversity with a focus on social and political concerns and relationships. This book may also be used as a tool in reframing teacher preparation programs.

This volume is organized to facilitate its use as a textbook. The focus questions at the beginning of each chapter assist the reader in identifying complex issues to be examined. The discussion in the chapter is not intended to provide complete and final answers to the questions posed, but rather to generate discussion, critical thinking, and further investigation. The chapter summary provides a quick review of the main topics presented. The suggested learning experiences have been selected for their value in expanding preservice teachers' understanding of specific questions and issues raised in the chapter. Articles and books listed as critical reading extend the text to treat important issues in greater depth. References listed at the end of the volume are materials I used in writing the text, but may also be of interest to the reader.

New Features in this Edition

- New emphasis is placed on the power of social ideology in framing teachers' thinking and school practices.
- The relationship of core values and other important social values common in the United States to school practices is explicitly discussed.
- Discussion of racism includes an explanation of the relationship between institutionalized racism and personal beliefs and actions.
- Approaches to understanding and evaluating curriculum have been expanded to include different genres and dimensions of multicultural education.
- A framework for understanding cultural diversity in the classroom is presented.
- New emphasis is placed on participating in a community of practice.

Acknowledgments

I am greatly indebted to many people for their advice, encouragement, and support during the writing of this book. I am especially grateful to my editor, Naomi Silverman, who convinced me to write this book. Her wonderful skills as an editor guided me through the initial process. I am grateful to Curtis Branch and Irving McPhail for reading early versions of the manuscript. Their comments and suggestions were invaluable. I am also especially indebted to my two daughters, Kimberly and Karla, for reading the earliest versions of the manuscript, as well as all revisions. Their feedback, patience, and support were inspirational.

I am grateful to California State University at Hayward for providing a Research, Scholarship, and Creative Activity award that supported release time for me to work on the first edition of this book and to the University of Southern California for granting a sabbatical leave that provided time for completing the second edition.

Etta R. Hollins

CHAPTER 1

The Centrality of Culture and Social Ideology in School Learning

Focus Questions

1. What is the relationship among social ideology, social change, and school practices?
2. How do social ideology and understanding the meaning of culture converge in influences on learning to teach and teaching practices?

Introduction

Long before the early European settlers arrived on the continent of North America it was inhabited by groups of people from diverse cultural traditions, who spoke different languages, held different world views, and who lived in societies that were governed and structured differently. The Cherokee, Navajo, Chippewa, Sioux, Pueblo and others referred to as tribes were separate nations who engaged in the trade of goods and services and in territorial conflicts or wars just as we see in the world today. The early European settlers themselves came from different nations, with different cultural traditions, and spoke different languages. This situation formed the context for the evolution of a social ideology aimed at building relationships among people from diverse cultural traditions and languages that would provide a basis for living together in harmony and unity in one nation.

The primary goal of this social ideology was to foster a socialization process by which a society comprised of people from diverse cultural and experiential backgrounds could be united into one nation with shared traditions and values. This process has evolved through several iterations including the Americanization/assimilation ideology evident in Native American education at the beginning of the twentieth century, cultural pluralism which emerged during the early twentieth century in response to immigration from southern and eastern Europe, intergroup relations which emerged during the 1940s as a way to facilitate understanding and racial harmony after several violent race riots, and contemporary multicultural education which emerged as a product of the Civil Rights Movement of the 1950s and 1960s.

The central purpose of this chapter is to discuss the evolution of the ideology that has guided the economic, education, and social policies that influence the life conditions and goods and services available to the diverse populations that comprise the United States; and to provide you with an opportunity to examine the consistency and persistence of this ideology in teaching and school practices. The first part of this chapter presents an overview of the evolution of major iterations of social ideology related to diversity along with a brief explanation of the origin and application of each. The second part of the chapter presents a typology of teachers' perceptions of culture, social ideology, and school practices. This part of the chapter gives you an opportunity to examine your own perception of the relationship between culture and school learning.

Social Ideology and Diversity

Americanization/Assimilation

Adams (1988) discussed the ideology and policies that framed schooling for Native American youth from 1880 to 1900. He argues that there were three interconnected perspectives that were fundamental in informing policymakers' decisions concerning Native American schooling—the Protestant ideology, the civilization–savagism paradigm, and the quest for land by Whites. The Protestant ideology embraced the concepts of Bible reading, individual salvation, and personal morality which were directly linked to more secular values found in capitalism such as "personal industry, the sanctity of private property, and the ideal of 'success' " (p. 4). The civilization–savagism paradigm received scholarly support from a cultural evolutionist named Lewis Henry Morgan in 1877, where he made the claim that societies evolved through seven stages from savagery to civilization. He placed the Indians at middle savagery. Policymakers believed that this stage of savagery placed the Indians at risk for extinction and the only way to prevent this was through assimilation or Americanization. According to Adams' analysis, the Protestant ideology and the civilization–savagism paradigm demanded that the Whites divest the Indians of the land as a way of protecting them from an otherwise inevitable fate of extinction.

The tenets of the framework for schooling for Native American youth that emerged from the ideology that prevailed from 1880 to 1900 included Protestantism, individualization, and Americanization. As actualized in school practices, the conversion from native religions to Christianity, with a preference for Protestantism, was carried out in the form of Bible reading, memorizing Bible verses, classroom prayers, and singing hymns. Individualization was intended to replace the communal perspectives and practices of Native American cultures. Individualization as embraced in schooling for Native American youth included the values of self-reliance, self-sufficiency, the work ethic, and the celebration of personal accomplishments. The primary aim for Americanization was the elimination of the Indian's political sovereignty. The goal of these school practices was to divest Native American youth of their cultural heritage, their language, their personal identity, and political sovereignty—to Americanize them.

Cultural Pluralism

The Americanization process that was part of Native American schooling as described by Adams (1988) was part of the image of the emerging nation as a "melting pot" where different races contributed to the character of the nation. This analogy was well established in social ideology during the nineteenth century; however, it was popularized by a novel written and published by Israel Zangwill in 1908 entitled *The Melting Pot*. The vision of the United States as a melting pot changed in response to a massive wave of nearly thirteen million immigrants, most of whom were from southern and eastern Europe, who arrived between 1890 and 1914. Most of these immigrants were poor, had little education, had limited skills for the labor market, and as a result lived in the low-income areas of the cities. In 1915 Horace M. Kallen coined the term "cultural pluralism." According to Ratner (1984), in Kallen's view:

> Americanization in the most liberal sense of the term involved not the destruction of all the distinctive cultural group traits other than those of the dominant Anglo-Saxons, but the cherishing and preserving of every ethnic group's cultural heritage—language, art, literature, music, customs—within the overarching framework of a common use of the English language and adherence to the prevailing political and economic system. (p. 187)

Social Justice/Multicultural Education

Kallen's view of cultural pluralism was primarily aimed at European immigrants and did not adequately address the economic, political, and social plight of people of color living in the United States. However, African American scholarship on history, politics, and social commentary had already begun to emerge with publications by George Washington Williams (1882, 1883/1989), W. E. B. Du Bois (1889, 1896/1973); and later works by Carter G. Woodson (1919/1968, 1921), Horace Mann Bond (1939), and Charles H. Wesley (1935/1969). This scholarship was the foundation for other social movements concerned with race relations and social justice such as the Intergroup Education Movement, the Ethnic Studies Movement on college and university campuses, and multicultural education. The Intergroup Education Movement was aimed at improving cross-cultural understanding and improving relationships among different ethnic and racial groups as a response to the violent race riots of the 1940s. Both the Ethnic Studies Movement on college and university campuses and multicultural education were an outgrowth of the Civil Rights Movement and likewise incorporated a social justice ideology. Also, each of these movements incorporated the fundamental ideas of cultural pluralism.

Multicultural education is based on the core values of democracy, equity, human rights, and social justice. According to Bennett (2001):

> This ideal vision of society affirms the democratic right of each ethnic group to retain its own heritage. It envisions a society based on core values of equity and social justice, respect for human dignity and universal human rights, and freedom to maintain one's language and culture, provided the human dignity and rights of others are not violated. (p. 173)

Multicultural education has evolved into a well-established discipline based on the work of scholars and researchers committed to its vision and basic principles. Bennett (2001) describes four clusters of research and theory in multicultural education that include curriculum revision and reform, equity pedagogy, multicultural competence, and societal equity. Curriculum revision and reform involves rethinking the traditionally Eurocentric school curriculum to incorporate knowledge and perspectives that have been previously omitted. The aim of equity pedagogy is to provide fair and equal access to learning, knowledge, and the development of cognitive and applied skills for all students. Cultural competence is concerned with developing the ability of each citizen to function as part of a diverse society with the knowledge and skills necessary to accept, communicate, and interact with those from different cultural and ethnic groups with an attitude of cooperation, respect, and support. Societal equity addresses issues related to inequitable social and economic policies, biased and inequitable representation in the media, and interventions that prepare students at different levels in their education to become social change agents.

The proponents of multicultural education, just as those of previous social movements concerned with relationships among different ethnic and racial groups, have viewed schooling as an important part of the process for enculturation, socialization, and the institutionalization of the supporting ideology. The ideology for each social movement has been incorporated into the preparation of teachers, teaching, and school practices.

Learning to Teach, Teaching, and Contemporary Social Ideology

Learning to teach in a culturally diverse society with students from different cultural and experiential backgrounds remains a challenge. This challenge encompasses questions based on ideology, the purpose of schooling, and teaching competence. One of the goals of multicultural education is to ensure the preparation of teachers for a diverse student population. Today, the National Council for the Accreditation of Teacher Education (NCATE) and almost every state in the United States require that teacher education programs address student diversity; however, what Kennedy (1991) found in her research study continues to be true for many teacher education programs. Kennedy reported that:

> Almost all the programs we studied, at every level, included courses designed to help teachers better understand the cultures of various groups they might eventually teach. However, these courses did not enhance teachers' ability to teach children who are members of these different groups. Despite a variety of attempts to prepare them for diverse students, few teachers and teacher candidates in our sample could move beyond the two contradictory moral imperatives of teaching—that teachers should treat all children equally and that they should individualize. (p. 15)

As Kennedy pointed out, many beginning teachers leave their teacher preparation programs not knowing how to teach students from different cultural and experiential backgrounds; yet, it is apparent that children learn in different ways and, as a consequence of socialization and other factors, they develop different learning preferences and strengths. Traditionally, school practices have been consistent with how some students have been socialized in their home-culture and with the learning preferences and strengths they have developed. These students are more successful than underserved populations of students for whom this is not the case. Planning productive learning experiences for youngsters from underserved populations requires understanding how to make linkages between students' home-culture and classroom practices. Why is it difficult for preservice teachers to learn to make such linkages while in a teacher education program? A partial answer to this question can be found in the ideology that guides preservice teachers' thinking and frames appropriation of what is learned in teacher education courses. This was evident in an investigation conducted by a team of faculty researchers at the University of Missouri–Columbia (Cockrell, Placier, Cockrell, and Middleton, 1999).

Cockrell *et al.* (1999) conducted a study of 24 preservice teachers randomly selected from among 126 full-time candidates enrolled in four sections of a foundations course in a teacher education program. The candidates were majority White and female, and most had limited experiences with people different from themselves. These researchers found that among the candidates were three ways of thinking about the purpose of schooling: school as cultural transmitter, school as cultural mediator, and school as cultural transformer. Each of these conceptualizations addressed a central purpose for schooling—what was believed to be an appropriate focus for multicultural education, what was believed to be or should be the impact of multicultural education, and school practices that support the purpose of schooling (see Table 1.1). In each of these categories there is evidence of elements of the ideologies discussed earlier in this chapter. For

Table 1.1 Framing the Conceptualization of School Learning

	Type I	Type II	Type III
Definition of culture	Artifact and behavior	Social and political relationships	Affect, behavior, and intellect
Ideological stance	Dominance of Western culture	Social reconstruction	Self-determinism
	Common culture in the United States	Cultural pluralism	Social reconstruction
	Assimilation— status quo		Cultural pluralism
Conceptualization of learning	Universalistic traditional theories are accepted	Influenced by experiential background	Culturally mediated cognition
		Traditional theories are not challenged	Traditional theories are challenged

example, the ideas in the cultural transmitter stance are much like those of the Americanization/assimilation ideology; the cultural mediator stance has elements of the Intergroup Relations Movement; and the cultural transformer stance is much like that of the multicultural/social justice movement. These ideologies influence how teachers perceive their role in the classroom, how they perceive their students, and what they anticipate will be the immediate and long-term effects of classroom instruction.

Teachers' Perspectives on Culture, Learning, and Ideology

When you are hired as a classroom teacher, you will bring your own cultural and experiential background into your professional practice. The extent to which your teaching behavior will become an extension of your own experiences or will incorporate the cultures of the students you teach may be influenced by your perception of the relationship between culture and school practices, your ideological stance, and your conceptualization of school learning (see Table 1.1). The typology of perceptions presented in this chapter illustrates the interaction among these three factors in pedagogical practice, the framing of curriculum content, and context for learning (see Table 1.2). The typology consists of three positions (Type I,

Table 1.2 Perspectives in Pedagogical Practices

	Type I	Type II	Type III
Curriculum content	Dominant group perspective	Multiple perspectives	Culturally valued knowledge
	Common heritage	Integration of multiethnic heritage	Knowledge about culture
	Multicultural contributions	Common heritage	Cultural knowledge
Instructional approaches	Generic teaching strategies	Learning styles	Culturally mediated instruction
	Individualization Remediation = repetition	Background experiences Individualization	Cultural accommodation
			Personalization
Social context for learning	Teacher-directed	Teacher-facilitated	Teacher-facilitated
		Cooperative learning	Collaborative learning
		Less competitive	Non-competitive

Type II, and Type III) and six categories of indicators that vary across positions (definition of culture, political beliefs, conceptualization of learning, curriculum content, instructional approaches, and social context for learning).

Type I: Culture as Artifact and Behavior

Defining Culture – It is likely that the applied definition of culture for Type I teachers is that of observable phenomena primarily related to behaviors such as social interaction patterns including rituals and ceremonies, traditional dress, and cultural artifacts including visual and performing arts and culinary practices. It is important to point out that this applied definition of culture may be different from what would be present in oral or written discussions.

Ideological Stance – Type I teachers are likely to take an assimilationist stance in their classroom practices. This is based on a traditional perspective of culture as supporting continuity and maintaining the status quo. Examples of the traditional perspective include support of and participation in promoting a national curriculum designed to provide students with the language, knowledge, and values necessary to preserve the essential traditions of Western civilization; opposing affirmative action; supporting legislation such as that establishing English as the official language of California passed in 1986 (see Stalker, 1988); and believing that multiculturalism is divisive for the nation (see Ravitch, 1990).

Conceptualization of School Learning – Type I teachers may view learning from a universalistic perspective. This perspective may have been implicit in university courses on theories of learning where culture was not addressed in a significant way, or discussions of culture may have been avoided or omitted. This universalistic perspective may partially account for the observation made by Kennedy (1991) that "few teachers and teacher candidates in our sample could move beyond the two contradictory moral imperatives of teaching—that teachers should treat all children equally and that they should individualize" (p. 15). There is clearly an emphasis on individualization in traditional school practices. Type I teachers are likely to maintain tight control in their classrooms, requiring direction or permission for any type of interaction among students. This ensures that each individual student will independently complete all assignments to be graded and is solely responsible for the quality of the work produced.

When universalistic notions of learning are applied in classrooms where all students receive the same instruction, there is a need to explain discrepancies in outcomes for different groups of students. These explanations tend to locate the problem in the learner. For example, explanations based on notions of deprivation, disadvantage, and learning disabilities point to deficiencies in the learner rather than problems with the instructional approach. Teachers subscribing to these ideas are likely to retain their approach to instruction and try to change the learner by using remediation or other techniques.

Research described in subsequent chapters in this book provides evidence of cultural and individual differences in learning strengths and preferences; however, you may agree with the argument presented by some traditionalists who believe identifying cultural patterns of learning is a form of stereotyping. Certainly, there is variation in learning strengths and preferences within any group; however, the publication of standardized test scores and other measures of academic achievement revealing discrepancies in performance based on race and ethnicity are more likely to lead to harmful stereotyping than appropriate adjustments to instruction that incorporate aspects of students' home-culture. The latter is more likely to improve the performance of underserved populations than maintaining existing approaches because of concern for misunderstanding and misinterpretations.

Approaches to Instruction – Type I teachers may plan instruction for ethnic minority, low-income, and English-language learners focused on remediation or acceleration in the acquisition of basic skills using traditional approaches and paying close attention to pacing and monitoring instruction, precisely sequenced objectives, employing carefully delineated steps, with little or no attention to the social and cultural needs of the youngsters. They may not be aware of, or may not give particular attention to, the cultural knowledge ethnic minority learners bring to school.

Type I teachers' instruction may be aimed at preparing youngsters for acceptance in mainstream society. They may want to ensure that every student learns to use standard English in oral and written communication, and displays appropriate social interaction skills and behaviors. Such goals are acceptable when the students' home-culture is accepted and they are supported in becoming bicultural. When the goal is to minimize or eliminate practices from the students' home-culture and foster a preference for mainstream culture, active participation in cultural hegemony may be the outcome. Some students are likely to resist this type of forced acculturation. Their resistance can be mistaken for a lack of interest in learning and evidence of cultural deprivation.

Framing the Curriculum – Type I teachers are likely to advocate a "contributionist" perspective in curriculum design. This means that the "contributions" to the larger society made by ethnic minorities are included as an appendage to mainstream curriculum. This is consistent with a traditionalist perspective advocating a school curriculum focused on a rich common heritage reflecting the contributions of all Americans. However, there is little or no discussion of the perspective from which this common heritage is to be presented or the role of schools in shaping personal and group identity for its students. Certainly, the enslavement of Africans is part of the American heritage; however, when told from a Euro-American perspective in the nation's elementary and secondary schools, there are no slave revolts and only a few Africans escaped slavery by running away from it, usually with the help of a few Euro-American sympathizers. The African American perspective of this story is quite different (see historical accounts written by Lerone Bennet and Benjamin Quarles).

Ravitch (1991/1992) argued that "under no circumstances should the curriculum be patterned to stir ethnocentric pride or to make children feel that their self-worth as human beings is derived from their race or ethnic origin" (p. 11). Ravitch argued that

> it is not the role of public schools to teach children the customs and folkways of their ethnic and racial groups; that is, as it has always been, the role of the family, the church, and the local community. Nor is it the role of the public school to encapsulate children in the confines of their family's inherited culture. (p. 8)

Yet, Lasch (1979) clearly described the preservation of culture through the schooling process. He stated that:

> in dealing with their children, they insist not only on their own authority but on the authority of the past. Rich families invent historical legends about themselves, which the young internalize. In many ways the most important thing they give their children is the sense of generational continuity so rarely encountered elsewhere in American society. (p. 219)

Lasch referred to rich families; however, this practice is apparent in the Eurocentric perspective in the public school curriculum where there is limited inclusion of ethnic minorities.

Type II: Culture as Social and Political Relationships

Defining Culture – Nieto (1992) defined *culture* as "the ever-changing values, traditions, social and political relationships, and world view shared by a group of people bound together by a combination of factors that can include a common history, geographic location, language, social class, and/or region" (p. 306). This definition may be evident in the professional practice of Type II teachers. It is broader, more abstract, and includes more political referents than the Type I definition.

Ideological Stance – Type II teachers subscribe to a multicultural perspective. Proponents of this perspective advocate social reconstruction. Examples of ideas included in the multicultural perspective are promoting egalitarianism and pluralism rather than assimilation (Banks, 1991), reframing and expanding the school curriculum to include multiple perspectives (Banks, 1991), and education for social change (Sleeter, 1989). The multicultural perspective is primarily associated with reconstructing the society to be more egalitarian and inclusive of all citizens and their cultural orientations.

Conceptualization of School Learning – Type II teachers may reject a universalistic perspective of learning without having a well-formed conceptualization of their own. They may be willing to admit that there are cultural and individual differences in approaches to learning, although the controversy this idea engenders may be uncomfortable for them. They are likely to be open to trying different approaches to instruction for different learners and to encourage input and collaboration among students.

Approaches to Instruction – Type II teachers want instruction to be responsive to student diversity. This is based on the belief that patterns of learning result from early socialization during the acquisition of one's own culture. Type II teachers may believe that many young and immature learners fail in school because the environment is made inflexible and children lack the experience and skill to adapt to the instructional process. These beliefs may lead Type II teachers to try to identify and use what works for a given student or population of students.

Framing the Curriculum – Type II teachers are likely to oppose reproducing the society as it presently exists. They do not wish to have their classrooms reflect the injustices presently existing in the society. They may argue that schools should be directly involved in social change. Schools should not only prepare students for economic productivity, but should prepare them to live harmoniously in a culturally diverse society. This would directly involve educators in teaching about the history and culture of the different populations that comprise the nation and about the social ills that need to be remedied. Multicultural education is intended to serve this purpose.

Banks (1989) identified four levels in the integration of ethnic content into the school curriculum: (a) the contributions approach (focuses on heroes, holidays, and discrete cultural elements); (b) the additive approach (content, concepts, themes, and perspectives are added to the curriculum without changing its structure); (c) the transformation approach (the structure of the curriculum is changed to enable students to view concepts, issues, events, and themes from the perspectives of diverse ethnic and cultural groups); and (d) the social action approach (students make decisions on important social issues and take actions to help solve them). The fourth level represents the most comprehensive level in the integration of multicultural education in to the school curriculum. Teachers may find their own practices at one of these levels.

Type III: Culture as Affect, Behavior, and Intellect

Defining Culture – Saravia-Shore and Arvizu (1992) described the function of culture as guiding "people in their thinking, feeling, and acting . . . [and serving] . . . as a road map in an evolving journey of survival or as a river bed that creates its own form and direction over time due to a variety of influences" (p. xxvii). Type III teachers are more likely to reflect this definition, which is more abstract, flexible, and encompassing than that held by Type I or Type II teachers. This definition portrays a more centralized function of culture in human existence.

Ideological Stance – The ideological position held by Type III teachers is of the reconstructionist–egalitarian and social justice mode. However, less emphasis is given to schooling as a vehicle for fostering a pre-determined direction for social change, and more as a process for empowering youngsters with the knowledge, skills, and cultural values for self-determination and active and responsible social participation.

Conceptualization of School Learning – Type III teachers are likely to agree with educational philosophers such as John Dewey who long ago postulated that school practices should build on and extend what the child learns in the home. Type III teachers strive to make linkages between the home-culture and school learning for students from different cultural and ethnic backgrounds.

Approaches to Instruction – Type III teachers are likely to engage in critical analysis of the relationship among approaches to classroom instruction, students' social and cultural backgrounds, and prior school learning. They identify or develop instructional approaches that build on and extend what students learn outside of school in their homes and communities. Within the classroom, students learn from and with each other. This means that Type III teachers encourage and facilitate collaboration among students.

Framing the Curriculum – Type III teachers may view the school curriculum as including cultural knowledge and knowledge about culture. Cultural knowledge includes those understandings, values, and behaviors acquired in the socialization or enculturation process within the home-culture. Children begin formal schooling with "learning in progress." They have learned the language, behaviors, perceptions, and values appropriate within the home-culture from their families, friends, and other significant people in their lives. Meaningful school learning is directly linked to that already in progress in ways that extend and build on the knowledge that has already been acquired as well as that being processed. Knowledge about culture includes the history, beliefs, customs, practices, traditions, and accomplishments of a particular group and how others have benefited from the group's experiences. Valid knowledge about culture is accurate in representing perspective and contextual factors influencing the values and practices of a particular cultural group. The inclusion of valid knowledge about culture and cultural knowledge for different cultural and ethnic groups is inconsistent within the existing school curriculum.

The Interrelatedness of Indicators Within Each Position on the Typology

In the typology of teachers' perception of culture, there is interrelatedness among the indicators for each of the positions. For example, in Type I the definition of culture is focused on surface features, which does not direct attention to exploring the relationship between culture and learning, nor does it situate learning within a cultural context. In this view, the value of culture is in the common heritage shared by members of a particular group. Acknowledging another group's heritage is one way of showing acceptance and respect for differences among people. However, considering only the surface features of culture might suggest that little harm would result from eliminating aspects of culture during the process of acculturation or assimilation. In the assimilation process, school practices are grounded in the host culture, which is viewed as the norm, thereby promoting a universalistic perspective on learning. There is an interactive response among the indicators that supports and reinforces this Type I position. When the perception of culture, learning, and ideology in this position is linked with instructional practices, the social context for learning, and curriculum content, there is a reciprocal reinforcing effect. The instructional practices reflect the universalistic view of learning as detached from culture and are not connected to prior learning outside of school, the social context does not incorporate ways of communicating and interacting found in the students' home-culture, and the curriculum content reflects only the surface features of culture.

In the Type II position, the concept of culture is abstract and broadly defined to capture the history, social, and political context within which different groups of people live and interact. The focus is on a social and political perspective that emphasizes relationships among and between groups. This perspective supports a multicultural, social justice ideological stance that encourages acceptance and appreciation for differences among groups and individuals. Individual differences among learners are recognized and, to some extent, addressed; however, instructional practices are not based on a view of cognition and learning as aspects of socialization within a particular culture. There is an interactive response among the indicators that supports and reinforces this Type II position. When the perception of culture, learning, and ideology in this position is linked with instructional practices, the social context for learning, and curriculum content, there is a reciprocal reinforcing effect. In the social justice perspective, schooling is viewed as an essential part of constructing a more just and equitable society. This perspective is reflected in instructional practices that incorporate a variety of approaches, curriculum framed to incorporate multiple perspectives and to include the heritage of a diverse population, and a social context for learning that supports diversity.

In the Type III position, culture is defined as a guide for feeling, thinking, and behaving. In this perspective, school learning is an extension of learning originating in the home-culture. The purpose for schooling is to empower students with the knowledge and skills necessary for self-determination and active and responsible participation in the society. This ideological perspective embraces social reconstruction as an outcome for self-determination. There is an interactive response among the indicators that supports and reinforces this Type III position. When the perception of culture, learning, and ideology in this position is linked with instructional practices, the social context for learning, and curriculum content, there is a reciprocal reinforcing effect. In the ideological perspective where self-determination is the basis for social reconstruction and culture is viewed as the guide for feeling, thinking, and behaving, culture is central to school learning. Classroom practices incorporate culturally mediated cognition, culturally mediated instruction, culturally valued knowledge in the curriculum, and culturally based social discourse. The ultimate goal for teachers in this position is to foster in their students the ability to think deeply, critically, and analytically; to be sensitive and responsive to others; and to actively and responsibly participate in improving the society and the human condition.

Chapter Summary

This chapter addressed the centrality of social ideology in school practices and in teachers' perceptions. The first part of the chapter described the evolution of social ideology that guided social policies and practices in a society comprised of diverse people. The early social ideology was grounded in an Americanization/assimilation perspective where the host culture was the norm into which diverse groups of people were socialized. Early schooling for Native Americans reflected this perspective. The massive wave of immigrants who arrived from southern and eastern Europe between 1890 and 1914 provided the impetus for the development of the cultural pluralism perspective, where each group was expected to retain distinctive features of their own culture while participating in the common culture of the United States. Multicultural education evolved from the cultural pluralism perspective and was a response to the Civil Rights Movement of the 1950s and 1960s.

The second part of the chapter presents a typology of teachers' perceptions where culture and social ideology form the core for classroom practices. The typology consists of three positions (Type I, Type II, and Type III) and six indicators that vary across positions (definition of culture, ideological stance, conceptualization of learning, curriculum content, instructional approaches, and social context). There is a reciprocal and reinforcing effect among the indicators within a position that supports continuity and consistency.

Suggested Learning Experiences

1. Collect several textbooks from different foundations and methods courses usually taught in teacher credential programs. Use the typology presented in this chapter to determine the working definition of culture employed.

2. Collect several definitions of culture from different sources. Note how the authors use the definitions. Save these definitions of culture for reference as you begin to develop your own working definition of culture.

3. Based on your reading of this chapter, begin to formulate your own working definition of culture. This definition should help identify and translate the cognitive functions of culture into curriculum perspectives and instructional approaches for a culturally diverse student population.

Critical Reading

Adams, D. W. (1988). Fundamental considerations: The deep meaning of Native American schooling, 1880–1900. *Harvard Educational Review, 58*(1), 1–28.

This author discusses the social ideology that framed policies and, ultimately, influenced practices in schooling for Native American youth from 1880 to 1990. The author discusses the Protestant ideology that embraced Americanization/ assimilation, the civilization–savagism paradigm, and the quest for Indian land as the perspectives framing school policies for Native American youth.

Bennett, C. (2001). Genres of research in multicultural education. *Review of Educational Research,* 71(2), 171–217.

This author presents a conceptual framework for organizing the research and theory in multicultural education. She has identified four clusters and twelve genres. This reading will help you understand the significance and value of the work in multicultural education in promoting equal access to learning and developing cognitive abilities and applied skills for all students.

CHAPTER 2

The Deep Meaning of Culture

Focus Questions

1. How do ethnic and racial differences influence experiences and perspectives related to the core values shared among different groups within the United States?
2. What have been the major impediments to actualizing the core values of the society in the United States? What have been the limitations of the efforts that have been implemented to overcome these impediments?
3. To what extent will the core values and cultural discontinuity found in the larger society influence your work as a classroom teacher?

Introduction

There is no such thing as a neutral educational process. Education either functions as an instrument which is used to facilitate the integration of the younger generation into the logic of the present system and bring about conformity to it, or it becomes "the practice of freedom," the means by which men and women participate in the transformation of their world.

(Shaul, 1970, p. 15)

It is evident that schools serve the purpose of the society for which they have been constructed and that social and political forces shape the practice and purpose of schooling. However, the cultural factors supporting social and political forces may be less evident. This chapter provides the reader an opportunity to objectify and explore the deep meaning of culture by examining aspects of the national culture in the United States. The reader will continue constructing a working definition of culture to inform classroom practices.

Defining Culture

Culture is difficult to define because it is the essence of who we are and how we exist in the world. It is derived from understandings acquired by people through experience and observation (at times speculation) about how to live together as a community, how to interact with the physical environment, and knowledge or beliefs about their relationships or positions within the universe. Many anthropologists and other researchers have provided definitions for culture as the underlying phenomenon guiding humanity. Barrett (1984) defined culture as "the body of learned beliefs, traditions, and guides for behavior that are shared among members of any human society" (p. 54). Hall (1977) succinctly described the function of culture in the following statement:

> Culture is man's medium; there is not one aspect of human life that is not touched and altered by culture. This means personality, how people express themselves (including shows of emotion), the way they think, how they move, how problems are solved, how their cities are planned and laid out, how transportation systems function and are organized, as well as how economic and government systems are put together and function. However, like the purloined letter, it is frequently the most obvious and taken-for-granted and therefore the least studied aspects of culture that influence behavior in the deepest and most subtle ways. (p. 16)

Carter (2000) defines culture simply as "learned patterns of thought and behavior that are passed from one generation to another and are experienced as distinct to a particular group" (p. 865). These descriptions of culture seem to capture the essence of definitions provided by social scientists. Yet, they seem insufficient for understanding the deep meaning of culture in school learning.

The systemic and complex integration of cultural norms into the psychological, sociological, and spiritual make-up of human beings contributes to a culture-bound existence that renders it difficult to understand one's own culture as well as that of others. One approach to overcoming this situation is to objectify culture by critical examination of specific aspects of the national culture. This approach will also support the quest for understanding the deep meaning of culture in school learning within the United States.

Culture in the United States

The population in the United States is comprised of people from different cultural, ethnic, and racial origins; however, within the society core values are shared among diverse groups of people. As was discussed in Chapter 1, the core values in our society (democracy, freedom, equality, justice, and human rights) are based on the ideological concepts of Protestantism, capitalism, and republicanism. According to Adams (1988)

> ideology is seen as a set of interconnected and mutually reinforcing beliefs and values that provide members of a given society with a sense of who they are as a collective cultural enterprise and where they fit into the historical scheme of things. (p. 4)

The Protestant ideology was especially evident in the common-school movement in the first half of the nineteenth century, where classroom activities included Bible reading, hymn singing, and prayer. Protestantism was directly linked to the capitalist values of the work ethic, private property, self-reliance or individual success, and competition. The common-school movement also emphasized individualization and Americanization. The Americanization process forced immigrants and Native Americans to abandon their own culture in favor of that of the northern Europeans. Individualization was linked to Americanization for immigrants from cultures with communalism as a primary value. Republicanism based on a constitutional democracy replaced other forms of societal governance.

Core Values

Core values such as freedom, equality, justice, and diversity are considered important enough to be legally protected. Although these are national core values, there are subtle variations in how they are actualized in response to the status of different groups within the society and how group status influences the perception of national values.

Freedom – The high value placed on freedom emanates, at least partially, from the historical origins of the early settlers from England, and their desire to be free of the constraints placed on them by the government that prevented or inhibited certain freedoms such as freedom of speech and religious choice. Individual freedom is an essential characteristic of constitutional democracy.

The high value placed on personal freedom includes the right to live in dignity and security and to seek fulfillment as an individual or as a member of a group without arbitrary constraints or sanctions brought by the government or other citizens. The Supreme Court has interpreted the freedoms of the First, Fifth, and Fourteenth Amendments to the Constitution to protect personal freedom of choice in such private matters as birth control and abortion. The famous case of *Roe v. Wade* (1973) legalizing abortion and its subsequent limitation in *Webster v. Reproductive Health Services* (1989) triggered nationwide political campaigns engaging bitter debate and polarizing the nation.

Public freedoms include the intellectual and political rights of individuals to participate in the democratic process of government. The First, Fifth, and Fourteenth Amendments protect the rights of freedom of speech, press, assembly, and petition that are basic to maintenance of a democratic society.

Other values associated with freedom are individualism, self-reliance, and autonomy. Bellah, Madsen, Sullivan, Swindler, and Tipton (1985) pointed out the centrality of these values in the following statement:

> We [the society at large] believe in the dignity, indeed the sacredness, of the individual. Anything that would violate our rights to think for ourselves, judge for ourselves, make our own decisions, live our lives as we see fit, is not only morally wrong, it is sacrilegious. (p. 142)

The importance of protecting individual freedom is reinforced by the Bill of Rights.

Americans strive for self-reliance and autonomy. Yet, this deep desire to protect individual uniqueness is tempered by the need to belong to a group or a community, the need to "fit in," and the need to be included in other people's lives. The conflict between individualism and conformity is one of the contradictions in U.S. culture. This contradiction is evident in the schooling process where students are simultaneously encouraged to act individually and to conform to group norms. For example, a common instructional practice is to assign a group of students homework that is to be completed in the same way by each individual within the group, rather than each individual determining an appropriate response to the assignment based on personal insight. In this example, students work individually to complete an assignment according to an established group norm. Such practices limit individual freedom.

Equality – There is a basic belief in U.S. society that all citizens should have equal rights economically, legally, politically, and socially. These ideals have been difficult to attain, partly because of the inequities inherent in a democratic system. In a democratic society, individuals are free to choose different avenues for pursuing "life, liberty, and happiness." This means choosing different lifestyles and different ways of providing for one's livelihood. Some of the choices individuals make are more valued by society than others, and result in greater personal recognition and financial reward. Other reasons for inequities in society include unequal access to education, wealth, and power; and biases such as prejudice, racism, and sexism that influence access and the distribution of goods and services available in the society.

According to the Constitution, every citizen has a right to equal protection under the law. In practice, many cases tried in the nation's courts require the time and skill of a private attorney to ensure a fair trial and to protect the rights of the accused. Those who cannot afford a private attorney are provided a public defender. In many urban areas, public defenders are too overloaded with cases to devote the time to the investigation and preparation necessary for effective counsel and an appropriate defense in court. Thus, financially disabled citizens may not receive legal protection equal to that of wealthier citizens. Many Americans accept such discontinuities between values and practices as a fact of life.

Political equality is another ideal that has been difficult to realize. Every qualified adult citizen has a right to vote in a political election. This means that every adult has an equal right to vote regardless of economic status or group membership. Every qualified voter also has the right to run for political office. In practice, the cost of political campaigns frequently limits participation to those with financial resources or with membership in a network capable of generating the necessary finances for an election.

Social equality has been among the most elusive of ideals and values. Ideally, in a society that values equality the laws and policies enacted to govern would provide equal access to benefits and fair administration of sanctions so as to avoid creating a legitimated class structure or a privileged class. It is apparent that in the United States a class structure exists where there is a privileged class with members receiving benefits not available to non-members. For example, data from the U.S. Department of Labor reported in 2002 showed workers of African American and Hispanic descent to have a higher unemployment rate than their Euro-American counterparts and a disproportionately lower household income.

Economic inequality is thought by many to be a natural outcome of a democratic society where citizens make choices affecting the rewards and recognition they receive. The unequal distribution of wealth in the nation is far more complex and is inextricably tied to social inequality and the advantages provided to a privileged class.

Justice – Equality and justice are interrelated and interdependent concepts. It is difficult to envision one without the other. Both equality and justice incorporate a sense of fairness and respect for the legal and personal rights of others. In our society, justice is a complex concept involving privileges, responsibilities, rewards, constraints, and consequences. The laws and policies developed to govern the society are intended to be purposeful, necessary, and fair in maintaining order in the society and protecting all citizens' rights and privileges. A persistent problem in our society has been the challenge of maintaining a fair and equitable justice system related to constraints and consequences. This is evident in the disproportionate percentages of certain groups incarcerated in the prison system.

Presently, there are more than 2 million people incarcerated in prison in the United States. Census data for 2000 indicates that, while African Americans make up about 12 percent of the total population in the United States, 44 percent of all prisoners are African American. The rate of imprisonment for African American men is more than seven times that for white men. This racial disparity in imprisonment has little relationship to frequency and type of offenses committed by African American men. Frequently, in cases where African American and white men are convicted of similar crimes, the penalty for African American men is much more severe. Recent laws enacted for crime prevention such as the "war on drugs" and the "three strikes" law in California, have disproportionately impacted people of color, especially African American men. Nicholson-Crotty and Meier (2003) found that environmental, political, and structural factors within the society are related to these differences in incarceration rates and length of sentences. These authors concluded that "Blacks are arrested at disproportionately high rates because the poverty and disorganization of their communities make it easier and less expensive to target those areas, particularly for drug arrests" (pp. 124–125). These authors further conclude that "the publicity associated with the war on drugs, and the high unemployment in urban minority communities, create the perception of a 'black crime problem' that results in harsher sanctions at all levels of the criminal justice system" (p. 125).

Diversity – The United States is characterized by great economic, ethnic, political, racial, religious, and social diversity. The Constitution protects citizens' rights to be different and to choose their own lifestyles, group memberships, and personal preferences within the limits of established laws intended to provide the maximum of personal and group freedom, yet maintain relative peace and order. Despite carefully planned laws and public policy, aspects of diversity such as particular cultural practices remain problematic, including language. Proponents of the English Only Movement of the 1980s have argued that English is the official language of the nation and should be learned by all immigrants. Presently, 25 states have laws specifying English as the official language. These laws can be identified as part of the English Only Movement given that 24 of the 25 were passed between 1975 and 2005. The United States federal government does not specify an official language; however, all official federal documents are written in English.

Providing instruction for students who are English language learners has been particularly contentious. In a case originating in the San Francisco Unified School District, *Lau v. Nichols* (1974), the U. S. Supreme Court mandated instructional support for English language learners across the nation. However, the English Only Movement muted the impact of this new mandate. In 1998, Proposition 227 was passed by the California voters that mandated teaching English as efficiently and rapidly as possibly to all students. This mandate withdrew support for bilingual education that was intended to maintain the home language while students learned English as a second language (Katz, 2000).

Other Shared Values

Values that support the Protestant ideology, capitalism, and republicanism, such as competition and success, are informally accepted as a part of our way of life. Competition and success are two values in U.S. culture that are difficult to separate. Idealistically, Americans tend to describe success as satisfaction in one's work and in service to the community (Bellah *et al.*, 1985). The phenomenon of competition is present in both of these areas of success. Individuals compete to get the best jobs and gain the highest level of recognition within their own communities. Competition is evident in all aspects of life, whether economic, educational, or political.

Through an extensive series of interviews in a study of U.S. culture, Bellah *et al.* (1985) made the following observation:

> One is successful to the extent that one personally comes out ahead in a fair competition with other individuals. Most of those we talked to emphasized that they attained their present status in life through their own hard work, seldom mentioning the part played by their family, schooling, or the advantages that came to them from being middle class to start with. (p. 198)

This further underscores the belief in competition and success based on individual achievement.

Diversity in Cultural Perspectives

Ethnic groups living in the United States emigrated from different parts of the world during different time periods. The original culture of each ethnic group had a deep structure that included primary ideologies and interrelated beliefs and values. Most ethnic groups have a history that predates arrival in the United States. The history of Native Americans predates the arrival of Europeans. The degree to which different ethnic groups have retained aspects of their original culture is influenced by assimilation, acculturation, and social and economic experiences after their arrival in the United States.

Euro-Americans, when compared to other ethnic groups, view national values within U.S. culture, such as success and upward mobility, differently. For example, Ogbu (1988) pointed out that among middle-class Euro-Americans,

> the culturally approved strategy for upward social mobility, or the strategy for getting ahead, stresses individual competition, drive, and initiative. These qualities are expected and rewarded at home, at school, and in the workplace ... [and] ... also constitute an important part of the values underlying the child-rearing practices of White middle-class parents and other socialization agents. (p. 14)

For middle-class Euro-American parents, education is the key to success and upward mobility. Those with the best education are believed to have a competitive edge over those with less education. In contrast, Bachtold (1984) pointed out that despite acculturation and acceptance of some Euro-American values, most Native American tribes do not view

> work as a virtue in itself, nor as a source of prestige ... [and] ... most Indian groups have retained enough of their traditional cultures to prevent them from total acceptance of the white American attitudes toward education as a means of occupational achievement and social mobility. (p. 217)

Bachtold further pointed out that the Hupa Indians'

> history of "harmony with the universe," of cooperative solutions rather than competitive resolutions and of negotiation rather than aggression, is continuing not only in parental expectancies for their children's behavior, but in the social interaction of the children themselves. (p. 229)

The Hupa Indians' focus on intimacy and cooperation among individuals and groups is antithetical to Euro-American individualism and competitiveness. Thus, success defined in individual terms is not a Hupa Indian value.

The high value placed on individualism in the Euro-American culture is not necessarily shared by African Americans. Hill (2001) argues that African American parents share the core values of the American society, including the strong work ethic and the high value placed on achievement. However, Hill also found evidence in multiple research studies that strong kinship bonds and participation in mutual aid involving an extended family that mitigate against a strong individualistic achievement orientation continue to exist. Upwardly mobile middle-class African American families tend to continue their strong extended family ties and kinship-help patterns.

Independence and self-reliance are aspects of individualism not shared by several ethnic groups in the United States. For example, research indicates that the relationship between one group of Mexican American mothers and their children supports the development of dependence rather than independence (Escovar and Lazarus, 1982).

Cultural Discontinuity

Cultural discontinuity exists in the national culture in the form of conflicting beliefs, values, and practices. For example, the ideologies of Protestantism, capitalism, and republicanism are in conflict with oppression, racism, classism, and sexism.

Oppression – One need only look at the make-up of the cities, towns, suburbs, and communities across this nation to see visible signs of racial and economic stratification. The urban inner cities have become increasingly poor and populated by ethnic minority groups. The suburbs of the cities have remained predominantly Euro-American and middle class. Communities in the suburbs are developing into lifestyle enclaves further delineating social class status. According to Hodge (1990), this type of stratification is based on oppression that he described as occurring when:

> the members of a group are restricted by others so that the group's members typically have fewer rights or less power than those who restrict them. Those who restrict the group are its oppressors. Others who do not actively contribute to this oppression may nonetheless benefit from it. (p. 90)

Hodge described two extremes of oppression: (a) violent oppression employing murder and physical brutality against the oppressed, such as that involved in slavery in the United States, and (b) peaceful oppression that is legally imposed, such as de jure segregation in public facilities (overturned by *Brown v. Topeka*, 1954), and continued unequal funding of public schools that ensures a lower quality of education for poor and minority children, guaranteeing that they will remain disproportionately poor. It is peaceful legalized oppression, and the institutions that maintain and perpetuate it in the United States continue to be troublesome.

Oppression contributes to unnecessary human suffering and threatens the survival of the oppressed. Data from the Children's Defense Fund (May 19, 2006) describes the disproportionately high percentages of children from ethnic minority groups living in poverty, the lack of pre-natal care given poor mothers, poor health care provided for children and youth, the rapid deterioration of the family structure among the poor, and high rates of homicide and imprisonment among low-income African American males. Data from the Children's Defense Fund (May 19, 2006) shows that there are more than 13 million children living in poverty in the United States. This is an increase of 12.8 percent since 2000. The number of Latino children living in poverty has increased by 23 percent, African American children by 8.4 percent, and White children by 7.7 percent.

Hodge believes that oppression is rooted in the dualism of Western logic based on moral values of good and evil or good and bad. In dualistic thinking, good is associated with reason, law, and rationality. Bad is associated with emotion, chance, spontaneity, and nature. Even in the dualism of Western thinking, inflicting unnecessary human suffering and pain is immoral. However, justification for the pain and suffering of oppressed groups is based on a view of one's own group as good and those that are different as bad or inferior. According to Hodge, "given dualism, it is considered reasonable to reward with more power and rights those who are seen as closer to the good; similarly, it is reasonable to restrict the power and rights of those seen as less good" (p. 97). This logic generates a type of xenophobia as well as racism, ageism, sexism, and mistreatment of those with emotional, mental, or physical challenges.

Race/Racism – A fundamental principle of oppression is the power one group has over other groups within the society. Some scholars define racism as an institutionalized system of power that is not dependent on personal prejudice, but that is supported by personal actions and participation that promote and perpetuate advantages for one racial group and disadvantages for another (Blum, 1999). For example, state governments establish laws and policies regulating funding for public schools and high school graduation requirements. Frequently, these laws and policies have a disproportionately negative impact on different groups based on ethnicity, race, and social class. The individuals who implement these laws and policies may be well-intentioned, but their actions in carrying out their job responsibilities support and perpetuate institutional racism and its negative impact on particular groups. On the other hand, there is evidence that individuals, consciously or not, enable hurtful acts of prejudice and racism against others. For example, Lewis (2003) found in her study many instances where teachers participated in discriminatory practices against students from ethnic minority groups in ways that denied full access to learning and social interaction in the classroom, and situations in which teachers ignored students' deliberate acts of prejudice and discrimination against peers from particular groups.

Race is an essential concept that supports social stratification and the empowerment of one group over others. Carter (2000) defines race as "the sociopolitical designation that is assigned on the basis of perceived skin color, physical features, and in some cases, language (e.g., Hispanic)" (p. 865). Carter further points out that "racial group designation has been associated with presumptions about cultural characteristics as well" (p. 865). Lewis (2003) points out that "racial categorizations are used to decide who is similar and different; opportunities and resources are then distributed along racial lines as people are included in or excluded from a range of institutions, activities, or opportunities because of their categorization" (p. 152).

Goldberg (1990) warned against taking a simplistic view of how racism is maintained and perpetuated. He described racism as entwined within a racist discourse that permeates the entire society in forms that are scientific, linguistic, economic, bureaucratic, legal, philosophical, and religious. Goldberg (1990) stated that:

> Adoption of racist discourse has been widespread. It has been assumed across classes, nations, social and ethnic groups; in different places, at different times, and under widely varying conditions. This cannot be explained solely in socioeconomic, political, or historical terms. Such explanations are singular in ignoring a central feature: the persuasiveness of racist discourse, that is, its compelling character for agents. Similarly, the prevailing presumptions of racism's irrationality, and of the "false consciousness" of racists, stress the psychosis of the racist personality rather than his or her persuasion, conscious belief and conviction, or rational willingness. To comprehend this widespread domestication of racist discourse, the question of human agency and the formation of subjectivity must be addressed. (pp. 308–309)

Racist discourse creates a perception of humankind that allows for classification and description resulting in hierarchies that denigrate those who are culturally and racially different.

In an article appearing in the *San Francisco Chronicle*, titled " 'Warlords' and White Lies," Lester (1993) described contemporary uses of "the vocabulary of hatred." For example, she contended that *warlords* is "a term reserved for Asians and Africans" and that "Europeans in a similar feudal

role were 'lords of the manor'—or, if especially warlike, 'knights' "
(p. A–23). The term *warlords* equates political conflict in Somalia to that
of gang violence in the United States. Ethnic clashes in Eastern Europe are
not described as tribal warfare or "White-on-White" violence. In racist
discourse, categorical differences form the basis for determining relationships with those who are different. Racism sustained by racist discourse
can foster and maintain societal arrangements such as apartheid and de
jure and de facto segregation in housing and schools.

Classism – Society in the United States is comprised of a class structure
that maintains and reproduces itself through social institutions and
agencies. Members of the middle- and upper-class strata have economic,
educational, political, and social privileges not available to lower-class
citizens. Discrepancies in funding "public" schools in affluent and poor
neighborhoods is one example of how the social class structure is maintained and perpetuated. Children from affluent families are provided a
better quality of education than children from poor families. Children
from affluent families who receive a good education are prepared for
jobs that will allow them to retain the social class status of their parents.
Likewise, children from poor families who receive an inadequate education
are prepared for jobs that limit them to the social class status of their
parents.

Although there are increasing numbers of ethnic minorities who attain
middle- and upper-class income levels, the percentage remaining in
poverty is still disproportionately high when compared to Euro-
Americans. Edelman (1987) pointed out that African American children
are three times more likely to live in poverty than Euro-American children.
Members of ethnic minority cultures who acquire middle- and upper-class
status seldom have access to all the privileges of power and prestige
granted their Euro-American counterparts (Close, 1993).

Sexism – The subordination of women to men is another form of oppression that is problematic within the society. Male domination permeates
the social, political, economic, and educational structures of the nation.
Male attitudes and behaviors are valued as those of authority, power, and
leadership. Female attitudes and behaviors are often viewed as more
nurturing, and, consequently, more suited for home life and childrearing.
Female attitudes and behaviors are less valued in leadership roles in the
society and the workplace.

Traditionally, women have been relegated to the more "feminine" and
lower-paying jobs in the workplace. Households headed by single women
are much more likely to be low income than those headed by single men.
Such biases against females have influenced their socialization during

childhood and youth, their education and occupational aspirations, and the general freedom of choice women exercise.

Historically, women have struggled for political, social, and economic rights. Women's rights activist groups have taken on issues ranging from the right to vote to abortion. In essence, women's struggle for freedom and equality within the society has included rights of full citizenship as well as those involving choice in matters of personal health.

The low status of women in the society has led some women activists and academicians to equate their treatment with that of ethnic minority populations. The claim has been made that Euro-American women are treated like minorities in the sense of their low social status, powerlessness, and economic oppression. The argument is frequently made that women from ethnic minority groups experience double jeopardy in the society and should therefore join the struggle for women's rights in order to improve their own status. However, a less common argument is that Euro-American women should band with oppressed cultural groups in their struggle for freedom and equality.

Evidence of inequities in employment based on race and sex is apparent in the national unemployment rate. A 2002 report from the Bureau of Labor Statistics showed men with college degrees earn more than women at the same educational level. Also, it was reported that Euro-American women are gaining parity with Euro-American men in management and professional positions as well as in the unemployment rate. The national unemployment rate for Euro-American men over 20 years of age in 2002 was 4.7 percent, while that for Euro-American women in the same age group was 4.4 percent. In contrast, the unemployment rate for African American and Latino men over twenty years of age was 9.5 percent and 6.4 percent respectively. African American and Latina women over twenty years of age had unemployment rates of 8.8 percent and 7.2 percent respectively. These race and gender differences are evident in salaries as well. These data suggest significant gains in employment for Euro-American women, but lower gains for men and women from ethnic minority groups. These data further suggest that race is as significant as gender in determining the rate of unemployment.

A salient issue in the women's rights movement has been equal access to higher-paying jobs. Data from the Bureau of Labor Statistics showed that in 2005 the median weekly earnings for full-time wage and salary for Euro-American men was higher than that for Euro-American women and ethnic minority men and women. Euro-American women earned more than African American or Latino men. This provides evidence that Euro-American men tend to hold higher-paying jobs than Euro-American women and ethnic minority men and women.

Many higher-paying jobs are found in supervisory positions. Maume (1999) used "the glass ceiling" and "the glass escalator" as metaphors to describe how discrimination inhibits employment in supervisory positions for Euro-American women and ethnic minority men and women; and in situations where there is a high concentration of Euro-American women and/or ethnic minorities, opportunities for employment in supervisory positions are accelerated for Euro-American men.

Identifying Solutions for Societal Problems

Prospects of substantial change in the national culture have met with resistance in the form of hostility, acts of terrorism, racial hatred, and at times more restrictive legislation. Historically, individuals involved in hate crimes and related negative behavior have aimed to further legitimize cultural domination and intimidate and discredit groups posing a threat to the status quo. Examples of intimidation and terrorism aimed at protecting the national culture include such acts as the formation of the Immigration Restriction League in 1884 and the lynching of eleven Italians in New Orleans in 1891. Examples of legislation enacted to protect the national culture include the Emergency Quota Act of 1921, which limited immigration for each nationality to 3 percent of that group's foreign-born population living in the United States in 1910; and the National Origins Act of 1924, which reduced the quota of new immigrants from 3 percent to 2 percent of those present in 1890. A recent example of restrictive legislation to protect the national culture is the California official-English constitutional amendment passed in 1986 that prohibits printing ballots in any language other than English.

The Melting Pot Myth – Between 1870 and 1920 there was a significant increase in immigration from southern and eastern Europe, Asia, and Central America. These groups came in larger numbers than before; thus it was easier for them to form ethnic group enclaves and continue the cultures of their homelands. These new immigrants were less responsive to assimilation. Thus, a modified form of cultural assimilation symbolized by the melting pot was introduced. The immigrants were no longer expected to totally abandon their native culture and assume the majority culture. A new common culture was to be formed that would include the best attributes from all cultures present in the society. Although the rhetoric was different, the process was the same. With the exception of a few recognized "contributions and influences" from the nation's diverse cultures, the institutionalized culture has remained predominantly northern European. Most of the official agencies and institutions that govern the nation and serve the people are fundamentally bound by northern European cultural values and practices or those most acceptable to members of that population.

Cultural Pluralism – Cultural pluralism, as described in Chapter 1, is a paradigm that provides parameters for explanations of social, political, and economic conditions and relationships among the diverse people within the United States. This paradigm provides ways of conceptualizing power relationships between and among culturally diverse groups.

Cultural pluralism is a theory advocating a society wherein multiple cultures coexist by maintaining distinct identities, yet sharing equal social, economic, and political status. However, other forms of pluralism exist (Smolicz, 1996). Democratic pluralism describes a balance of power between competing and blended religious, cultural, ethnic, economic, and geographical groupings. Insular pluralism refers to a situation where different cultural groups live in relative isolation from one another. In insular pluralism each group controls and limits the association its members have with outsiders. Structural pluralism exists where social contact between various ethnic or cultural groups is kept at a minimum and is limited to that occurring in occupational, political, and civic encounters.

Cultural pluralism as an ideology emerged during the colonial period when English-speaking settlers felt the need to maintain, protect, and promote their cultural dominance in the face of increasing numbers of immigrants from southern and eastern Europe. Initially, insular pluralism was practiced in the colonies where different European groups were separated geographically.

Insular pluralism of the colonial period provided privileges for Europeans only and should not be confused with the rebirth of the theory of cultural pluralism in the early 1960s and 1970s. From the colonial period until the 1954 *Brown v. Board of Education* Supreme Court decision, laws existed regulating the status and level of participation of people of color in the society. De jure segregation and other laws restricting legal rights of citizenship were not exclusively aimed at African Americans. For example, in 1906 the San Francisco Board of Education took action that restricted Asian children's school attendance to Oriental schools. In 1892, passage of the Geary Act excluded Chinese laborers and took away most of the Chinese immigrants' legal rights. In 1913, the California legislature passed a land bill making it difficult for Japanese immigrants to lease land; and in 1920, the California legislature passed a bill prohibiting Japanese immigrants from securing land. The new pluralism emerged as a form of resistance to exclusionary structural pluralism and cultural imperialism in which people of color were socially and politically segregated from the Euro-Americans, received a limited share of the goods and services of the society; yet, they were required to abandon their own cultural practices in favor of the national culture.

Multiculturalism, the new pluralism of the 1960s and 1970s, might best be described as democratic pluralism. The multiculturalists sought to eliminate insular and structural pluralism, replacing it with a more democratic pluralism wherein there would be a balance of power between competing and blended cultural, economic, ethnic, geographic, and religious groupings. Democratic pluralism was intended to eliminate cultural imperialism and to promote cultural diversity as a desirable condition for life in the United States.

The new cultural pluralism was intended to move away from assimilation as incorporated in Americanization processes such as those in the melting pot myth. Although the new pluralists advocated the right of each cultural group to practice and maintain its own culture, there was also concern for creating increased national unity through the recognition, acceptance, and celebration of cultural diversity as a national asset. The national culture under the new pluralist ideal would not be dominated by one cultural group, but rather, it would address the needs, ideals, and aspirations of all citizens. The majority group would not select the best attributes from among the diverse cultures for inclusion in a common culture, as in the melting pot myth. The new pluralism was to represent a more democratic ideal in which more egalitarian processes would be employed to establish values and practices for the common good that could be included in a national culture.

Impetus for Contemporary Change – An important impetus for change in contemporary U.S. culture is derived from demographic shifts in the nation's population not unlike that during the 1870–1920 period. Eighty percent of the 14 million immigrants arriving in this country during the 1980s were from Asia and South America. In the mid–1990s, ethnic minorities comprised one fourth of the population of the United States. By the year 2010, ethnic minorities are expected to make up one third of the national population. Hodgkinson (1991) predicted a regional shift in the nation's population such that by the year 2010

> [Twelve] states and the District of Columbia will contain 30 million of our 62 million young people, with the percentages of minority youths as follows:
> Washington, D. C., 93.2 percent; Hawaii, 79.5 percent; New Mexico, 76.5 percent; Texas, 56.9 percent; California, 56.9 percent; Florida, 53.4 percent; New York, 52.8 percent; Louisiana, 50.3 percent; Mississippi, 49.9 percent; New Jersey, 45.7 percent; Maryland, 42.7

percent; Illinois, 41.7 percent; South Carolina, 40.1 percent; U.S. total, 38.7 percent. (p. 12)

There are several reasons for these demographic shifts in the nation's population. First, there is a declining birthrate among Euro-Americans as compared to an increasing or stable birthrate among most other ethnic groups. The estimated birthrate for Euro-Americans in the mid–1990s is 1.7 children per female; for Puerto Ricans, 2.1; for African Americans, 2.4; and for Mexican Americans, 2.9. Second, there is an increase in the percentage of immigrants from Asia and South America. Third, the U.S. population is aging rapidly. The population over the age of 65 is larger than that of teenagers (Hodgkinson, 1991). The school-aged population reflects these changing demographics.

Another important reason for change is globalization. According to Suarez-Orozco (2001), "globalization has three pillars: (1) new information and communication technologies; (2) the emergence of global markets and post-national knowledge-intensive economies; and (3) unprecedented levels of immigration and displacement" (p. 345). The pillars are inter-related and they are fueled by advances in technology. Digitization, the internet, and high-speed data networks have made it possible to do many types of knowledge work almost anywhere. The outsourcing of jobs from the United States to developing countries began in the 1980s with manu-facturing shoes, cheap electronics, and toys. The next phase of outsourcing included service work such as processing credit card receipts, and writing software codes. Today, high-paying jobs requiring advanced degrees are being outsourced, partially because of the high cost of wages in the United States as compared to that in other countries. This has improved the econ-omy in some developing countries and has worsened conditions for others. Some scholars argue that outsourcing has made it more difficult for many citizens in the United States who seek employment in the areas being outsourced. The emergence of global markets has made the distribution of goods and services international. Transnational companies are a way of life. The impact of the final pillar to which Suarez-Orozco refers, immigra-tion and displacement, is felt throughout the world and is influenced by war and the global economy. These factors of globalization have important implications for schooling in a diverse society where citizens experience and perceive core values differently based on race and ethnicity and where cultural discontinuity already poses many challenges.

School Practices Reflect Cultural Norms

Schools are shaped by cultural practices and values and reflect the norms of the society for which they have been developed. The ideologies undergirding culture in the United States are apparent as interrelated beliefs and values in the culture of schooling. The culture of schooling described by Taba (1955) still exists today in:

> the patterns of acceptance and rejection, the methods of gaining status and leadership, the ways of using authority and allocating belonging, the ideas about individuality and conformity, about what constitutes success and worth expressed in the formal and informal rules of conduct [that] offer daily lessons for personal and group conduct. This culture teaches concepts and attitudes about life and relationships, good or bad, depending on what patterns and values it follows. (p. vi)

The existence of the culture of schooling can be inferred from the uniformity of values and practices across school districts. For example, the hierarchical system of governance of schools across the nation, the grouping and batch processing of students by age and grade level in the elementary schools, the ability grouping in both elementary and secondary schools, the uniformity of the school curriculum, similarities in practices of student control including suspension and expulsion, and the ringing of bells to move students from one module of instruction to another are all part of the culture of schooling. It is rather easy to see that this hierarchical structure in the governance of schools reflects the bureaucratic governmental structure of the nation and that the interconnected beliefs and values associated with Protestantism, capitalism, and republicanism are present in the focus on individualism, competition, and equality. Those cultural discontinuities that exist in the larger society are also present in the schools in the form of differences in the treatment of students, and at times differences in the quality of education provided, based on classism, racism, and sexism.

Other Ways of Revealing the Deep Meaning of Culture

In this chapter we have linked the primary ideology underlying U.S. culture with core values and beliefs as a way of revealing the deep meaning of culture. There are other approaches to revealing the deep meaning of culture that are equally valid, such as childrearing practices, communication, and social interaction practices. Childrearing is particularly revealing.

Childrearing can be viewed as a mirror of cultural ideologies as well as practices and values. According to Ogbu (1981), parents prepare their children for the society and the world as they know and have experienced it. LeVine (1988) extended this idea to a model of adaptive parental behavior aimed at protecting and ensuring the survival of the young that, over generations, develops into childrearing practices that are intuitive cultural codes embedded in folk wisdom that descendants may not be able to consciously explain. Members of the same cultural group living in different strata may experience the society differently and may alter their values and practices to accommodate the existing environmental circumstances. Thus childrearing practices may vary within cultural groups for a variety of reasons.

According to Escovar and Lazarus (1982):

> The bulk of child-rearing research has led to two conclusions. First, social class cuts across ethnic groups in determining many child-rearing practices. That is, there are variations in child-rearing practices that are strictly due to SES [socioeconomic status] and are not discrete, vertical cultural values. Second, when social class is controlled, there remains a variation in childrearing . . . that can be said to be typical of a culture regardless of SES. These culture-specific effects are not easily overshadowed by social class. (p. 144)

In essence, the factors of political power, resources, time, and education have an effect on values, practices, and perceptions, but there are those elements of culture that are embedded deeply enough to endure these environmental influences. In many instances those considered the most acculturated continue some of the childrearing practices passed on from their ancestral heritage.

Chapter Summary

Schools are shaped by the core values and practices of the society, although the deep meaning of culture in school learning may not be apparent to educators, students, or parents. Definitions of culture employed by anthropologists provide insights into its integral influence on human behavior and thought; however, these definitions may be insufficient references for designing school learning experiences in culturally diverse settings. Thus, preservice teachers are encouraged to systematically construct a working definition of culture that will guide decision making in planning instruction for different populations of students.

In this chapter, objectifying culture is presented as the initial step in the process of constructing a working definition of culture that can be used to guide planning school-learning experiences. Objectifying culture is the process of depersonalization that supports critical examination of the ideology supporting accepted behaviors and practices. Ideologies reflect aspects of the deep meaning of culture.

Schools reflect the cultural norms of the larger society. These cultural norms are reflected in overall operations of schools including interactions among students and between students and teachers, and in the reward and punishment systems instituted.

Examining ideologies and interconnected beliefs and values represents one way to reveal the deep meaning of culture. Other ways of revealing the deep meaning of culture include examining communication, social interaction patterns, and childrearing practices.

Suggested Learning Experiences

1. Read the articles by Banks and Ravitch listed in Critical Reading. Develop your own position statement on multicultural education.
2. Read Hodge's theory of Western logic and propose an alternative explanation for the phenomenon he identified.
3. Conduct a review of the literature on childrearing practices for a particular ethnic group. Identify the primary ideologies and interrelated beliefs and values present.
4. Construct an initial working definition of culture that will guide planning for school learning in a culturally diverse setting.

Critical Reading

Banks, J. A. (1991). Multicultural education: For freedom's sake. *Educational Leadership*, 49(4), 32–36.
The author, a strong proponent for multicultural education, presents an argument for establishing a common ground of understanding between conservatives and multiculturalists.

Hodge, J. L. (1990). Equality: Beyond dualism and oppression. In D. T. Goldberg (ed.), *Anatomy of racism*. Minneapolis: University of Minnesota Press.
The author presents a theory of Western logic explaining the antecedents of oppression in all forms including racism, classism, and sexism.

Lewis, A. E. (2003). *Race in the Schoolyard: Negotiating the color line in classrooms and communities*. New Brunswick, NJ: Rutgers University Press.
The author reports a study that explored how race and racial inequality are reproduced in schools and the role of administrators, counselors, and teachers in consciously or unconsciously enabling this reproduction.

Ogbu, J. (1988). Cultural diversity and human development. *New Directions for Child Development*, 42, 11–25.
The author argues that members of a specific culture acquire the cognitive, communicative, motivational, socioemotional, and affective competencies characteristic of that culture.

Ravitch, D. (1991). A culture in common. *Educational Leadership*, 49(4), 8–11.
The author, a conservative anti-multiculturalist, argues that schools should teach the common culture rather than about our separate cultures.

CHAPTER 3

Personalizing Cultural Diversity

Focus Questions

1. Why is racial identity important, and to what extent does it influence relationships among groups and the lives of individuals living in the United States?
2. The motto of the United States is *E Pluribus Unum*, one out of many—a reference to national unity. What is the relationship between national unity and ethnic and cultural diversity?
3. Why is it that Euro-Americans are often excluded from discussions of culturally diverse populations within the United States?

Introduction

In summary we can say that the journey inward becomes an ongoing process that leads outward to a more complete understanding of the human condition. Self-understanding is not merely a reflection on what we are but on what we are in relation to the world. Self-understanding comes to us via our unique perceptions of the world which are dependent on our inherent individual abilities as well as on our particular socio-cultural histories.

(Krall, 1988, p. 467)

The journey inward can be uncomfortable for many different reasons, particularly when it deals with the roots of socialization that have defined who we are in relationship to our own reference groups and to other groups within the society. The journey inward can elicit feeling the need to defend and protect one's own status and that of family and friends. The journey can elicit memories of encounters and situations, both pleasant and unpleasant, with individuals and groups different from ourselves. It can bring into question our own status of privilege or oppression within the society. However, an important aspect of personal growth is taking the journey inward.

The journey inward is a way of acquiring personal agency through acquiring a level of personal and social awareness that empowers individuals to make conscious decisions about how to participate and contribute to the society. It has been pointed out in the previous chapters that schools are tools for the support and maintenance of the prevailing social ideology, and that individuals serve as institutional agents for this purpose. Participation in perpetuating the prevailing social ideology may or may not be intentional, depending on the level of self-understanding and social awareness an individual has acquired. In part, the probability of different cultural groups living together in harmony is influenced by the self-perception held by group members, how members of one group perceive members of another group, and the differences in the belief systems held by each group. These perceptions and beliefs may be culturally based or grounded in the prevailing ideology—both depend on socialization of the young into the beliefs and practices of adults with whom they are affiliated.

The pervasive nature of culture and socialization in our daily lives was discussed in the previous chapter. The purpose of this chapter is to present a heuristic for reflecting on personal perceptions and responses to beliefs about culture and race, and another for positioning one's self in a culturally diverse society. These heuristics are intended to empower individuals to make conscious decisions about how to behave, feel, and think about those who are different from themselves. The discussion in this chapter is not intended to elicit feelings of anxiety, guilt, or hostility from members of any cultural, ethnic, or racial group. However, considering the hypothesis that racial identity is dynamic and an individual can move from one status of identity development to another may be helpful in understanding such feelings.

The Importance of Personal Awareness

There are several important reasons for teachers to be aware of their own thoughts about culture and race, and how they respond to members of their own culture and those who are from other cultural backgrounds. First, teachers are the product of their own socialization into a particular culture, ethnic group, or social ideology. When teachers and students share the same or a similar background with common perceptions and values, communication and learning are facilitated. In cases where teachers and their students are from different cultural and experiential backgrounds, even when a common language is shared, communication and learning may be a challenge. Data presented in the previous chapter show demographic trends of increasing cultural diversity in public schools. Teachers who are aware of their own thoughts and behaviors in cross-cultural interaction are better prepared to respond in ways that will improve teaching and learning in culturally diverse classroom settings.

Second, teachers are tremendously significant and powerful individuals in the lives of their students. What an individual teacher projects has a profound impact on students' self-perception, self-confidence, and academic performance. In a preliminary study conducted by Hollins and Spencer (1990), it was found that African American students from Grades 1 through 12 identified as their favorite teachers those with whom they had positive interactions, and who acknowledged aspects of their lives outside the classroom. These same teachers tended to be interested in the students' opinions during class, further increasing students' interest and preference for the subject matter they taught. Third, in many cases the curriculum content and materials used in schools do not reflect the multicultural perspectives of the populations taught. Teachers need to be able to identify the value perspective of the material used in teaching, as well as that presented in professional publications and at conferences and workshop sessions.

Classifying and Labeling People

Classifying and labeling individuals and groups according to "race" is a common practice in the United States. Public schools regularly make reports of their racial composition to the state and federal government. Employers request race identification from job applicants as a way of monitoring equity in the job market. The national census is reported by race. The U.S. Department of Labor reports unemployment by race. The notion of classifying groups by race is not inherently negative. However, there are negative consequences when the classification is treated as hierarchical or used to separate groups for economic, political, or social reasons. Race as it is used in the United States is a social and political designation referring to national origin and status in the society that incorporates physical features. Until recently, African Americans and Euro-Americans were the only groups consistently classified by color rather than place of national origin. In the past, Asian Americans and Mexican Americans have been classified as "other Whites." Both groups are now classified as people of color, a non-White classification. The classification by race used in the United States consistently separates "Whites" from "non-Whites." This need to differentiate between Whites and non-Whites has been particularly troublesome because of thinly veiled practices of preferential treatment for those classified as White and exclusion and discrimination against those labeled non-White.

Presently, understanding diverse cultures and including culturally diverse perspectives in the school curriculum and instructional approaches is subject to controversy. In many cases, the history and culture of diverse populations are added to the existing school or university curriculum, or carefully integrated into what is referred to as the regular curriculum without identifying its cultural underpinnings. A good example is the conspicuous absence of Euro-American history and culture in departments of ethnic studies at major universities. Euro-American history is not usually referred to as an ethnic history, but rather as American history. This mainstream treatment of Euro-American heritage has contributed to attitudes of superiority that support prejudice and discrimination against those perceived as inferior.

Euro-American Racial Identity

By whiteness, I refer to a set of meanings and practices that provide white people with a perspective through which they experience the world. This lived standpoint is discursively constructed in relation to ideologies of privilege and domination.

(Proweller, 1999, p. 777)

Proweller (1999) reported a study of White racial identity development among a group of adolescent girls attending a predominantly White elite private school. This researcher found that when

asked to locate themselves racially, white youth construct their analyses through a language of othering, decidedly positioning themselves in relation to an "other." In order to articulate whiteness as a lived part of their everyday experience, they must find a language that inscribes *who they are* racially in terms of *who they are not.* (p. 781)

At this school Whiteness is institutionalized by an approach to race management carried out by students and teachers that is tied to a "white, liberal, middle-class agenda [where] liberal epistemologies *white out* differences through a language of tolerance and respect for cultural differences" (p. 788). When approached individually, students of color were aware of the race management process and were, to some extent, uncomfortable with it, but accepted it as the way things were at the school.

The need to create racial boundaries, manage race, and establish a position for Whiteness has been evident since the arrival of the early European settlers. During the colonial period, Euro-Americans were separated into at least two different racial groups. Immigrants from southern and eastern Europe and those from northern and western Europe were considered racially distinct. Immigrants from southern and eastern Europe came to North America as a source of cheap labor that benefited those from northern and western Europe. Many came as indentured servants.

Alba (1990) believes the ethnic identity that polarized early immigrants has all but disappeared and has been replaced by a new ethnicity referred to as Euro-American. This new ethnic group includes anyone from anywhere in Europe. An important point is that Euro-Americans continue to be racially classified as White. Marable (1990) argued that, "to be white in the United States says nothing directly about an individual's culture, ethnic heritage, or biological background" (p. 16). Marable further argued that White culture does not exist and that White racial identity is based on the victimization of people of color. Even if we accept Marable's argument, we are left with two perplexing problems: first, that of understanding exactly how the White racial identity he described is sustained without cultural transmission and, second, the relationship between racial identity for Whites and non-Whites.

In the previous chapter, insular pluralism was described as the prevailing mode in U.S. society, which means that interaction between members of different cultural groups is likely to exclude frequent social contact (Pratte, 1979). If White racial identity is based on the victimization of people of color, how is this identity formed in the absence of direct contact? Helms (1990) postulated that Euro-Americans become aware of African Americans either vicariously, being told about them by their parents or peers, or directly, by personal contact. In the case of vicarious contact, individuals learn from their parents and peers how they are to think about and respond to persons who are members of groups other than their own. More specifically, Helms postulated that through this socialization process, Euro-Americans learn to fear and devalue African Americans in particular. Even when direct personal contact with other groups is positive, "gatekeepers" may use personal and group pressure to reinforce the socialization process that teaches a White person how to behave as a member of the White racial group. This suggests that a culture does exist in some form and that cultural transmission is part of the process for sustaining a White racial identity.

If White racial identity is based on the victimization of non-Whites, what influence does this have on the racial identity of non-Whites? In an article in *Newsweek* magazine, Whitaker (1993) described identity as one of "the dozen demons" of race with which professional African Americans struggle. He described the case of an African American who found it necessary to avoid being typecast as Black in order to become vice president one of America's largest companies. This meant disassociating himself from "any hint of a racial agenda," and included remaining silent when confronted with apparent racist behavior (p. 61). The price for such a choice is social and cultural isolation. Such self-effacing behavior did not bring full acceptance in Euro-American social circles and it alienated other African Americans who labeled him an "Uncle Tom."

In reality, racial identity is ascribed by societal norms. Every citizen is either White or non-White. The dichotomy of racial identity victimizes all citizens socially and psychologically by establishing artificial boundaries that prevent natural human bonding. Consequently, the society is wrought with racial conflict resulting in violent confrontations and social unrest, with many people living in fear while others are unjustly and disproportionately imprisoned. The progress of the nation is affected by the loss of valuable human resources. Human energy expended in maintaining racial boundaries could be better used to improve the quality of human life.

Depolarizing Racial Identity

The polarization of racial identity can be partially reconciled by empowering individuals to understand and make conscious decisions about their response to personal and group identity. *Status theory* (Helms, 1995) is a promising heuristic for developing a positive racial identity. In her discussion of what she referred to in 1990 as stage theory, Helms postulated that "the evolution of a positive White racial identity consists of two processes, the abandonment of racism and the development of a non-racist White identity" (p. 49). Helms is primarily concerned with the development of White racial identity as a response to the presence of African Americans.

Similar considerations can be given to developing a positive racial identity for other people of color. An essential problem in developing a positive non-racist White racial identity is that Whiteness has been normalized and institutionalized within the society. The fact that individuals serve as agents for institutionalizing Whiteness provides opportunities for change. Helms' (1995) model of White racial identity holds promise as a viable tool for change at the individual level. *The discussion of White racial identity may be uncomfortable for you just as it was for the adolescent girls in Proweller's (1999) study; however, your experience and maturity should enable you to see the value of the process.* The process of examining racial identity is valuable to the extent that it encourages self-awareness—increases capacity for introspection and reflection; increases awareness of personal interaction with those different from oneself; increases the awareness of the experiences of others; and increases awareness of one's role as an institutional agent maintaining a particular ideology and social structure.

White Racial Identity Status

Helms (1995) presented a model of White racial identity consisting of six statuses. Five of the six statuses may be either terminal or transformative. Individuals may advance in the frequency and quality of their experiences with people of color. They may acquire substantial academic knowledge about the history and culture of these groups without advancing from one status to the next in White racial identity. Actually, it is possible for such increases in experience and knowledge to increase cleavage to a negative White identity. Awareness of the different statuses of racial identity can facilitate self-understanding and the type of reflection that increases the potential for personal growth that is particularly important for classroom teachers. Racial identity is especially significant in culturally diverse classroom settings. Thus, Helms' description of White racial identity has been extended to include discussion of important aspects in the dynamics of teacher–student interaction.

Contact Status – This is the point at which Whites have had limited interaction with African Americans or other people of color. This has primarily included those posturing White behaviors and values. This contact may have been with individuals in positions where acceptance or advancement required conformity to White behaviors and values. At this status, individuals may deny that race matters within the society or that race is personally meaningful.

Teachers in this status of development expect all of their students to conform to White behaviors and values. Those who do not conform are likely to face negative consequences. For example, Gilmore (1985) reported a study in which teachers describe African American students as having an "attitude" when they participate in practices from their own culture. These students were excluded from the Academic Plus Program because of their "attitude" when they were otherwise qualified. These teachers may not recognize their unwillingness to accept the fact that people of color actually have a different culture that is valid and vital to their existence, and is potentially meaningful in the classroom. Students of color are likely to perceive White teachers in this status of racial identity as racist and employing discriminatory practices because of their apparent preference for students who conform or assimilate.

Disintegration Status – At this status, White individuals begin to question what they have been socialized to believe about members of other racial, ethnic, and cultural groups. It is during this status that many Whites first become aware that "justice and equality for all" is an ideal rather than truth, and that people of color do not have access to the same privileges as Whites of similar educational and occupational status. Such realities are countered with overt and covert pressure from within the White culture to deny such realities and conform to established norms for thinking about, interacting with, and treating non-Whites. These conflicting realities are likely to lead individuals to the next status, reintegration.

Conflicting realities and in-group pressures may cause teachers at the disintegration status to be inconsistent in their treatment of students of color. At times they may seem fair and at other times they may seem unusually biased in their judgments.

Reintegration Status – Reintegration is the point at which the individual consciously acknowledges a White identity and accepts the myths of White superiority and the innate inferiority of African Americans and other people of color. These individuals believe White privilege is justified on the basis that it has been earned. Feelings of guilt and anxiety resulting from the conflicting realities of personal experience with people of color and group pressure to conform may be replaced with feelings of anger, blame, and fear. At this point, individuals may feel personally threatened to the extent that they act violently toward people of color without specific or immediate provocation. During this status, individuals may take action believed to be in the best interest of Whites as a group.

Teachers at this status may consciously deny students of color equal treatment in the classroom. Certain privileges and recognition may be reserved for White students only. Teachers at this status may intentionally create situations that perpetuate the perception of White student superiority. For example, situations may be created where only Whites receive recognition for outstanding performance.

Pseudo-Independence Status – This is the status at which White individuals begin to redefine White racial identity. At this point individuals seriously question their group-reinforced views of people of color as innately inferior. These individuals begin to acknowledge the role Whites play in perpetuating racism and oppression and their personal responsibility for covert or overt participation. During this status, White individuals become uncomfortable with a racist White identity and begin to seek accurate information about other groups. These individuals recognize that negative perceptions of people of color are central to the group-reinforced views of White identity. During this status White individuals may act with zeal to decrease or eliminate racism and oppression. People of color may respond with skepticism, and some Whites may view this behavior as violating cultural norms.

Classroom teachers in Status IV are likely to be very conscientious in attending to the needs of their students of color. They may be very enthusiastic about including the history and culture of diverse populations in the curriculum. These teachers may put forth extra effort to learn about new immigrant students enrolled in their classes or in the school where they teach. They may openly espouse philosophies such as critical pedagogy and multicultural education.

Immersion/Emersion Status – This is the point at which White individuals replace stereotypes about their own and other ethnic groups with accurate information. Individuals at this status begin to concentrate on their own personal and group identity. They question who they are and who they wish to become. Individuals who are successful at this status experience a catharsis where past negative feelings that may have been denied are acknowledged and examined.

Teachers at this status of development have a more balanced and authentic response to differences among their students. They have a basis for better understanding and making use of information about their students in a natural and humanistic way. For example, the teacher may increase options for projects and assignments, allowing students to personalize their work. This has potential for naturally increasing the cultural relevance of instruction.

Autonomy Status – At this point, White individuals internalize a new and more positive definition of Whiteness evolved through the previous five statuses. The term *race* has been replaced with concepts of culture and ethnicity. Persons at this status are open to understanding and accepting human diversity in its many forms. There is no evidence of the need to respond to in-group pressure to conform and accept established norms. Persons who have internalized a new White identity are prepared to live harmoniously with the culturally diverse groups who make up the nation and the world.

Teachers at this status are open to discover new ways to teach their students on the basis of knowledge about their cultural and experiential backgrounds. For example, these teachers may begin to spend more time in the students' home-community and may be observed using new information from such experiences in their classrooms.

Each status of White racial identity described by Helms (1995) includes behaviors and ideology that can be experienced and clearly observed by outsiders. Likewise, insiders with a keen sense of self-awareness who seek to understand the experiences and perceptions of others can make similar observations about behaviors and ideology associated with racial identity. This awareness enables individuals to monitor their own behavior and interactions with others.

Racial Identity Status for People of Color

There is a reciprocal relationship between White racial identity and that of people of color. Negative White racial identity and the associated attitudes, beliefs, and behaviors have an adverse effect on racial identity, behaviors, and attitudes of people of color. For example, Whitaker (1993) pointed out that:

> knowing that race can undermine status, African-Americans frequently take aggressive countermeasures in order to avoid embarrassment. One woman, a Harvard-educated lawyer, carries a Bally bag when going to certain exclusive shops. Like a sorceress warding off evil with a wand, she holds the bag in front of her to rebuff racial assumptions, in the hope that the clerk will take it as proof that she is fit to enter. (p. 58)

The countermeasures to which Whitaker referred are those employed by professional African Americans who have acquired a level of sophistication that may be less characteristic of the working class. Such experiences are not limited to African Americans and can be viewed as representative of the experiences of other people of color.

Research studies involving different racial and ethnic groups of people of color reveal similar experiences with oppression and racism in the society, and similar interpersonal and intrapsychic responses for coping with internalized racism and achieving a positive racial identity and self-concept (Asher, 2002; French et al., 2006; Lee, 2001). The conditions under which these diverse groups of people of color experience racism and oppression vary for groups and individuals within groups. Based on this type of evidence, Helms (1995) presented six statuses of racial identity development for people of color (African, Asian, Latino, and Native American) in the United States: conformity, dissonance, immersion, emersion, internalization, and integrative awareness.

Conformity Status – At this point, individuals believe that if they conform to White behaviors and values they will be fully accepted into the White group. The conformity status has been divided into two phases: active and passive. During the active phase, individuals idealize the White culture while denigrating their own. This conformity status is also characterized by disassociation where individuals identify with a White reference group rather than with their own ethnic or racial group. In the passive phase of conformity, an individual's orientation is reinforced by, and so closely matches that of, the White racial group that this phase may be difficult to recognize. There is also considerable peer support from others in the same phase. Individuals in this phase believe strongly in individualism and internal causation and deny that race influences their behavior or life choices.

Teachers of color in holding this status may identify more with White students than with those more like themselves. They are likely to show the same preferences and behaviors as teachers in the early status of White racial identity. For example, teachers of color at this status may reject students of color when they participate in practices from their own cultural or ethnic group.

Dissonance Status – At this point, individuals realize that people of color are not likely to be accepted as part of the White establishment. Individuals realize that values and perceptions belonging to a White racial identity are not functional for themselves, and they begin to seek a new identity and reference group. Individuals experience a wide range of emotions during this transformation from dissonance to increased awareness. Emotions may include feelings of anxiety, confusion, depression, hopelessness, and ultimately anger and euphoria. The person begins to develop a new identity tied to his or her own ethnic group resulting in transition to a new status of racial identity.

Teachers of color when holding this status begin to make a conscious effort to relate to students from their own ethnic group. Their behavior may be inconsistent, fluctuating between the developing ethnic identity and the old racial identity. For example, they may send mixed signals to students of color. On one day they might compliment and encourage the wearing of ethnic attire; the next day they might encourage conformity to mainstream standards of dress and behavior without reference to particular situations, events, or conditions.

Immersion Status – At this status, individuals withdraw into their own ethnicity. Attempts are made to find authenticity within their own ethnic group. Individuals may display a sort of generalized anger toward Whites for their role in racial oppression and at themselves for having participated in its perpetuation. Ethnicity is not yet internalized. Individuals appear to conform to an idealized or stereotypical ethnic behavior.

Teachers of color holding this status may transform the curriculum to focus on the history and culture of their own ethnic group. The inclusion of specific ethnic practices and values are likely to be apparent in their classrooms. They may actively exclude or denigrate White culture and history.

Emersion Status – This is the point at which individuals develop a positive non-stereotypical ethnic identity. Persons holding this status reach a balance in perspective and emotional responses to ethnicity, oppression, and racism. Ethnic stereotypes no longer influence feelings of self-worth. Individuals begin to sort out the strengths and weaknesses of their own ethnic group. Persons at this status gain an increased sense of personal control and begin to move toward internalizing their own ethnicity.

Teachers at this status begin to develop a more balanced approach to ethnic culture and history in the curriculum. They have a tendency to be inclusive rather than exclusive.

Internalization Status – At this status, individuals define the relevance of their own racial identity. There is a blending of personal and ascribed identity. Individuals accept their ascribed racial identity, but reject external determination of its meaning. Persons who have internalized and personalized their own racial identity, and its meaning, operate from a position of greater strength in relating to racism and oppression. At this point it is possible to ascertain the authenticity of White individuals initiating alliances with people of color. These individuals are able to avoid exploitation and further dehumanization.

Teachers of color who understand their own identity are better able to work with all children and provide a balanced perspective in curriculum content. However, understanding one's identity in relationship to society within the United States may not be enough. Well-balanced individuals understand their own identity beyond the boundaries of a race-conscious society. They understand their personal heritage; their cultural, economic, political, and social existence in the world; and their interconnectedness to the past, present, and future. This knowledge of self and the world provides hope for the future. It also allows teachers of color to help their students maintain hope for the future.

Integrative Awareness Status – At this status individuals are comfortable with themselves and their racial identity. They are self-defining and self-affirming in terms of their personal and group identity. Individuals at this status are able to integrate their racial identity with membership in other reference groups related to ethnicity, gender, sexual orientation, and social class status as parts of a holistic self-identity. There is acceptance of others.

Teachers of color at this status of integrative awareness are able to project this sense of a holistic self-identity in their relationships with their students.

As in the case of White racial identity, each status of racial identity for people of color includes behaviors and ideology observable by outsiders and by insiders who have developed a keen sense of awareness. Awareness of racial identity status enables one to avoid counterproductive behaviors and negative social interactions. The basic intent of this discussion on racial identity is to enable teachers to be more aware of the influence of societal norms on personal perspectives and values, individual behaviors, and classroom practices. Hopefully, this will enable classroom teachers to be more self-aware and more aware of their interactions with students in their classrooms and colleagues with whom they work.

E Pluribus Unum (One Out of Many)

The motto of the United States is *E Pluribus Unum*, which translates into "one out of many." Fostering unity in the midst of diversity is a complex undertaking. It is not difficult to point out that the United States is a culturally diverse society and to identify visible ethnic groups, particularly people of color. However, including one's self in this multicultural mosaic is more difficult for some people than for others. The characterization of race as White and non-White has contributed to some Euro-Americans viewing themselves as a collective group of Americans without an ethnic identity or cultural group membership. On the other hand, people of color have been required to justify their worthiness for inclusion in the society, and the benefits and rewards of citizenship have been parceled out to them on the basis of acceptable ethnic group performance.

The requirement that people of color justify worthiness for inclusion in the society has fostered competition among these groups for acceptance, recognition, and rewards from the Euro-American community. The Euro-American community responded by setting standards and rating the acceptability of the performance of the different groups of people of color. For example, Asian Americans have been stereotyped as the "model minorities" and African Americans have received the least favorable ratings from the Euro-American community. Evaluation of the per-formance of these different ethnic and racial groups for the rewards of a favorable rating has served to reinforce ethnic and racial group boundaries and to restrict cross-cultural contact. The racial polarization of the society has not fostered a perception of the commonality and interrelatedness of human experiences, particularly across racial lines. The separation of the society into Whites and non-Whites can be partially ameliorated through groups from both sides developing a positive racial identity, as previously discussed, and by including Whites not as the "norm" against which all other groups are measured, but as one among many groups in the cultural diversity that comprises the nation.

People of color have expended energy trying to attain approval from the Euro-American community that could have been directed towards gaining cultural understanding. The history and culture of different ethnic groups has often been the subject of comparative analysis by Euro-Americans rather than a vehicle for better human understanding. In order to change this situation, all groups must see themselves as part of the cultural diversity that comprises the society. Each group needs to accept and appreciate its own ethnic heritage as well as that of others. It is important for each group to recognize that the struggles of all our foreparents are historically intertwined with the development of this nation. When individuals are in contact with their own heritage and feel their own sense of identity they are better able to understand, accept, and include others as equally deserving citizens of the United States.

This is supported by my own experience as a university professor. The procedure I used in my social foundations course is presented here as a heuristic for a group process where ethnic group identity is a vehicle for understanding the interconnectedness of humanity. This process addresses the issues raised in the debate described in Chapter 1 between the proponents of multicultural education and the traditionalists. The proponents of multicultural education are concerned with allowing ethnic groups to retain their identity while sharing in a national culture. Traditionalists believe multiculturalism is divisive. Examples of students' responses to the group process used in my course are presented to demonstrate that reclaiming ethnic identity can foster linkages of common human experiences and reduce divisiveness. The group process described here can unlock the mysteries of shared human experiences and contribute to actualizing the nation's motto, *E Pluribus Unum.*

Cultural Inclusion in a Diverse Society

The majority of students in my courses were Euro-Americans. At the outset of the course, these preservice teachers described themselves as American while describing the students they would soon teach as African American, Asian American, Mexican American, and Native American according to their geographic origins. The students described themselves by ethnicity, rather than as American. These preservice teachers frequently spoke of the experiences of these other Americans as alien to themselves. It was easy for some of my students to view these other Americans as not deserving certain privileges that they enjoyed.

At the outset of the course, my students were asked to describe personal attributes or experiences that might be helpful to them in a culturally diverse school or classroom setting. They had the option of responding verbally as part of the class discussion or limiting their responses to notes in journals kept for the course. The assignment that followed the initial class discussion included research on a surname selected because of a personal, legal, or biological connection to it. This assignment was not the same as constructing a chart of family lineage or constructing a simple family history. It was much richer and more complex. *This assignment was about looking at the meaning of a name; its origin and its social value; its sustainability, modification, or replacement; and patterns in the values, practices, social and political experiences of those who held certain family names.* At the end of the chapter are guidelines for doing this activity yourself.

Reclaiming Ethnic Group Identity – At the class meeting following the surname research, I focused the discussion by asking the students what thoughts and feelings they had as they organized the information on a particular surname. The students were not asked to share personal or specific information from their research, although many shared humorous, perplexing, and even tragic stories from their past. Discussions began slowly, but gained momentum and even enthusiasm as students began to recognize common aspects of their histories and different perceptions and responses to similar situations. By the end of the class meeting it was apparent that students had begun to reclaim their ethnic identity and felt more connected with each other than they had prior to the class discussion. In reflecting on the assignment and the class discussion one student made the following notation in his journal:

> The professor asked: What do you bring to teaching that enhances your effectiveness in a culturally diverse setting? I wished I wasn't so damned White. I immediately used my maleness as a way to be different, to give myself credentials to understand minority status. After all, the whole field of education is female dominated; therefore, I must be special because I choose to be a teacher. I really felt the need to identify with an oppressed group in order to be knowledgeable enough to personally contribute to a quality multicultural learning experience. After discussing our family histories in class, I am not so sure I need to have a special status, or maybe, I already do and it comes from my personal history. What I realized from our classroom discussions, is that everyone sees the world through his or her own cultural lens. The ethical and progressive way to look at the multicultural world is by remembering my own cultural lens and to

imagine what the other cultural lenses are like too. This is new and exciting.

This student recognized the need to have an ethnic group identity and had begun the process of reclaiming his own heritage. Through the experience and insight gained in researching and discussing his heritage with peers, his self-understanding began to increase and expanded his capacity to understand the life experiences of the youngsters he will teach.

In relation to the surname research another student noted in her journal:

> I avoided starting the assignment because searching out information about my childhood meant that I would have to relive painful child-hood memories. I had no ties to my blood family on either parent's side. I was raised by foster parents from 2 years old until I married. Even though I have a relationship with my mother now, there are still many emotional scars on both sides. The foster parents were very prejudiced and being Italian was not very acceptable. As a matter of fact, I was continuously reminded that my parents were not very "good" people. Part of me wanted to claim my Italian heritage and the other was very hesitant to make waves. I greatly appreciated having done this assignment. I feel as if I have been reborn. I had no idea that having an identity was so important to me. I put myself in contact with a long lost relative and in touch with my roots. I see the relevance of learning more about ourselves. We can't respond to others' needs if we don't have a better understanding of our own. This assignment also reminded me that each of us brings something different to the profession of teaching.

The history my students studied in their undergraduate programs had apparently been too far removed from their own lives to be personally meaningful. These students had not seen those who struggled with various forms of prejudice and oppression in the new land as their own relatives. Many had pushed from their minds the humiliation their grandparents, parents, and in some cases they themselves, had suffered due to a heritage from the wrong location in Europe. Many of my students had forgotten or never knew the price some of their ancestors paid for inclusion in mainstream America.

Making Personal Connection with the Past – The students found recon-necting with their own heritage particularly meaningful. One student described her reconnecting experience this way:

> I even found a newspaper clipping that told about my father chan-ging his name. If he had changed his name because he thought it

would be easier to spell that might have been alright. But, he didn't do it for that reason. He did it because he wanted to deny who he was, to totally assimilate into the American culture. Following our discussion in class today, I finally realize how important that was to my father, and why he did what he did. He wanted to be accepted as a true American citizen. The only way to do that, according to the attitudes of this society, was to give up all or part of one's previous identity in order to "fit in" with the "American way." I can't begin to say that I understand those kinds of feelings. I can only hope that I will be more aware that these feelings do exist, and understand some of the reasons why.

At the beginning of the course many students believed African Americans were the only people whose surnames had been lost. During class discussion they found that other groups shared this experience as well.

Connecting With Other People's Experiences – In the process of the surname research assignment, Euro-American students were able to make linkages among the experiences of their parents and foreparents during earlier periods of immigration and contemporary experiences described by their peers. For example, a Vietnamese student made the following observation about contemporary Americanization:

> I recall going through transcripts and lists of names of [high school] students graduating in Spring. I wondered why many of the Vietnamese names were followed by a name in parenthesis, usually a name of such Western origin as Johnny or Cathy. For the sake of convenience, for the sake of the laziness of the Western tongue, and for the sake of American pomposity we have bastardized the Vietnamese language. I remember asking a Vietnamese student how to pronounce her name, and when she said it, it was such a beautiful sound, as if it were a sung whisper. Yet so many immigrants take on English names, compromising both their true names and their culture. Is there a loss of identity, of heritage in such an action? There has to be. It is said that the most beautiful sound in the world is the sound of hearing one's own name in a positive context. Is this occurring at the moment Xiang Zhuang responds as someone calls, "John"?

This comment about the contemporary Americanization of Vietnamese students' names, when compared to changes in Euro-American names during the nineteenth and early twentieth centuries, juxtaposes historical and contemporary events in a way that helps make connections between the past and present, and between Euro-American experiences and those of other ethnic groups.

Understanding Prejudice and Discrimination – When Euro-American students acknowledge and grapple with understanding the prejudice and discrimination many of their ancestors faced as immigrants to the United States, they are better prepared to understand the experiences of other ethnic groups. Many of my students had not reckoned with the idea that people of color continue to struggle for the same inclusion as many early immigrants from southern and eastern Europe, but face an insurmountable racial barrier. An Asian American student described her encounter with racism in the following way:

> I hesitated in class that night. It stirred me—the discussion on racism disturbed me because I didn't want to remember. I didn't want to remember . . . But I remembered. I remembered the dark, musty hallways and classrooms with wooden floors that echoed. I remember the doors and the windows that seemed never to allow light into the stifling grimness. I remember the harsh voice of a teacher, telling me what to do and scolding me for following directions. I remember understanding or coming to understand that the directions she gave were for the class, not for the tiny, frightened little Asian girl in the corner. The little one who was just learning that she was Asian. I remember that damned game—"Even-Steven"—a game I played with everyday during recess, taking it off the shelf and sitting on the floor with it—red and orange plastic pegs. A boring game, way below my skill level, but it was the only game on the shelf that a child could play by herself. But I remember not really playing it—it was a silly game—I only pretended to play it so my body looked busy while my mind pondered my aloneness. Then came lunch time. I remember sitting in the cafeteria with my sisters. It wasn't dark in the cafeteria, the lights seemed blaring and focused on us. I don't remember ever ingesting food. I remember them circling us. I remember them circling us, staring at us, laughing at us and taunting us. I couldn't understand because I didn't know what the word was that they were yelling at us. I had never heard the word "CHINK." But now I was hearing it over and over and over. And I couldn't understand. I didn't know then. But now I know. And it still hurts.

Euro-American students were better prepared to understand and empathize with the Asian American student's story after personal reflections on their own heritage. The Asian American student felt less alone when the Euro-American students shared their personal histories.

Prejudice and discrimination were understood from different perspectives by students from different cultural and ethnic backgrounds.

Unveiling the Mysteries of Shared Human Experiences – Researching one's own heritage is egocentric in that it brings personal pride in family history, struggles, and accomplishments. However, through the experience of constructing a personal history we can learn to laugh at the humorous side of our own family histories, to lament the tragedies, and to understand, accept, and empathize with situations and events in other people's lives. The mysteries of shared human experiences that are overshadowed by preoccupation with racial classifications and cultural encapsulation can be unveiled through the process of forming a positive personal and group identity that fosters better understanding of others. Some basic ideas and generalizations concerning common cross-cultural experiences that have been shrouded in mystery include the following:

1. A monolithic White culture does not exist within the United States. People classified as White immigrated to the United States from different countries with distinctive cultures in Europe. These differences caused conflict among those from the same continent. Vestiges of cultural values and practices from the old country still exist in family values, practices, and traditions.
2. There are cycles of education, ignorance, oppression, poverty, and power within the history of a single family or those affiliated with a particular surname. These cycles are similar for different families and various cultural and ethnic groups during different historical periods and in societies around the world.
3. Members of many groups viewed as outside the mainstream have attempted to change their identity to be included. Some have changed their names, and others, for whom changing names would make little difference, have tried to camouflage their identity by changing their behavior, language, or appearance. These attempts at identity changes have caused losses in family history, cultural traditions, and the sense of interrelatedness with other cultural and ethnic groups within and outside the United States.
4. Life experiences and personal and family histories can serve as a basic source for subsequent learning and sharing.

Surnames as Part of the Journey Inward

The journey inward through identification with a surname that locates one within a particular group, itself part of a racialized society that places higher value on one group than another, is an approach that supports developing a positive ethnic/racial identity while developing acceptance and appreciation for those different from oneself. The process for taking this journey need not be extremely time-consuming. A good place to begin is with a single surname. The surname selected may be matrilineal, patrilineal, or related to a lineage you acquired through marriage or adoption. The initial approach to collecting information about the surname you have chosen may be to prepare an anecdotal account by acquiring as much informal knowledge as possible through conversing with family members and examining family records and documents. The family Bible can be an excellent source of information. Other helpful records include certificates of birth, death, and marriage. These certificates can be acquired from a county or state office of vital statistics by submitting a letter of request stating the reason you want the information and including your relative's name, location of the event, and approximate date. A nominal fee is charged for each certificate requested.

In conducting interviews with family members it is important to have in mind the exact questions you want to ask. These questions should include inquiries about when and where the family first arrived on the continent of North America, the country of their origin, the interviewee's personal relationship to these early immigrants, the conditions they left behind, the conditions they found in their new homeland, as well as how they were affected by significant historical events and changes in living conditions. It is important to know the social relationships among and reactions to the immigrant group of which your family was a part. You should make note of occupational trends and family health problems. You might also want to ask about the origin of family customs, traditions, and beliefs. It is interesting to keep records of amusing and tragic family stories and legends.

Researching the geographic origin and meaning of the name and examining the history and living patterns of those to whom the name has been ascribed can provide academic knowledge about a particular surname. It is possible to identify interesting patterns in the geographic distribution of particular surnames. When a surname is shared with historically prominent personalities it may be possible to get more published information. Many books have been published on the origin of European surnames. A few books have been written on other surnames. Your local reference librarian can assist you in locating specific genealogical materials.

In cases where a genealogical record has been established, the procedure may be to review and expand what already exists. Expansion may include updating family lineage charts and adding recent events in the lives of family members.

Constructing your own personal family history can be tremendously beneficial. Knowledge of personal history can provide a sense of personal and group identity and serve as a vehicle for integrating the past and the present. Constructing a personal family history can provide avenues for individuals to link their own life experiences to an ethnic heritage and, ultimately, to the history of the world. Personal family history can reveal painful memories that we may think are best forgotten, but that continue to haunt us. Sharing these experiences with peers may be too difficult. Some negative experiences may deal with conflict, love, and tragedy. These are elements of shared human experiences that link people across culture, ethnicity, history, and race. Putting these memories into a sociological and historical perspective seems to help alleviate the pain and connect us with others who share similar experiences.

Chapter Summary

The discussion in this chapter has focused on personalizing cultural diversity, which includes acquiring a positive racial identity, reclaiming an ethnic identity, and connecting with shared human experiences that transcend cultural, ethnic, and racial boundaries.

Helms' work on the status of an individual's racial identity development is presented as a heuristic for developing a positive racial identity. The statuses of White racial identity include:

1. Contact (Whites have limited interaction with non-Whites).
2. Disintegration (Whites question their beliefs about non-Whites).
3. Reintegration (Whites accept the myth of their own superiority over non-Whites).
4. Pseudo-independent (a redefinition of White racial identity is initiated).
5. Immersion (White individuals replace stereotypes with accurate information).
6. Autonomy (White individuals internalize a positive racial identity).

The statuses of racial identity for people of color include:

1. Conformity (an active phase where White culture is idealized and a passive phase where there is a strong belief in individualism and internal causation).
2. Dissonance (people of color realize they are not part of the White establishment).
3. Immersion (individuals withdraw into their own ethnicity).
4. Emersion (a positive non-stereotypical ethnic identity is developed).
5. Internalization (individuals define the relevance of their own ethnic identity).

6. Integrative awareness (individuals are self-defining and self-affirming in terms of their personal and group identity).

A group process using surnames as a way to reveal family heritage is presented as a heuristic for facilitating inclusion in a culturally diverse society. The group process facilitates reclaiming ethnic identity, making personal connection with the past, connecting with other people's experiences, understanding prejudice and discrimination, and unveiling the mysteries of shared human experiences.

A general approach to constructing a personal family history by researching a surname that is matrilineal, patrilineal, or acquired through adoption or marriage is presented.

Suggested Learning Experiences

1. Review the status of racial identity development for Whites and people of color. Do a self-assessment to determine your own status of development. Determine what this means for you and your students in a culturally diverse school setting.
2. Conduct a study of a surname in your family as a way to better understand your self, your values, and perspectives.
3. Re-examine your working definition of culture. Make revisions based on the new insights you have gained so far.

Critical Reading

Alba, R. D. (1990). *Ethnic identity: The transformation of White America.* New Haven: Yale University Press.

The author presents the results of a research study of the nature of ethnicity among Whites in the contemporary society of the United States.

Helms, J. E. (ed.). (1990). *Black and White racial identity: Theory, research, and practice.* New York: Greenwood Press.

The author examines the meaning of racial identity in the United States. This book reviews the literature on racial identity and presents status theory as it has been applied to the development of racial identity.

Proweller, A. (1999). Shifting identities in private education: Reconstructing race at/in the cultural center. *Teachers College Record,* 100(4), 776–808.

The author reported a study of White racial identity development among a group of adolescent girls attending a predominantly White elite private school.

CHAPTER 4

Learning About Diverse Populations of Students

Focus Questions

1. What do classroom teachers need to know about students from different cultural and ethnic backgrounds and how might this knowledge inform their teaching?
2. Are there unique skills and knowledge acquired by students through their ethnic heritage or status in the society that may have implications for teaching and learning?
3. What are the best ways for teachers to acquire the knowledge they most need about the students they teach?
4. How are teachers to deal with the ethical responsibility of having extensive knowledge about individual students?

Introduction

Teachers have no choice but to inquire into each student's unique culture and learning history, to determine what instructional materials might best be used, and to determine when a student's cultural and life experiences are compatible, or potentially incompatible, with instruction. To do less is to build emotional blocks to communication in an already complicated instructional situation.

(Berliner, 1986, p. 29)

The heuristics for depolarizing racial identity and facilitating inclusion in a culturally diverse society presented in the previous chapter provide an important basis for reducing cultural encapsulation and preparing you to inquire into your students' culture, life experiences, and learning history. Such inquiry is important to providing productive learning experiences, creating a supportive context for learning, and making curriculum content meaningful.

This chapter is focused on inquiring and reflecting on teaching practices for students from diverse cultural backgrounds. The central question framing inquiry in this chapter is: How can teachers expand their knowledge and make sense of the complex and divergent experiences and the social and cultural milieu of the diverse students they teach in ways that support teaching and learning within and outside the classroom? The primary assumption underlying this question is that the background experiences, cultural knowledge, and competencies students acquire outside of school are important in making sense of school learning. As a classroom teacher, you need to understand the nature of the experiences that students bring to school in order to make connections and provide reciprocal support between learning within and outside of school.

Traditionally, the purpose of schooling, pedagogical practices, curriculum content, and the social context of school learning are based on middle-class Euro-American culture. The perceptions, practices, and values on which schooling is based are not necessarily shared by all populations that make up the society. There is sufficient evidence to suggest that some degree of continuity between the experiential background of the students and school learning is more than helpful. In some instances, when acquiring basic knowledge and skills this connection between the students' experiential background and the content and process of instruction determine the quality of academic performance.

You cannot learn from university courses all you need to know about the students you will teach, but you can learn a process for acquiring, interpreting, and transforming knowledge about students for pedagogical practice. One approach for doing this is what I call reflective–interpretive–inquiry (RIQ). This is a process whereby educational practitioners construct meaning by reflecting on their own practice and their students' experiential backgrounds in ways that facilitate focused and strategic inquiry concerned with improving professional competence and the benefits provided their students. The application of RIQ requires educators to engage in strategic planning of learning experiences for student growth, to be systematic in executing planned learning experiences, to reflect on and document students' responses to the learning experiences provided, to interpret the meaning of students' responses in terms of the appropriateness and effectiveness of the learning experiences, and to translate this interpretation into questions for inquiry that will extend professional understanding and improve practice.

As a beginning teacher, you are not expected to immediately collect data in all of the RIQ categories for all of your students. Gathering the type of data described in this chapter should be an ongoing part of professional development. This is a slow process that can take several years. However, as a preservice teacher, you should begin the process in order to become familiar with the techniques, and to understand the usefulness of the data collected. At the outset you are not expected to study all of your students simultaneously. Initially, you might elect to study a small group of students such as those performing least well in the classroom. As you gain more experience with the process of data collection, you become more adept at studying more of your students' attributes simultaneously.

The primary purpose for adopting RIQ as a classroom teacher is to develop competence in relating knowledge about learners to instruction and creating an appropriate approach and social context for learning. Many teachers who are effective in culturally diverse settings have learned to reflect on and grow from their own practice. These teachers have learned to examine the context in which they teach, and to connect the content they teach and the learning experiences they provide with their students' daily lives and their cultural values, practices, and perceptions.

The Ethics of Data Collection

The quality of the data gathered and the conclusions and inferences drawn are influenced by the perceptions and values of the teacher involved in the inquiry. Examining the cultural background of students requires some degree of objectivity. An egocentric or ethnocentric perspective in data collection is counterproductive. You must be able to examine the cultures of your students without making value judgments based on your own personal or cultural experiences. The only legitimate reason for collecting data about the background and experiences of students is for improving classroom instruction. Teachers who are convinced that their instruction is appropriate and should not change, although it does not serve some groups of students well, and who blame the students or their life conditions for instructional failures, probably would not benefit from collecting data about their students. For these teachers, there is the probability that data collection will reinforce negative beliefs about their students.

If you want to improve your instruction to better serve your students, you should proceed ethically and responsibly with data collection. That is, you must assume the legal and moral responsibilities associated with such investigation. Legally, information about individual students, their parents, and life circumstances cannot be shared with or disclosed to others in any form without written permission. Also, individuals about whom information is collected have a legal right to review the information upon request. The state and federal government place rigid constraints on research and experimentation with human subjects. Assuming moral responsibility requires you to maintain confidentiality and protect the privacy of individuals who act as informants or about whom data are gathered. The protection of research subjects is particularly important if you plan to publish your findings. Data collected solely for instructional purposes may not need approval from an institutional review board, but you do need to follow the same ethical standards related to confidentiality and privacy. To be certain you comply with such regulations, you should contact the institutional review board for your school district or that of a local college or university. You can learn more about regulations and policy guidelines for research involving human subjects at the website for the United States Department of Health and Human Services, Office for Human Research Protection (http://www.hhs.gov/ohrp/).

Organizing for Data Collection

You need to be well organized and systematic in data gathering and record keeping. It is highly recommended that you keep your notes organized in an electronic file, a three-ring binder, or a file box. The notes you take need to be clearly identified with the time, place, content being taught, situation/event, condition, and clear identification of persons involved. The description of the situation or event should be clear, concise, as objective as possible, and clearly separated from your personal response or interpretation. Objectivity in documentation is important for later interpretation, the identification of patterns, and drawing conclusions. It is very important to document your personal responses and interpretations. However, they must be clearly labeled. By documenting your personal responses you can monitor your own professional growth and can bring to the forefront your own biases and begin to eliminate some of them.

A teaching portfolio is one way to manage your data. The artifacts of data collection can be placed in a cardboard file box with dividers. The file may be organized in the following way:

I. Demographic/sociological context
   A. The larger societal and political context
   B. The local community
   C. Ethnic and cultural groups
II. Student experiential background
   A. Significant experiences outside of school

      B. Significant experiences within school
   III. Student work samples
      A. Course/content area (e.g. science)
         1. Individual exhibits appropriately labeled by date, class period, objective
      B. Course/content area (e.g. English)
         1. Individual exhibits appropriately labeled by date, class period, objective

Strategies for Data Collection

The data gathering for the RIQ is similar to the grounded theory approach used in qualitative research. However, your purpose is different from that of a researcher whose goal is to answer specific questions and contribute to the published research literature in a particular area. Your purpose for collecting data on your students is to better understand how to plan instructional experiences that will foster the desired learning outcomes within a predetermined time frame. Your approach to data analysis will be more informal, although your data collection strategies are quite similar to those used in qualitative research studies.

The strategies you will use for data gathering include: (a) participant-observer note-taking, (b) questionnaires, (c) formal and informal interviews, (d) life history or biographical accounts, and (e) documentation of academic performance. Collecting data from multiple sources provides opportunities for triangulation, a method of confirming findings in qualitative research studies. You will use triangulation as a way to confirm the importance of particular student attributes, experiences, and values. For example, in investigating students' preferences for particular curriculum content, you might examine data from interviews with students and their parents, review report cards and anecdotal notes from previous teachers, and examine standardized test scores. Each of these sources of data can provide information about preferences for curriculum content that, when combined, provides greater insight.

Participant Observer

Your role as a participant observer is to make careful observations and to take notes while actively engaging in teaching and planning for teaching. You will make careful observations about how your students respond to learning experiences, their peers, and to you as their teacher. In your notes about how students or a particular student responded to instruction you should be as specific as possible. For example, if there was something the students did not understand or if they seemed confused, note the specific part of the experience that caused the problem and the nature of the attempts and errors made by the students. If the lesson went as planned, note the points at which the students were highly engaged and points when they were less engaged. A helpful way to format your note-taking is to divide a sheet of paper in half. Label the left side of the page "my observations" and the right half "my thoughts." Keeping your observations and thoughts separate will be helpful when you begin to look at patterns in your data. Your observations should be a documentation of a situation or event as it happened. Your thoughts are your interpretation of and reflection on your observation. Your thoughts may include possible explanations of the observation or a tentative interpretation of the meaning for teaching and learning. Keep your notes organized sequentially, preferably in an electronic file or three-ring binder.

Questionnaires

A questionnaire is a convenient and efficient way to collect data where personal communication is not the most expedient approach or a viable option. The items on a good questionnaire are characterized by clarity in language usage, absence of ambiguity, and well-defined terminology; and are framed to elicit responses that will provide specific information and, when analyzed, provide specific insights for addressing specific challenges or issues. Teachers can use questionnaires to elicit beliefs, opinions, past experiences, and expectations for the future from their students to support planning meaningful and productive classroom instruction. The data from questionnaires may be analyzed to identify relationships among different student attributes and experiences. Tables 4.1 through 4.5 are examples of questionnaires used to solicit information for instructional purposes.

Formal and Informal Interviews

Interviews involve direct contact with participants that allow the interviewer to clarify questions and probe responses. Interviews may be face to face, on the telephone, or on the internet. Interviews may be structured, semistructured, or informal; conducted with the entire population, a selected sample of the population, or key informants. Structured interviews have a clearly established purpose and predetermined questions or format. An interview may be structured by a questionnaire. A semistructured interview may include a verbal questionnaire as in the structured interview, but allows for flexibility in the use of probe and follow-up questions based on the participant's responses. Informal interviews have a general goal of data collection focused on a particular issue, rather than a well-established purpose and predetermined questions. An unstructured or informal interview may be scheduled or unscheduled; may result from planned open-ended discussions about a topic; or may emerge during casual conversations with individuals not sought out for data gathering. These informal interviews may provide more reliable data during an extended study than formal interviews where responses may be influenced by the situation.

The individuals interviewed may include all of the members of the particular population under study, a selected group, or key informants. In some instances, the population about whom the inquiry is conducted is small enough to allow for the inclusion of all members. For example, you may choose to study a group of students with similar academic performance, an ethnic group, or some other configuration within a class or across several classes.

In studying a large community, it can be helpful to select a sample group of individuals to interview who are representative of the total population or to utilize key informants. One advantage to selecting a sample population is that the interviewer can get a range of the ideas and responses within the community. The size of the sample can limit the depth and breadth of the information provided by any one individual. The use of a key informant allows for more depth and breadth in the interview process. A key informant is someone who is particularly well informed, representative of the population about which information is sought, and is highly articulate. There is the risk that a key informant may not be representative of the group studied.

Life Histories and Biographies

Life histories and biographical accounts may be acquired through publications found in local newspapers, books in local libraries, and documents in historical museums. Biographical data can be acquired during interviews with local residents appearing on talk shows on local radio or television stations. This information can provide an historical context for other information, a view of how individuals are affected by the local context over time, and a view of how individuals choose to portray their lives.

Academic Performance Data

Academic performance data is a rich source for those studying schooling for students from different ethnic groups. Such data collection might include standardized test results, performance on other commercial tests as well as teacher-made tests, and samples of students' work on specific tasks or assignments from coursework. Student work samples can be a source of valuable information for revealing and correcting biases in instruction. For the purpose of monitoring and achieving effective instruction for all students, you can collect work samples from assignments that illustrate outstanding work, that which is representative of the class as a whole, and the worst work. The idea is to use the questions in RIQ Category 2 to analyze these data and to develop approaches that provide equal access to instruction for all students. Such data should be a routine part of the teaching portfolio.

Formulating Questions That Reveal the Big Picture

Ideally, before classroom instruction begins, you will have acquired knowledge about the students you will teach from examining their records, talking with the students and their parents, and conducting a study of the ethnic or cultural groups of which the students are members, as well as the larger community. The constraints of practice very often dictate that you begin inquiry with your own students in the classroom and that you initially employ traditionally designed approaches to curriculum and instruction. These constraints further dictate that those who have not had the luxury of compiling a profile of their students prior to beginning instruction act as teacher researchers or participant observers in collecting qualitative data. Your inquiry should be guided by a set of questions that frame data collection and that generate additional questions. The quality of the questions asked influences the data collected and the conclusions and inferences drawn. The questions that follow may be helpful in guiding inquiry.

Category 1: Teacher Beliefs About Students

You can begin the process of RIQ by reflecting on your own beliefs about the students you will teach. Teachers consciously or unconsciously hold beliefs about their students that influence the type of instruction provided and the performance and behaviors expected. Questions that may help you examine your beliefs include the following:

1. What do I believe or think I know about my students' experiential backgrounds?
2. What do I believe about the relationship between my students' experiential background and successful teaching and learning?
3. How are these beliefs revealed in my teaching practices?
4. Do I hold different beliefs for students from various ethnic backgrounds and social strata?

It is important for you to take time to produce written responses to these questions. Your responses will form the basis of future reflection. Your initial responses will be confirmed, altered, or discarded. It is important for you to monitor your own thinking and progress in acquiring and utilizing information about your students' experiential backgrounds.

Category 2: Teacher Beliefs About Instruction

The second category of questions for RIQ addresses your beliefs about instructional practices. These questions are intended to help you identify and correct biases in your own instructional practices that support students with certain attributes and provide very little support for other students. This does not mean reducing support for some students while increasing it for others, but rather, that you should consciously work to improve instruction for all students. Questions that guide RIQ in this category include the following:

1. What do I believe constitutes good teaching?
2. What are the attributes of a good student?
3. Are my instructional approaches more suitable for some students than for others?
4. What are the attributes of the students for whom my instructional approaches are most suitable?
5. Do students for whom my instructional approaches are less suited have particular attributes?
6. How can I consider the attributes of both groups in planning instruction that will generate superior outcomes for all the students?
7. How can my instruction be altered to change poor students into good students?

Category 3: Teacher Beliefs About the Social Context of Instruction

The third category of questions in RIQ considers the social context of instruction. Most students do their best learning in situations where they feel comfortable and supported. How students feel is not always apparent. Students who are attentive, quiet, orderly, and on-task are not necessarily comfortable in the classroom. Some students may feel personal rejection from the teacher or from peers. The structure of the classroom may be intimidating to some students. Your behavior may be in conflict with the home-cultural norms for adult–child relationships. The questions in this category of RIQ are intended to help you examine your personal views about the social context of learning in your classroom. These questions include the following:

1. What is the role of the classroom teacher?
2. What do I believe should be the relationship between teachers and students?
3. What should be the relationship among students?

4. What social conditions within and outside the school influence relationships among students and between students and teachers?
5. How can I employ aspects of the social/cultural milieu of the students within and outside of school to create a comfortable and supportive context for learning?
6. What views of relationships within the classroom are evident in the routines and procedures in my classroom?

Category 4: Ethnic and Cultural Groups

The fourth category of questions for RIQ is concerned with acquiring knowledge about the ethnic and cultural groups of which the students are members and a sense of the cultural knowledge and competencies they might have acquired. Youngsters from groups traditionally underserved in the nation's public schools acquire some knowledge and competencies different from those of middle-class Euro-Americans for three primary reasons. First, some students are from ethnic groups that choose to maintain their culture intact. Second, those who are members of underrepresented cultural groups are excluded from full participation in the society and are socialized into their own ethnic groups out of political and social necessity. Third, how youngsters from under-represented cultures experience the society is different from that of most middle-class Euro-American youngsters because of their political and social status.

The questions that guide inquiry in the fourth category include the following:

1. Would a population distribution map of the city in which your school is located reveal ethnic, cultural, or social class enclaves?
2. To what extent is the population distribution within the community represented in your classroom?
3. If the students are active members of a particular ethnic or cultural group, what are the customs, perceptions, practices, traditions, and values that are fundamental to their culture?
4. What aspects of the students' culture are evident in their social inter-action, the perceptions they express, the language they use, and the expectations they hold for the schooling process?
5. How can aspects of the students' cultural orientation be utilized to inform classroom practices?
6. How does the cultural knowledge students acquire through socialization within an ethnic group manifest itself and how can it be used to enhance school learning?
7. Are the history and culture of the ethnic groups that make up

the school represented in the curriculum and social context of the school?

Category 5: The Local Community

The fifth category of questions for RIQ deals with understanding the community in which the students reside. The community in which the students live frames their existence and has an impact on their perceptions and values. The questions for this type of inquiry include the following:

1. What are the major social and political divisions or segments within the community?
2. How do people from the different segments of the community relate to each other?
3. From your observations, do you get the sense that political power and economic resources are fairly distributed among the different groups within the community?
4. Do residents of the community feel reasonably protected from economic and political exploitation, social isolation, and physical and psychological violence from within and outside?
5. Are there adequate opportunities within the community for residents from different segments of the population to participate in social activities, recreation, cultural activities and experiences, and to receive adequate health care?
6. To what extent does the makeup of your class reflect the composition of the community where the school is located?
7. What impact does community life have on students' aspirations, values, perceptions, behavior, and learning in school?
8. Are the history and culture of the local community evident in the school curriculum and the social context within the school?
9. What resources are available in the local community that can be used to support classroom learning?

Category 6: Societal Context

The sixth category of questions for RIQ deals with fitting it all together into the larger societal context. Significant aspects of society within the United States were covered in previous chapters of this book. For the purposes of inquiry and formulating questions for this category it is sufficient to simply point out that the students, their ethnic groups, and their communities are all part of a larger society that has political and social norms that support and constrain activities. Questions for inquiry into the relationship between the larger society and the behaviors and perceptions of students include:

1. What image of the local community is portrayed in the media? Does this image appear distorted or stereotypical?
2. Do the residents of the local community have equal access to and derive equal benefits from national resources?
3. Is the local school district adequately funded to provide the necessary resources for quality education for the children served, or are the funds limited due to the low economic and political status of the local residents?
4. From personal observations or systematic investigation, do you get the sense that the community is internally or externally controlled? That is, do the local residents have the power to determine what happens in the community?

Category 7: Students' Experiential Background

The seventh category of questions for RIQ deals with understanding the personalized and unique qualities of each student's experiential background and the implications for learning in school. In essence, these questions will help you gain insights necessary for making links between the students' experiences in and out of school in ways that support and facilitate learning. Such questions include the following:

1. What significant experiences and social contacts have individual students had within and outside of school that frame behavior, learning, and perceptions within school?
2. How can knowledge of these significant experiences and social contacts be utilized to support meaningful learning in the classroom?

Collecting Data on Students

Students as Primary Source

Students are frequently overlooked as a primary source of information about teaching and learning in school, yet they have specific expectations and desires for the outcomes of attending school for any given year. Their expectations may be influenced by their prior experiences and may not be as positive as you might hope. Students who have experienced many disappointments or a number of failures in school tend not to have the same positive expectations as those who have experienced success. Frequently, these students are simply categorized by their teachers as unmotivated. The fact is that most people who experience repeated failure at a particular task will eventually lose the motivation to persist. You need to solicit from your students the type of information that will allow you to understand their experiences, expectations, and desires related to school in general and to specific subject areas, if possible. The broader the database, the more meaningful it will be for you.

Students' Expectations and Desires – One way in which you can acquire the data you need on students' expectations and desires is to develop meaningful questionnaires that can be used in an interview or as part of the work you assign in class. For the best results, these questionnaires should contain open-ended items that solicit specific information. The questionnaire in Table 4.1 is an example of a data-gathering instrument that can also serve as a writing assignment in an English or language arts class.

Question 1 in Table 4.1 allows even the student who has become turned off academically to engage in introspection to determine what he or she would like to get out of school. For those who are the most turned off, you might need to use probe questions that help these students transcend negative experiences and identify what they really want from school. For example, you might ask: "If you could design a school to teach anything you wanted, what would you include first and how would you benefit from that particular knowledge or skill?" Probe questions should lead to introspection rather than to what you want to hear.

Information about what students want to learn will be helpful to you in planning an approach to the curriculum and for selecting or developing learning experiences. The curriculum may be predetermined by local school boards or the state department of education. However, as a teacher, you have the responsibility to make the curriculum accessible to the students you teach. One way to do this is to incorporate a perspective that connects with what students most want to gain from school and to plan learning experiences that emanate from the students themselves. Do not be surprised if what an individual student most wants to gain from school is not academic.

The second question in Table 4.1 asks for positive disclosure of what would be helpful to the student in learning the desired content or skills.

Table 4.1 Data-Gathering Instrument that Serves as a Writing Assignment

What I Want Most from School This Year

1. What I want most from school this year is . . .
2. It would be helpful to me in getting what I want most from school if . . .
3. The biggest problem I expect to have in getting what I want most from school is . . .
4. I might be able to overcome this problem if . . . or by . . .
5. Some places I might go for help include . . .
6. I really believe I can get what I want from school if . . .

Information coming from responses to this question can provide insight into how to support students' learning. This open-ended question allows for discussion of a wide range of topics that may include peer relationships or support, approaches to learning, teacher–student interaction, broader issues within the school such as scheduling problems or preferences, or concerns outside of school. You will need to sort through the responses to identify those unique to individuals and those common within the group. You will need to decide which issues to incorporate in planning and which are beyond the scope of the classroom. Some issues may be shared with parents when deemed appropriate.

The third question on Table 4.1 is more direct in asking the student to disclose anticipated problems in attaining what is desired from school. Responses to this question can reveal prior experiences with school. Students' perceptions of anticipated problems should be taken seriously regardless of how they may appear to you. Many students may have had experiences with teachers and peers in school that you find unimaginable. However, their experiences are valid. Like most people, they learn what to expect in the world from their lived experiences. Teachers can do grave harm to students by disregarding their concerns, experiences, and perceptions.

Question 4 on Table 4.1 asks the student to think about possible ways to overcome whatever problems he or she has identified. Some students will view themselves as having the power to solve problems and will identify options and alternatives. Others may view themselves as powerless to control or influence the situation. These perceptions should be examined carefully. In many instances, students have experienced conditions where adults assume all the authority and power, and consequently, they have had little practice in identifying options and alternatives for solving problems and will need support and direction from the teacher in this area.

Question 5 on Table 4.1 asks the student to examine resources within the school, home, or community and determine which are most appropriate in helping to attain desired outcomes. Some students may be able to identify appropriate resources quickly. Others will need to be asked probe questions to facilitate their thinking in this area. Some students limit their desired learning outcomes to what they already know and can do, and do not seek help from others. These students need to be encouraged to utilize the resources around them. It takes time for some students to become comfortable with collaborative learning. Some students might feel quite comfortable talking with another individual who is working on the same or a similar task or in seeking assistance from the librarian or another adult resource person in locating information. In some instances students are hesitant because they have not learned to verbalize their needs or feel they have not learned how to ask appropriate questions for getting the information they need.

Question 6 puts the locus of control directly with the student, by asking each student to look within him or herself to determine what action he or she can take to ensure achievement of the desired outcomes from school. Some students will find this question difficult to answer, particularly those who view the locus of control as external from themselves. These students might need a great deal of assistance in examining options and alternatives for their own action.

Although there are other ways to approach data collection on students' expectations and desires, a questionnaire such as this, presented as an assignment, has several advantages: (a) students tend to find it less threatening than some other approaches; (b) students are not likely to interpret it as an intrusion into their private thoughts; (c) students can take time for reflection; (d) you will find it less time-consuming and more convenient to conduct than individual interviews or case studies; and (e) you can easily file the data in each student's portfolio.

The analysis of the data collected using the questions in Table 4.1 should be part of the individual student's profile as well as a profile for the class as a whole. Individual student profiles are helpful in supporting learning for particular students. A profile of the class is helpful in planning collaborative learning experiences and whole-class activities.

Interview Questions – In cases where you want to initiate personal contact and build relationships with students individually or where students' literacy skills are not well developed, it might be more appropriate to conduct personal interviews. The questions in Table 4.1 can be modified slightly and used in personal interviews with students. In personal interviews, the questions may be less formal. For example, the first question might be changed to, "Tell me what you most want from school this year." A tape recording of the interview can be used to support notetaking. However, parental permission is required and the ethical procedures discussed earlier in this chapter must be followed. In an interview, notetaking should not interrupt the flow of the conversation. The student needs to feel comfortable talking to the interviewer rather than feeling studied or examined. Personal interviews provide numerous advantages. For example, personal contact with the students allows you to make general observations about such things as how comfortable the student is or the student's verbal ability. Students who have difficulty writing their responses may be better able to express their ideas verbally or ask for clarification about items and issues. Some students may take a personal interview more seriously than a written questionnaire.

Personal Experiences in School – Children within the same school have very different experiences and perceive the school differently. Most students have a combination of positive and negative experiences. You can build on both types of prior school experiences to create a more supportive learning environment for students.

A school or a classroom that provides positive experiences for one child may provide negative ones for another child. Students may have positive or negative experiences academically or socially, or in both areas. Some students may have negative experiences with specific content, or with both content and social interaction within a particular classroom or the school in general. Students may not have acquired the knowledge or skill necessary to succeed with certain academic content. Students may not have acquired the social skills necessary for positive interaction with peers and teachers or they may be rejected because of their physical appearance, poor hygiene, or a personality quirk.

Some of the experiences students have in school may be related to their status in the local community. For example, students whose parents are prominent personalities in the local community due to political affiliation or personal wealth may hold a privileged status in the school context. Other students may have negative experiences due to their economic, ethnic, or social status in the local community. That is, some students experience privileged or discriminatory treatment from their teachers and peers based on their status relative to the Euro-American community. Negative experiences are real and very often painful regardless of the source.

As a teacher, you have a major responsibility to make every effort to create a comfortable learning environment for every student. Table 4.2 provides examples of items teachers can use to learn about their students' personal experiences in school. Recalling your own experiences in elementary and secondary school is likely to bring forth both positive and negative memories. Your memories can be helpful to you in understanding the experiences some students have had. Although you cannot change your students' past negative experiences, you can use what they share with you to create a more comfortable and supportive environment in your classroom. For example, students who have felt isolated or alone can be supported in developing meaningful relationships with others through collaboration on projects where common interests are shared.

The questions in Table 4.2 are open-ended and allow the students to choose their responses from among their many and varied experiences in school. The first item asks students to reflect on past experiences with school and to describe what immediately comes to mind. This provides a wide range of possibilities. Some students may give short or superficial

Table 4.2 Items Teachers Use to Learn about Students' Personal School Experiences

When I Think about School

1. When I think about school my first thoughts are about . . .
2. My most memorable experiences in school are . . .
3. What I like most about my present school is . . .
4. My most painful or disappointing experience in school was . . .
5. My favorite subject is . . . because . . .
6. The kind of teacher I like most is one who . . .

responses requiring probe questions to help clarify and develop their statements.

The second item in Table 4.2 is a deliberate rewording of the first item. The second item is intentionally more direct in soliciting a positive experience. Students who have described unusually painful experiences in responding to the first item may have an opportunity to recover. Those for whom school has been an unusually traumatic experience might respond to both items with negative thoughts. In this case, the third item is even more direct in soliciting a positive experience. Even this item may not elicit positive thoughts about school from some students. Should this happen, the student's response should be accepted as a valid perception of his or her experiences.

The fourth item on the questionnaire in Table 4.2 solicits the most painful or disappointing experiences each student has had at school. You should not be surprised if some of these experiences involve other teachers in situations that are unimaginable. It is important to keep in mind the fact that different individuals interpret situations differently. Questioning the validity of a student's perception is not an appropriate response at this time. The student's interpretation is of the utmost value in this data-gathering process. The goal is to compile data that will provide insights for developing a positive and supportive learning environment for students.

The fifth item in Table 4.2 is the first that directly addresses classroom instruction. The previous questions may elicit instructionally related responses, but are more likely to elicit responses related to social inter-actions. The fifth item asks the student to identify a favorite subject and to explain why it is a favorite. In this case, the student is likely to reveal something of his or her own learning preferences, particular skills or deficiencies, values, or other vital information directly related to teaching and learning.

The final item in Table 4.2 solicits information from the student about his or her response to teacher behavior. Again, the open-ended question is likely to elicit a wide range of responses. Students may respond by describing social interactions or their personal relationships with their favorite teachers. They may describe particular teaching strategies, personal demeanor in the classroom, classroom atmosphere, or other features of the teachers' approach to instruction.

Personal Experiences Outside School – Among those experiences students have outside school, which are most important for teachers to understand and relate to when planning classroom instruction? Which experiences and responses reveal important information about students' values, practices, and perceptions?

Table 4.3 presents open-ended items that allow students to give responses that reveal their choices, values, and perceptions about their world outside school. The first item in Table 4.3 asks the student to identify what he or she enjoys the most outside of school, and why. The student can describe anything that fits, whether it is travel, reading a book, cooking, or being with a special person. In asking probe questions, care should be taken not to give examples. Instead, you might want to say something like: "I know there is something you really enjoy doing when you are not at school or doing homework. What is that?" You can then leave the student thinking about his or her own experiences.

The second item is more directive in using the word "with," which to some students will suggest spending time "with" a particular person or group. In asking probe questions you should not over emphasize the inclusion of a person. For example, you might ask: "With what or whom do you spend most of your time when you are not in school?" Some students may not include a person in their response. This is acceptable because it gives information about the student. Some students spend a great deal of time alone and have learned to be independent and self-reliant. Thus, they may feel hesitant or uncomfortable working in groups. These students need experience working with others in dyads or triads on small tasks before being placed in "cooperative groups."

Table 4.3 Open-Ended Items That Allow Students to Reveal Feelings About the World Outside of School

When I Am Not at School

1. When I am not at school what I enjoy the most is . . . because . . .
2. When I am not in school I spend most of my time with . . . because . . .
3. Of *all* the people I know, the one person I admire the most is . . . because . . .
4. If I could have just one wish granted, I would wish for . . . because . . .
5. If I could live any place in the world I would choose . . . because . . .

The third item asks the student to reflect on all of the people he or she knows and identify the one person who is admired the most. A probe question to get students started can be something like: "Can you think of someone you believe is a genuinely good person? Can you think of someone you believe has some very good qualities? Who is the person and what are those good qualities?" These types of questions help students go beyond the superficial, provided they have the capacity to do so. Some students may have learned to examine only surface qualities such as beauty or wealth. The teacher can build on these values in constructing meaningful learning experiences. The teacher can also help students develop and add substance to their value perspectives.

The fourth item in Table 4.3 solicits responses that will reveal information about a student's value system and, perhaps, his or her stage of moral development. Those students who have attained an advanced stage of moral development may wish for those things that improve the quality of life for humanity or an individual who is suffering in some way that has not yet been resolved. They may wish for personal empowerment to resolve complex issues involving other people. Some students' responses may be more self-centered, personally indulgent, and superficial. For example, some students may wish for $1 million so they can do anything they want. When asked to describe what they would do with the money, their responses might be limited to the purchase of material things and travel for personal pleasure. These students should not be condemned for their responses because they have learned well what is presented in a materialistic society. The teacher should make special efforts to expand the students' thinking to include such ideas as acting responsibly to preserve and improve the quality of life on the planet.

The final item is intended to elicit responses related to how students view themselves in relationship to a larger world. Some students will identify a place more preferable than where they presently live. They may present an idealized view of this highly desirable place. This information reveals what the student might believe is missing from his or her present life situation. Some students will choose to remain in their present location because it is all they know. They express the need for security and stability. Both cases present information for the teacher to use in planning instruction and creating a comfortable and supportive context for learning.

In this section of the chapter we have explored the idea that students are the primary source for information about teaching and learning. Three categories of information that may be solicited from students have been examined: expectations, personal experiences in school, and personal experiences outside of school. This information is essential to teachers in creating or selecting meaningful learning experiences for their students, especially those from underserved populations. Much of the traditional instruction makes assumptions about students' experiences and perceptions that are not valid for those from different ethnic groups. You cannot learn all there is to know about every cultural group. However, learning to collect information and use it strategically will increase the likelihood that you will succeed in a culturally diverse classroom setting.

Parents as a Key Source

Parents are not only a child's first teacher, they serve as permanent guides throughout childhood and frequently serve as resource advisors into young adulthood. Ogbu (1985) pointed out that parents prepare their children for the world as they experience it. That is, much of how students come to view the world is taken from their parents' experiences. Most teachers would agree that students are more likely to succeed in school if their parents are knowledgeable, participate, and provide support. Often parental apathy is blamed for the failure of large numbers of students from particular ethnic groups. Some teachers believe many African American and Mexican American parents are not interested in their children's school work. These beliefs are not supported by real evidence. Many teachers do not understand how to involve parents in the schooling process nor do they understand or accept parents as a resource to inform planning for teaching and learning.

As a teacher, you need to identify ways to encourage parental participation and help parents feel comfortable in the school setting. An important way to include parents is to help them feel that the knowledge they have acquired over time about their particular child is valid and useful to you. Parents with limited education, limited verbal ability, or limited command of English should be helped to feel comfortable sharing their knowledge with you. At times this will mean providing an interpreter, translating questionnaires into the parents' first language, using tape recorders, conducting interviews or using whatever means are appropriate to solicit the necessary information from the parents. There will be times when it is most expedient to distribute a questionnaire at back-to-school night. When this happens, parents need to be allowed to take the questionnaire home and return it to the school office or the classroom teacher by a specific date. Parents will then have time to think about their responses or get the translation they need. Some parents may need the option of participating in an interview.

Parental Expectations – Parents have expectations for what their children should gain from school as well as reasons why they value certain information and skills over others. Parents and teachers do not necessarily have the same values relative to school learning. This is particularly true where cultural and ethnic differences exist between teachers and parents. The aim of this particular section of the chapter is not to try to bridge the gap between teacher and parental expectation, but rather to help the teacher gain specific information from parents that can be helpful in planning instruction.

The first item in Table 4.4 solicits from parents what they believe to be the student's educational needs. These will tend to be needs the parents feel the school should be able to meet. You will want to give very careful attention to the responses to this question because they can provide important information for many different aspects of teaching and learning. Parents may address needs in terms of students' academic weaknesses or ways to utilize a student's strengths to improve overall academic performance. Parents may identify psychological and social needs. For example, a student may experience serious conflict with peers due to more or less obvious factors. These factors may have to do with such things as language, personal appearance, hygiene, or idiosyncrasies of one kind or another. You may find it helpful to create specific learning situations that will facilitate acceptance or to work with the individual student to develop specific social skills. Telling a student to ignore the rude or inconsiderate behavior of his or her peers or blaming the victim does not help solve the problem. Students who create problems by acting rudely are exhibiting behavior that needs to be corrected, usually requiring something more than punishment. Correcting rude behavior requires the teacher's acceptance of the student, support, and instruction for correcting the behavior.

Parental Suggestions – The second item in Table 4.4 is an indirect request for parents' suggestions on how the teacher can help the student. What the parent suggests may be directly related to the needs described in the first item. Some suggestions may concern things as simple as clarity of homework or consistency of treatment in class. Parents may request additional support for a child in doing specific types of assignments.

Table 4.4 Parental Expectations of Students' Educational Needs

Parental Expectations

1. What . . . needs most from school this year is . . .
2. What I believe would be most helpful to . . . in school this year is . . .
3. The biggest school related problem I expect . . . to have this year is . . .
4. This problem can be avoided or solved by . . .
5. I really believe . . . will succeed in school this year if . . .

What parents suggest may not be under your control. In such cases, you must be candid in stating your desire to be helpful and in explaining your limitations. When appropriate, you might suggest agencies or individuals who are available to work with particular situations.

The third item in Table 4.4 allows the parents to describe the biggest school-related problem expected for their child, possibly revealing some history with the schooling process. Usually, this history relates directly to the child. At times, however, it can reflect the parents' personal experiences in going through school. In either case, you will need to give careful attention to the issues raised and determine their relationship to planning instruction. Problems anticipated by parents may be academic or social. Common problems may include the child neglecting to bring home his or her homework or not completing and returning it on time.

In the fourth item, the parents will propose some ways to avoid or solve the problems anticipated for their child. These solutions will reflect parental perceptions and values. Whatever is suggested should be treated seriously and politely. If the parents' culture is different from yours, their suggestions may appear strange. You must be careful not to communicate such reactions to parents. Your responses during conversations with parents can cause them to feel rejected and to withdraw their support for you. When parents feel they are not accepted they may appear to lack interest or concern for their children's education. One way to respond to unusual suggestions from parents is with questions related to the expected outcomes or about the feelings or responses of the child. You may also present an alternative and ask parents to respond to it.

The final item in Table 4.4 can reveal the faith parents have in their child's potential success and the school's ability to provide the needed education. If parents show little faith in the child and/or the school through a long history of failure, the teacher will have a great deal of work to do to engage parental support. Parents' lack of faith should not be taken personally. This type of parental response is natural when confronted with repeated failure. Parents should not be blamed or condemned for how they feel.

Soliciting Learning History from Parents – Parents have a history with their children that is not shared by classroom teachers. This history is vital to understanding students' responses to school and to learning in the classroom. Table 4.2 directly solicits from students information concerning their personal history with school. This information is from the student's perspective and is considered valid. A parental perspective might be quite different, yet equally valid.

Most parents have observed their children's learning from birth. Some have kept detailed records and samples of their children's work. Those who have not should be encouraged to do so. These files can be a good source of information for sharing with future teachers and can be used in planning learning experiences.

The first four items in Table 4.5 provide information about learning preferences that result from success or failure in school. You may be able to create more meaningful and effective learning experiences for an individual child by combining what parents report about successful school experiences and effective approaches used by other teachers. Teaching difficult skills through a student's favorite subject using familiar approaches may also enhance learning.

The last two items in Table 4.5 are more likely to be related to social interaction or the classroom context than the first four items. Children need to feel comfortable, safe, and supported in the classroom in order to do their best learning. Parents provide a source of information about how students feel in the classroom that may not be otherwise available to the teacher. This information can help you identify and correct whatever problems exist.

Data Analysis

The data you collect on students will be more useful when analyzed to reveal patterns that provide insights for planning instruction. One approach to analyzing the data from responses to the questions posed for interviews or written assignments is called selective data coding. Selective data coding in this instance means that the salient categories have been predetermined based on the questions posed to the students and parents and their value in planning meaningful instruction and creating a supportive social context for learning. Based on the questions posed, the data can be organized into five categories: (a) challenges that potentially interfere with success or comfort in school; (b) expectations for school

Table 4.5 Soliciting Students' Learning History from Parents

Parental Report of Student's History with School

1. . . . has been most successful in school when . . .

2. Learning in school has been most difficult for . . . when . . .

3. Teachers work best with . . . when they . . .

4. I believe . . .'s favorite subject is . . . because . . .

5. I believe . . .'s happiest time in school was when . . .

6. I believe . . .'s most disappointing time in school was when . . .

learning; (c) experiences within and outside of school that potentially influence learning; (d) preferences and values; and (e) relationships with peers and adults. These data are from three sources: students, parents, and the teacher. (See Table 4.6.) The responses from parents and students can be coded by identifying key words or phrases from their responses and placing each in one of the five categories. If you have been observing the students in class for several weeks you can code the data in your notes in the same way as the interview data. Once you have compiled the data for each student you have a good profile to support your work with the student. If you examine the data across several students or across all of the students in the class you can see patterns in their responses that will help you plan your work for the whole class.

If you are an elementary school teacher with a self-contained classroom, the procedures outlined here for data collection and analysis for individual students is much more manageable than if you teach high school where you have five or six different classes with a total of more than a hundred students. One approach to adapting the procedure in this situation is to present the questions to the students as an in-class written assignment. After the written assignment has been completed, organize the students into small groups where each group completes the student data chart. When compiled onto a single student data chart, this will give you a profile of the particular class. It will be important to collect all of the written responses and to more carefully analyze the responses from individual students who have faced serious challenges in their academic performance as indicated by their grades or diagnostic or standardized tests. These students may be uncomfortable sharing their concerns with the group and should not feel pressured to do so.

Once the data have been compiled and organized, they can be analyzed from different perspectives. For example, the challenges can be examined in subcategories related to situations within and outside of school, according to gender, relationships with adults or peers, and other factors. The other four categories in the student data chart can be analyzed in a

Table 4.6 Student Data Analysis Chart

Categories	Student	Parent	Teacher Observation
Challenges			
Expectations/Goals			
Experiences			
Preferences/Values			
Relationships			

similar way. This will help you focus your efforts in planning instruction and developing a supportive social context for learning in your classroom.

Chapter Summary

You cannot learn all you need to know about the students you will teach from university courses, but you can learn a process for acquiring, interpreting, and transforming knowledge about students for pedagogical practice. RIQ is a basic tool you can use to expand your knowledge and make sense of your students' complex and divergent experiences, and the social cultural milieu of the diverse students you will teach, in ways that support teaching and learning within and outside the classroom. The questioning format for RIQ is divided into seven categories that include:

1. Teacher beliefs about the students he or she teaches.
2. Teacher beliefs about instructional practices.
3. The social context of classroom instruction.
4. Students' ethnic and cultural backgrounds.
5. Understanding the community in which the students reside.
6. Understanding the students in relation to the larger societal context.
7. Students' personal and experiential backgrounds.

Data collection and analysis for RIQ is well organized and systematic. The basic instruments for data collection are the questions from the seven categories of the RIQ, teacher note-taking, and documents related to information on the local community and the society at large. The approach used in data collection and analysis is qualitative and involves you in the role of participant observer. The data collected on students are organized into five categories from three sources. The categories are challenges, expectations/goals, experiences, preferences/values, and relationships. The three data sources are students, parents, and the teacher.

The data-collection process described in this chapter should be an ongoing part of professional development for classroom teachers. It is not expected that all of the data will be collected immediately or simultaneously. Preservice teachers should begin the process to become familiar with the techniques involved and to understand the usefulness of the data collected.

Suggested Learning Experiences

1. Apply the RIQ process in developing a profile of students taking a class or at the grade level you will be teaching. It would be ideal to receive your student teaching assignment early enough to develop a profile of the students who will be in your particular class.

2. Develop a written analysis of your findings.
3. Re-examine your working definition of culture. Make revisions based on the new insights you have gained so far.

Critical Reading

Anyon, J. (1981). Social class and school knowledge. *Curriculum Inquiry*, 11(1), 3–42.

The author reports a case study of five elementary schools in contrasting social class settings in two school districts in New Jersey. She points out the similarities and differences in the curriculum provided.

Dillon, D. R. (1989). Showing them that I want them to learn and that I care about who they are: A microethnography of the social organization of a secondary low-track English-reading classroom. *American Educational Research Journal*, 26(2), 227–259.

The author reports on a case study in which a teacher's effectiveness with low-income students is determined by his ability to make instruction socially and culturally responsive.

Jordan, C. (1985). Translating culture: From ethnographic information to educational program. *Anthropology and Education Quarterly*, 16, 105–123.

The author describes how anthropological knowledge has been applied in the Kamehameha Elementary Education Program (KEEP), a successful language arts program for underachieving Native Hawaiian children.

Kowalski, T. J., Weaver, R. A., and Henson, K. T. (1990). *Case studies on teaching*. New York: Longman.

The authors present real cases of issues and needs faced by beginning teachers.

Polakow, V. (1985). Whose stories should we tell? A call to action. *Language Arts*, 62(8), 826–835.

The author provides vivid examples of insightful stories from children's lives.

Smyth, J. (1992). Teachers' work and the politics of reflection. *American Educational Research Journal*, 29(2), 267–300.

The author presents an insightful discussion of the process and content of teacher reflection that contributes to professional growth.

Wolcott, H. F. (1988). Ethnographic research in education. In R. M. Jaeger (ed.), *Complementary methods for research in education*. Washington, DC: American Educational Research Association.

The author provides a concise description of approaches to ethnographic study in education.

CHAPTER 5

Reframing the Curriculum

Focus Questions

1. How can the school curriculum validate, build on, and extend the life experiences of diverse learners?
2. How can a curriculum meet the particularistic needs of different groups within society and still provide a sense of national unity?
3. Is there an approach to curriculum development and organization that will meet the needs of a culturally diverse student population?

Introduction

The systematic data-gathering process recommended in Chapter 4 provides a basis for reframing curriculum for a specific population of students. To make curriculum meaningful, specific information is needed concerning students' knowledge, experiences, perceptions, and expectations; the expectations, perceptions, and desires of the students' parents or care-givers and significant others; the history and culture of the ethnic or cultural groups of which the students are members; the social, political, and economic climate of the community in which the students reside; and the status of their ethnic or cultural group within the local community as well as the larger society.

The purpose of this chapter is to present an approach to reframing the school curriculum for culturally diverse populations that is both inclusive and particularistic. The discussion in this chapter is focused on

85

characteristics of the existing school curriculum, characteristics of a meaningful curriculum for culturally diverse populations of students, an approach to organizing the curriculum for equitable access to learning, and an approach to curriculum validation.

A valid school curriculum includes both cultural knowledge and knowledge about culture. Cultural knowledge includes those understandings, values, and behaviors acquired in the socialization or enculturation process within the home-culture. Based on their experiences in the home and with caregivers, children have acquired a great deal of knowledge about the world. They have learned the language, behaviors, perceptions, and values appropriate within the home-culture from their families, friends, and other significant people in their lives. Meaningful school learning is directly linked to learning that is already in progress in ways that extend and build on the knowledge that has already been acquired as well as that being processed.

Knowledge about culture, on the other hand, includes the history, beliefs, customs, traditions, values, and accomplishments of a particular group and how others have benefited from the group's experiences. Valid knowledge about culture is accurate in representing perspectives and contextual factors influencing the values and practices of a particular cultural group.

A reliable curriculum consistently generates the desired outcomes. Because the inclusion of valid knowledge about culture and cultural knowledge for culturally diverse populations is often inconsistent within the existing school curriculum, learning outcomes are inconsistent as well.

The Existing School Curriculum

It is difficult to think about the elementary and secondary school curriculum without also thinking about the role of schools as agents of the society serving as conduits for prescribed norms for thought and behavior. The curriculum is in fact that package of knowledge, skills, and perspectives that prepares us to develop the attributes of thought and behavior that comply with the prescribed norms. The issue is not whether such norms exist, but what norms exist, promoted by whom, by what process, and to what end?

Curriculum as a Cultural Product

School curriculum is itself a cultural product. A particular cultural or ethnic group existing as part of a larger society, and that has retained sufficient power, is likely to develop a school curriculum that promotes its own (a) cultural values, practices, and perceptions; (b) psychological, social, economic, and political needs; and (c) elevated status within the larger society. There is usually an observable relationship between the school curriculum and the culture in power. Traditionally, the Euro-American middle-class culture is clearly observable as a pervasive force in the school curriculum. The emphasis on European settlement in North America, their world influence, and the marginalizing of other cultural and ethnic groups in the social studies curriculum is a good example of bias in perspective favoring Euro-American culture. Perhaps you can think of more specific examples from your own school experiences that include the distortion or exclusion of the history of specific cultural groups.

A research report by Cornbleth (1998) indicated that the traditional story of American history has been disrupted and replaced by three perspectives on American history: (a) America is an imperfect country with past mistakes and injustice, but is still the best country in the world; (b) the nation is multifaceted with partial and unconnected images that do not present a coherent story, leaving the impression that historical events and situations were chance occurrences; and (c) the nation is undergoing continuous change. However, at the outset of the report, Cornbleth acknowledged that "public schooling in the United States serves the purposes of Americanization and assimilation" (p. 622). She provides evidence to support this claim by pointing out that "all three of these teachers seemed to be encouraging, and students seemed for the most part accepting, identification with mainstream white America as if there were few if any significant social divisions" (p. 634). Additionally, it was found that more attention is given to individuals than to cultural, ethnic, or racial groups, or to gender and social class. Cornbleth argues that:

> Deflecting attention from group experiences and effects—and from critique generally—enables those who benefit from the status quo to sustain it. It also encourages those at the bottom to work within the system, reassuring them however falsely that they too can succeed if only they work hard enough. (p. 643)

The curriculum in urban, suburban, and rural schools with different populations of students tends to be similar and is established, maintained, and monitored by the prevailing cultural group. Students from different cultural and experiential backgrounds continue to be acculturated into the behaviors, values, perceptions, and practices of the culture in power. Students from white middle-class backgrounds find self-validation and develop a positive sense of appreciation for others like themselves. On the other hand, the curriculum fosters acculturation for youngsters from other cultural and ethnic backgrounds by encouraging them to accept Euro-American behaviors, values, perceptions, and practices as superior to those from their home-culture. In rejecting their home-culture in preference for the Euro-American culture, the children learn to reject themselves. This discontinuity between the home-culture and school learning ultimately disrupts the learning process for many children and the resulting failure may lead them to reject the Euro-American culture and school learning as well.

Dimensions of the Existing Curriculum

There are three dimensions to existing curriculum content: explicit, implicit (hidden), and null. The *explicit curriculum* is the content included in curriculum guides and textbooks available for visible inspection. The *implicit curriculum* consists of the beliefs and values taught through the curriculum that are not explicit and may not be obvious. The *null curriculum* refers to inferences made from omitted content.

The Explicit Curriculum

The explicit curriculum is that presented in state and school district standards, in textbooks, and on standardized tests administered in public schools. Traditionally, the explicit curriculum has been biased in content and perspective in favor of Euro-American culture (Cottrol, 1994/1995; Hilliard, 1991). This has been evident in the disparity in the test performance of Euro-American students when compared to those from certain ethnic minority groups. Multicultural education has been proposed as an approach that will provide more equitable access to learning for underserved students. Proponents of multicultural education such as Banks (1995), Bennett (2001), and Grant and Sleeter (1989) have identified approaches for including multiethnic and multicultural perspectives in the traditional explicit curriculum. Approaches to multicultural education address both research in the field and school practices.

Research in multicultural education is especially important because it helps teachers and administrators understand how to transform school practices to improve learning outcomes and the social context of schools for underserved students. Bennett (2001) developed a framework that organized research in multicultural education into four clusters: curriculum reform, equity pedagogy, multicultural competence, and societal equity. Each cluster is then subdivided into three genres. The four clusters are interrelated; however, our discussion is focused on the explicit curriculum which is directly related to the cluster on curriculum reform. The three genres identified for curriculum reform are historical inquiry, detecting bias in texts and instructional materials, and curriculum theory. In the genre on historical inquiry the author points out the need to rethink how history is presented; the need to incorporate multiple perspectives;

and to address issues related to race, ethnicity, culture, social class, and gender. Detecting bias in texts and instructional materials addresses issues of distortion and misrepresentation of historical events and situations in texts, omission of important information about the history and culture of those from diverse groups, and stereotyping of ethnic minority groups. The research on curriculum theory addresses concepts and principles, curriculum goals, rationale, models and recommendations for improvement. This body of research constitutes the knowledge base for curriculum reform for schooling in a culturally diverse society.

The five dimensions of multicultural education identified by Banks (1995) directly address transforming school practices, including the school curriculum. The five dimensions are: (a) content integration, (b) the knowledge construction process, (c) prejudice reduction, (d) equity pedagogy, and (e) an empowering school culture and social structure. Content integration refers to the approaches teachers use to incorporate cultural knowledge and knowledge about culture from diverse populations into the school curriculum. Knowledge construction refers to the approaches teachers use to engage students in the critical analysis of knowledge and the process of knowledge construction, the identification of assumptions underlying knowledge construction, and inquiry into the purposes for which knowledge is created and the specific interests served. Prejudice reduction is aimed at developing positive attitudes towards those from different cultural and experiential backgrounds, increasing awareness of personal and institutional racism, and supporting youngsters in developing a positive ethnic and racial identity. Equity pedagogy is an approach to contextualizing instruction for a particular population, in a particular setting, and learning under particular conditions by employing instructional strategies that incorporate aspects of their cultural and experiential backgrounds. An empowering school culture and social structure is one that embraces democratic principles and values, where the dignity and worth of every person and group are valued, where the purpose for learning is to improve the human condition, where learning is collaborative and reciprocal among all participants, and where shared responsibility is evident in daily practices. The purpose of these five dimensions of multicultural education is to transform schools and school practices to better serve all students, particularly those underserved by traditional school practices.

The Implicit Curriculum

The implicit or hidden curriculum is the subliminal transmission of the values, practices, and perceptions of the dominant culture that determine acceptable modes of communication, social interaction, ways of thinking and knowing, and ways of distributing power, status, and resources. The implicit curriculum can be divided into three categories of goals: (a) maintenance of the social class structure, (b) transmission of the dominant culture, and (c) cultural hegemony.

Maintenance of Social Class Structure – In a classic study, Anyon (1980) reported on the relationship of the implicit curriculum to the maintenance of social class status in an article titled "Social Class and the Hidden Curriculum of Work." Anyon described the working-class school as one in which assignments primarily consist of mechanical procedures with few options. Teachers do not routinely explain assignments, make connections between assignments, or explain underlying concepts, generalizations, laws, or principles. Textbooks are used irregularly. Teachers use dittoes and the chalkboard for presenting assignments. The children are instructed to follow the rules for completing assignments. Conforming to the procedure is more important than getting correct answers. Anyon's observations in classrooms led her to conclude that these children are being prepared for adult-level work that is mechanical and routine. They are not learning how to direct their own lives or to be decision makers. The children in this working-class school responded with resistance in the form of disruption and a lack of cooperation.

The middle-class schools in Anyon's study were found to be quite different from the working-class schools. Producing the right answer in doing assignments is the most important factor. Producing the right answer usually requires following the prescribed procedure; however, because it includes decision making, the children can exercise choice in identifying the steps to follow. Even written directions require deciphering to determine the steps to follow. Observations in the middle-class school led Anyon to conclude that children are being prepared for an adult life that requires functioning within a bureaucracy. These students are being prepared to handle paperwork, complete technical tasks, and interact with people in ways appropriate to positions in sales and social services.

In the third type of school described in Anyon's study, the affluent professional school, there are few rules and the children are encouraged to be creative and original. Individuality is encouraged. The emphasis is on learning to think and to express, expand, and illustrate ideas. Multiple forms of written expression are used. The children are guided in interpreting and making sense of the world. School work is evaluated on the basis of quality of design, accuracy in representing reality, quality of expression, and conceptualization of the task. Personal satisfaction may also be used as a criterion for evaluation. Anyon concluded that the children in the affluent professional school are acquiring the artistic, linguistic, and scientific skills needed to produce culture as represented in art, science, and other intellectual and creative endeavors.

In the fourth type of school described in Anyon's study, the executive elite school, children develop analytical intellectual powers through continuous exposure to opportunities for problem solving. The children learn to understand concepts, generalizations, principles, and rules that identify and describe relationships among and between ideas and phenomena. Children learn to analyze problems and apply principles and rules in identifying solutions.

Based on her description of executive elite schools, Anyon concluded:

> The executive elite school gives its children something that none of the other schools does: knowledge of and practice in manipulating the socially legitimated tools of analysis of systems. The children are given the opportunity to learn and to utilize the intellectually and socially prestigious grammatical, mathematical, and other vocabularies and rules by which elements are arranged. They are given the opportunity to use these skills in the analysis of society and in control situations. Such knowledge and skills are a most important kind of symbolic capital. They are necessary for control of a production system . . . Their schooling is helping them to develop the abilities necessary for ownership and control of physical capital and the means of production in society. (p. 89)

What Anyon's work shows is how the explicit curriculum may appear the same for all schools; however, the translation and implementation of the curriculum are altered in ways that maintain the social class structure within the society. A clear example of this can be readily observed in inner-city schools where the working-class curriculum is reduced even further and overt political and social behaviors within and outside the community lead to an even more restricted form of schooling.

How would you describe the elementary school you attended? Does your elementary school fit easily into one of Anyon's categories, or did you have a teacher whose practices fit one category and another who fit a different category?

Cultural Transmission – The approach to cultural transmission described by Freebody and Baker (1985) continues to be a goal of the implicit curriculum found in reading textbooks in elementary schools. These authors described the purpose and function of children's readers in the following way:

> Children's readers are designed to help teach the skills of reading. Because of their place in the educational enterprise, these books

inevitably perform two other related functions. First, they are the early harbingers of the culture of literacy. This is not merely a culture in which people can decode written language; it is also like an informal club or lodge with hidden stylistic signs, well-kept intellectual and social secrets, and obscure objects of reverence. For many children, this is a world in which they will always feel vaguely out of place, insecure, and perhaps inferior. They will see their more fortunate peers detect and soon actually produce the signs; learn, without ever having been explicitly taught, the ways of thinking; and display a genuine reverence for the objects with which they themselves can claim only an uncomfortable acquaintance. The second major function of children's readers is to present to the new school student a world which adults have officially sanctioned. This world is peopled by parents, kissable little girls, and energetic, gregarious boys. When the children in these books talk to other children and to adults, they are neither interrupted nor ignored: the dialogue is moderated, at grammatically convenient points, by an unobtrusive but omnipresent voice, and the children's utterances actually play a part in initiating activities. (p. 396)

The cultural transmission aspect of the implicit curriculum serves to reward members of the Euro-American culture and punishes those from other cultures who fail to assimilate quickly enough. The implicit curriculum can reinforce the notion of the superiority of one culture over another, reinforce stereotypes about ethnic groups, and encourage feelings of self-doubt and inferiority among students from different ethnic groups.

Cultural Hegemony – Roth (1984) described a third goal of the implicit school curriculum, cultural hegemony, found in reading textbooks in the elementary school. She described her findings in the following way:

Social/cultural control is tied directly to the structure of knowledge and symbols in schools and to the manner in which knowledge is presented in the schooling context. Schools, acting as agents for the culture, control the extent to which personal knowledge may enter into the public knowledge of school curriculum; they thus have a direct influence upon cultural continuity and change. In selecting what to teach and how it is to be taught and evaluated, schools reaffirm what the culture values as knowledge. This "valid" knowledge provides the "cultural capital" which works toward reestablishing pervading social groups. In school, as in society generally, this process of knowledge control may be consciously or unconsciously imposed and perpetuated. (p. 303)

Cultural hegemony involves the denial of the cultural knowledge valued by other cultures as well as the exclusion of valid knowledge about other cultures that gives them legitimacy. This prevents students outside the pervading culture from gaining a sense of personal and cultural identity and intergenerational continuity that gives them a sense of positioning in time and space. This can contribute to an absence of purpose and the inability to find meaning in school.

The Null Curriculum

The null curriculum is neither explicit nor implicit, but that content which by its omission influences the values, practices, and perceptions of the learners. Omitting the culture and history of a particular ethnic group can lead the reader to infer that its members have accomplished nothing of value. Omitting selected aspects of a particular ethnic group's history can promote biases and distortions. For example, a discussion of slavery that omits the form of resistance represented by Nat Turner presents a perception of Africans as passive and powerless, dependent on White abolitionists for their freedom. The absence of continuity in the history of many ethnic groups leaves the impression that their accomplishments are limited and less significant than those of European immigrants.

Curriculum for Culturally Diverse Populations

If we were to ask parents with school-aged children to explain the purpose of formal education, most would probably make some statement describing acquisition of the knowledge and skills most valued in the society. Thus, public school education is, for the most part, viewed as a conduit for the values, beliefs, and traditions of a society. Having successfully gone through the school system, an individual is expected to have acquired the appropriate behaviors and skills to function as a competent and productive adult in the society. In order to ensure that this is true for students from diverse cultural and experiential backgrounds, Stephens (2000) identified four elements of culturally responsive science curriculum: cultural relevance, best practices, standards-based, and assessment. When combined these four elements ensure that students from diverse cultural and experiential backgrounds have access to academic learning and culturally valued knowledge in the school curriculum.

A culturally responsive curriculum intended to develop academic competence, global awareness, and intercultural understanding must be simultaneously particularistic and inclusive. The particularistic aspect of the curriculum extends and validates the learner's culture and the learning already in progress. This aspect of the curriculum is omitted when the focus is on the common culture exclusively. The inclusive aspect of the curriculum addresses the common needs of all children in developing competencies for life within a highly technological and culturally diverse society and within a global community.

Particularistic Aspect

Children enter school with a repertoire of knowledge and skills acquired in the home-culture. This cultural knowledge provides children with a basis for making sense of the world within and outside of the home-culture. For some children, cultural knowledge is directly related to what will be learned in school, and for others there is virtually no relationship between the two. Where school learning builds on and extends what has been learned in the home-culture, children grow academically and do well in school. Where there is little or no relationship between knowledge acquired within and outside of school, learning is difficult and children are at risk for poor academic performance in school. Curriculum content should be appropriately linked to the home-culture of those taught so as to provide equitable schooling for all students. Examples of such linkages found in work done by Lipka and Moll are discussed at length in Chapter 7.

For young children, the particularistic aspect of the curriculum extends and validates the enculturation that is already in progress within the home-culture. For example, the child's home language is used as a basis for learning new communication skills. This personalizes learning and increases learning power by building on the familiar.

As the child matures, the particularistic aspect of the curriculum is formalized so that awareness of the home-culture is raised to the conscious level. For example, including expressions of meaning represented in traditions and artifacts from the child's culture helps the child better understand his or her own culture. This increases understanding of cultural influences on individual perception and behavior, improves the child's power of choice in personal decision making, and serves as preparation for understanding other cultures.

The particularistic aspect of the school curriculum provides for the unique needs of diverse populations by fostering (a) a strong sense of personal and group identity, (b) a balanced historical perspective, (c) a positive reality of ethnic group status, (d) a vision for the future, and (e) a desire for excellence in academic and intellectual preparation.

A Strong Sense of Personal and Group Identity – The curriculum should help students gain a positive identity as individuals. It should help each student develop a positive sense of who he or she is in relationship to others and confidence in his or her ability to maintain meaningful relationships. The curriculum should help each student develop a sense of self-worth and confidence in his or her ability to set and accomplish specific goals. The subject matter included in the curriculum should help students locate themselves within specific groups, including their own ethnic or cultural group.

A Balanced Historical Perspective – The school curriculum should provide students with a historical perspective that supports a sense of intergenerational continuity and pride in the accomplishments of their ancestors. McPhail (1987) captured this function in his statement that:

> Specifically, the reading of African and African-American history has enabled the voices of the past to speak to me personally, to call me by name, to ask me what I have done, what I am doing, and what I am prepared to do to ensure that the slaves and activists and martyrs did not dream and die in vain. (p. 9)

Students should be provided opportunities to examine the accomplishments and struggles of their foreparents in historical perspective and the influence of past generations on the present. Students need to understand the cultural knowledge that supported the political, social, economic, intellectual, and aesthetic accomplishments of their ancestors. They need opportunities to analyze the impact of the accomplishments of their foreparents locally as well as globally. The students should examine the interrelatedness of the struggles and accomplishments of their ancestors with those of other groups within the same society and in the larger world.

A Positive Reality of Ethnic Group Status – The school curriculum should provide students with a contemporary view that fosters a positive reality of their ethnic or cultural group's position within the society and the world socially, politically, and economically. Granted, the status of some ethnic groups in the United States is less than desirable; however, students should not be unduly burdened with negative realities to the point of hopelessness, distorted personal or group identity, or the loss of positive self-esteem. The curriculum should contain a balance of positive and negative trends in social, political, and economic gains and losses that foster hope for the future. Certainly, issues of racism and oppression need to be dealt with; however, perspective in presentation is very important. For example, a course in U.S. history may include information about the enslavement of Africans by European settlers without including the strategies employed by the slaves to resist captivity. This omission could lead students to perceive Africans as docile, lacking intelligence, and powerless, while perceiving Europeans as smart, confident, and powerful. African American youngsters exposed to such perceptions are at risk for negative responses such as a loss of self-esteem, distorted personal or group identity, active or passive resistance (loss of motivation might be an example of passive resistance), or peer problems.

Building a Vision for the Future – The school curriculum should provide students with a vision of the future that encourages hopefulness based on personal commitment to self-improvement, self-determination, and collaboration with others in determining and meeting personal and group goals and for assuming responsibility for active participation in bringing about positive change within the larger society. School knowledge must be linked with cultural knowledge in ways that validate significant aspects of what students from different ethnic groups value and have learned outside of school. For example, customs and traditions practiced outside of school can be placed in a positive historical context for a particular ethnic group. This brings authenticity and value to school knowledge. When the curriculum validates and extends what students learn outside of school it increases the likelihood that school will be viewed as a place for self-improvement. Self-determination is influenced by a personalized understanding of intergenerational continuity and the role of individuals in shaping their own future and life conditions, and in changing the course of history. Students from diverse ethnic groups need opportunities to work collaboratively in identifying probable solutions to societal problems. A sense of optimism is likely to result from students thinking and working collaboratively in areas of mutual concern and mutual benefit.

Academic and Intellectual Preparation – Students need to acquire the academic and intellectual preparation required for attaining personal and group goals, and for active participation in bringing about positive change within the larger society. Students need to acquire the knowledge and skills valued by their own culture as well as that valued by the society at large. Students need to acquire the knowledge and skills that will prepare them to become successful artists, intellectuals, legal authorities, scientists, technical experts, and members of other professions. Students need to acquire the level of communicative competence demanded at the most prestigious levels within the society. They need to understand the conceptual structure of the content knowledge provided in the school curriculum in ways that will allow them to manipulate and use it in practical and innovative ways to extend their own knowledge as consumers and to become producers of new knowledge. Students need to develop the intellectual skill necessary to analyze social, political, and economic systems.

Inclusive Aspect

This aspect of the curriculum addresses the common needs of all students. The particularistic aspect of the curriculum can be subsumed within the inclusive aspect. That is, the inclusive aspect of the curriculum can permit the learner to formalize understanding of his or her own cultural heritage, identify and acknowledge those characteristics of culture that are shared among the diverse groups that make up the United States, and gain understanding and appreciation for the uniqueness of the diverse cultures that comprise the society and heritage of the nation. The inclusive aspect of the school curriculum relates to developing the understandings and knowledge necessary for promoting national unity, improving the quality of life for all human beings, and for maintaining and improving the condition of the environment. The inclusive curriculum presents societal issues and problems in approachable and solvable ways; however, the students' work must be sorting through existing information and consulting with peers and authorities to identify options and alternatives for addressing societal issues and problems. The collective experiences of the past serve as resources that inform the present and the future.

The school curriculum should be designed to help all students acquire the competencies necessary for:

1. Finding meaning and purpose in their own lives and in the lives of other human beings.
2. Finding ways to reflect on, interpret, describe, and express the impressions, experiences, and meanings acquired through living.
3. Establishing familial and social bonds and connections that are intergenerational and between diverse peoples within the society and the world.
4. Identifying ways to improve the quality of life within this society and the world that include addressing human and societal problems, issues and concerns, and solving problems affecting the environment.

The curriculum can be organized in a way that supports all students in developing these necessary competencies that are both inclusive and particularistic.

A Framework for Organizing Curriculum for Equitable Access to Learning

The reauthorization of the Elementary and Secondary Education Act (ESEA) in 2002 initiated what is referred to as No Child Left Behind

(NCLB) with an overriding emphasis on accountability, testing, sanctions, rewards, and public school choice. A primary goal of NCLB is to reduce the achievement gap between white middle-class students and their traditionally underserved counterparts from low-income and ethnic minority groups. The mandatory testing of students required by NCLB to monitor progress towards this goal and the potential sanctions for schools that fail to meet goals for annual yearly progress has left teachers and administrators struggling to find ways to improve students' performance on standardized tests. What has resulted too often is teaching to the test and rote learning of decontextualized and disconnected concepts and skills that do not adequately support subsequent learning. In some cases test scores are temporarily elevated, but we see low scores for these same groups of students as they advance through the grade levels in school. Students need a well-designed and integrated curriculum in order to acquire knowledge and skills that will support subsequent learning.

An integrated curriculum provides important advantages for equitable access to learning. For example, inclusive and particularistic aspects can be combined in the organizational structure of the curriculum by making the central purpose explicit. This can occur in instances such as when the central purpose of the curriculum is improving the quality of life and issues related to individuals, ethnic groups, local communities, the nation, and the world are interrelated. When the curriculum is integrated across disciplines, students are better able to draw upon prior knowledge, learning preferences, and multiple resources to acquire new knowledge. The curriculum can be framed to allow students to utilize knowledge and skills that are well developed in one subject area to support development in another subject area.

The curriculum can be divided into two domains with three intersecting strands. The two domains, *descriptive* and *expressive*, are mutually supportive ways of understanding, or interpreting, and representing ideas in each of the three strands. The three intersecting strands (psychological, sociological, and health and environmental) comprise a content structure revealing patterns of reciprocal influences on how we understand and improve the quality of human life (see Figure 5.1).

This content structure helps students understand how individuals and groups participate in life processes, how they are influenced by changing situations and circumstances, and how physical and environmental conditions are affected by human actions.

Curriculum Domains

The focus of the *descriptive domain* is explanations and responses to issues, questions, and problems concerning life conditions and situations and

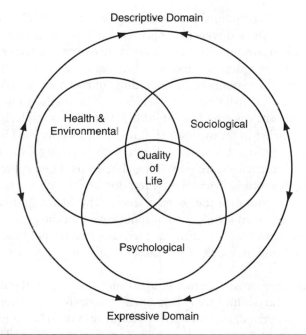

Figure 5.1 Reorganizing the Curriculum. The curriculum can be organized into two domains and three intersecting strands that support equitable access to purposeful learning for students with a variety of strengths and preferences.

living and non-living phenomena of the past, present, and future. Practices within the descriptive domain emphasize accuracy in quantitative data gathering, hypothesis formation, experimentation, and systematic documentation in ways that can be validated and replicated by others who have acquired the necessary craft tools and have access to the necessary information. The compilation and analysis of information collected for the United States census is an example of this type of data gathering. The primary goal of the descriptive artist is to increase understanding of phenomena within the universe and to preserve, protect, and improve the quality of all existing life. The descriptive artist usually prefers empirical–analytical means to study, document, invent, and describe phenomena, relationships among phenomena, conditions, situations, and events. Descriptive artists have traditionally been referred to as scientists because of the quantitative (empirical and analytical) qualities of the content and approaches apparent in their investigation and documentation.

The belief in pure objectivity in the descriptive arts is a myth. There is an apparent use of qualitative, creative, and intuitive approaches to describe phenomena, to identify problems and issues, and to invent responses and solutions. Descriptive artists bring to their work their own biases in values, perceptions, and points of view. They are also influenced by their peers, values of the larger society, and political and economic sanctions and constraints. Bias in the descriptive arts can frame or determine priorities, the questions and issues addressed, and the techniques or approaches used in responding and in finding solutions. Personal values and perceptions derived from culture, socialization, and education influence decisions about the value and use of information. For example, individuals with a strong belief in creationism tend not to be as interested in research supporting evolution. Likewise, societies with a strong Christian ethic would tend to restrict research involving aborted fetal tissue, even if it has obvious implications for revealing cures for serious diseases. A similar example can be found in the social sciences. The issues studied and the information presented are likely to benefit those with the greatest political and economic power. Individuals and groups lacking political and economic power find it much more difficult to bring their issues to the forefront.

The disciplines or subject matter areas included within the descriptive domain of the curriculum are referred to as descriptive arts. Those areas of the traditional curriculum that fit most readily into the descriptive domain include science, mathematics, history and the social sciences. These areas of the curriculum present formal and procedural knowledge derived from empirical sources that can be quantified or verified.

The *expressive domain*, like the descriptive domain, is concerned with explanations and responses to issues, questions, and problems concerning life and living and non-living phenomena of the past, present, and future. Practices within the expressive domain are aimed at capturing or interpreting, communicating, or representing personal or group ideas, perceptions, or responses to phenomena, events, circumstances, and situations that may be depicted as real or imagined, spiritual or carnal.

Practices in the expressive arts are intentionally subjective, although they tend to address the same issues, problems, and questions examined in less personalized ways in the descriptive arts. The subjectivity found in the expressive arts captures a wide range of human emotion, perception, and values that are important in understanding how people live and make sense of their world, as well as the spiritual world.

The disciplines or subject matter areas included within the expressive domain of the curriculum are referred to as expressive arts. Those areas of the traditional curriculum that fit most readily into the expressive domain include the visual and performing arts, philosophy, and literature. These subject-matter areas of the curriculum present informal and impressionistic knowledge intentionally derived from intuitive, subjective, and qualitative sources and procedures. The boundaries for the expressive arts are not absolute. Subject matter in the expressive arts may be derived from empirical–analytical sources as well. The work of expressive artists can be very valuable to descriptive artists. For example, literary forms such as novels and short stories may serve as primary sources for historical documentation and may provide important information about the use of living things or other natural phenomena useful in science.

The intersection of the descriptive and expressive domains of the curriculum is a source for creativity, discovery, invention, problem solving, and critical thinking (see Figure 5.2). None of these processes is exclusive to one curriculum domain. For example, if students are to solve real problems, identify new ways of thinking about phenomena, or produce new products for technological use, they must call on and combine different ways of understanding, or interpreting, and representing ideas. They must learn to employ informal, intuitive, and impressionistic ways of knowing and understanding as well as the formal, empirical–analytical, and procedural. When combined, these approaches to understanding and knowing increase the possibilities for developing new ideas.

The curriculum may reflect a balanced or unbalanced polarity within the field constituted by the two domains. That is, the curriculum may be designed or interpreted in ways that give more emphasis or value to one domain over another, without the benefit of the mutuality of these ways of

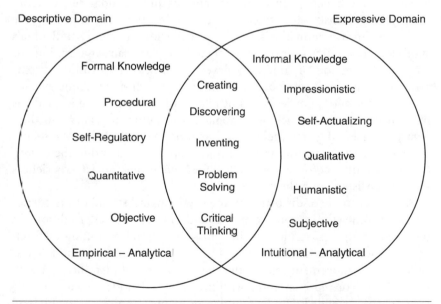

Figure 5.2 Curriculum Domains. The intersection of the two curriculum domains represents a potentially complex state of knowing and understanding that supports constructing new knowledge.

understanding and representing knowledge. This can lead to a situation where those with a predisposition to one domain are advantaged and those not predisposed to the domain being emphasized are disadvantaged. A balanced curriculum polarity provides for the development of students' intellectual abilities in both domains. An imbalanced curriculum may produce in students a sort of monocular vision that limits their ability to understand and represent ideas. Students from a particular cultural group may have been socialized in a way that gives preference to one domain over another.

Curriculum Strands

The curriculum can be divided into three strands that are directly related to understanding and improving the quality of life for all of humanity. These curriculum strands include: (a) psychological aspects that deal with personalized meanings related to personal and group identity, self-concept, perception, behavior, and belief systems that influence the quality of life for individuals; (b) sociological aspects that deal with cultural, historical, political, and social issues that influence the quality of life for groups of people; and (c) health and environmental issues with a potential physiological impact on the quality of life on earth (see Figure 5.3).

The psychological strand of the curriculum influences perceptions and attitudes towards personal and group identity, self-concept, social behaviors, and belief systems. The perceptions and attitudes derived from the psychological strand of the curriculum have a potential impact on the quality of life for individuals within and outside of school. Individuals subjected to a curriculum that is devoid of personalized meaning for an extended period of time may develop a lack of motivation, display poor academic performance, draw negative conclusions about self, or decide that school knowledge is not related to real life. Some individuals who encounter an absence of personalized meaning may abandon their own personal and group identity and assume that reflected in the school curriculum. Students from visible ethnic groups who abandon their identity may become confused or disillusioned when their social experiences are not consistent with their expectations.

A good example of distortion in the psychological strand of the curriculum for some ethnic groups can be found in social studies. Traditionally, the social studies curriculum is thought of as a spiral beginning with self and expanding to a more global world. For Euro-American middle-class children, this movement reflects their experiences and identification with U.S. culture. The representation of family in second grade does not usually include the extended family familiar to many ethnic-group children, but rather the nuclear family representative of Euro-American values and

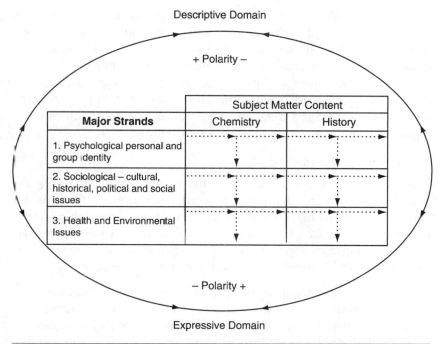

Figure 5.3 Interdisciplinary Curriculum. The two domains and three strands can be used to integrate the curriculum across disciplines.

practices. Fourth and fifth graders are particularly at risk. State history in Grade 4 is usually dominated by the exploration and settlement of an area by European immigrants with little attention given to the history and culture of indigenous people. The history of the United States as presented in Grade 5 is an ethnic history of the relocation, settlement, and creation of a new homeland for European immigrants. An updated multicultural history of the United States usually continues the traditional perspective but acknowledges the presence of non-European groups in a very cursory fashion. The omission of significant and relevant information about different cultural and ethnic groups is part of the null curriculum. In this instance, the null curriculum has a very negative effect on particular ethnic groups. Individuals in these populations become faceless and unable to find themselves in time, space, and location.

The *sociological strand* of the curriculum dealing with cultural, historical, political, and social issues is concerned with relationships within, between, and among groups of people that influence the quality of human life. These relationships are influenced by the distribution of power and wealth, patterns of social organization or stratification, cultural beliefs and values, technological advancement, political events and situations, history, and geography. The *health and environmental strand* of the curriculum is concerned with the physiological well-being of individuals, environmental conditions such as air and water pollution, scientific and technological advances, and natural phenomena that influence the quality of human life. In this case, the quality of life is influenced by physiological conditions derived from genetic and environmental sources affecting longevity, and the use of scientific and technological advances to support and extend a high quality of life physically and environmentally.

Interdisciplinary Curriculum

The foregoing discussion points out the importance of balancing the domains of the curriculum and the interrelatedness of the domains and strands. Balancing the curriculum can be done through an interdisciplinary approach. This approach relies heavily on your knowledge of specific subject matter. Shulman (1987) pointed out the critical importance of teachers' knowledge of subject matter and its structure:

> The teacher has special responsibilities in relation to content knowledge, serving as the primary source of student understanding of subject matter. The manner in which that understanding is communicated conveys to students what is essential about a subject and what is peripheral. In the face of student diversity, the teacher must have a flexible and multifaceted comprehension, adequate to impart alternative explanations of the same concepts or principles. The teacher also communicates, whether consciously or not, ideas about the ways in which "truth" is determined in a field and a set of attitudes and values that markedly influence student understanding. This responsibility places special demands on the teacher's own depth of understanding of structures of the subject matter, as well as on the teacher's attitudes toward and enthusiasms for what is being taught and learned. (p. 9)

In the present organizational structure of the school curriculum, subject matter for course content is derived from particular disciplines. Each discipline, in a broad sense, is comprised of principles, theories, laws, a conceptual structure, and procedures for inquiry that govern how knowledge is generated, validated, or invalidated. For example, the themes that form the conceptual structure for social studies include interdependence, change, culture, scarcity, and conflict. If you reflect on your study of U.S. history, you will recall a heavy emphasis on conflict, change, and scarcity. Here these themes are in the descriptive domain; however, they can be addressed in other subject-matter areas such as literature and music in the expressive domain in ways that directly relate to the study of

U.S. history. Each of these themes can be addressed in the three strands of the curriculum as well. You can use your knowledge of a particular discipline to begin to reorganize the curriculum into the two domains and three strands. It will be easier for you to integrate the curriculum across disciplines if you work with colleagues who have comprehensive knowledge of the structure of other disciplines.

Curriculum Validation

It was pointed out in the first part of this chapter that a valid curriculum contains both cultural knowledge and knowledge about culture. The reliability of the curriculum is directly related to the consistency with which both types of knowledge are included. A reliable curriculum consistently generates the desired outcomes and can be partially evaluated by examining student performance. One approach to curriculum validation is that of determining the extent to which it meets pre-established criteria. The following questions can be used to partially validate a curriculum for appropriateness to meet the needs of culturally diverse populations.

1. How does the content address the particularistic aspects of the curriculum?
   A. How does the content provide a positive historical perspective for the related accomplishments, values, and beliefs of a culturally diverse population?
   B. How does the content reflect the accomplishments of different ethnic groups in developing new knowledge in the field?
   C. Does the content allow for the use of cultural knowledge as well as knowledge about culture where possible or appropriate?
   D. How does the curriculum address the expectations and aspirations of the students and their caregivers?
2. How does the content address the inclusive aspect of the curriculum?
   A. Does the curriculum content promote a sense of interdependence, harmony, and national unity?
   B. How does the content help students find meaning in their own lives and in the lives of other human beings?
   C. How does the content help students learn to describe or interpret and express meaning acquired through their own experiences— real, vicarious, or imagined—as well as those of others?
   D. How does the content help students identify ways to improve the quality of life within this society and the world?
3. How does the subject-matter content provide a balanced polarity between the two curriculum domains?

    A. Are both the descriptive and expressive domains used for constructing new knowledge or making sense of what already exists?

    B. Do students use both quantitative and qualitative means of inquiry?

4. Are the three curriculum strands integrated into the subject-matter content?

    A. How is the subject-matter content related to the students personally?

    B. How do the issues addressed in the subject matter relate to or affect different groups within the society?

    C. What issues are addressed in the subject-matter content that relate to the health of individuals and groups of people?

5. Is the subject matter organized in a way that helps students understand the interrelatedness of the structure and major ideas across different disciplines?

Chapter Summary

This chapter focused on reframing the curriculum by comparing and contrasting the existing curriculum with one that might better serve the needs of culturally diverse populations. A framework for curriculum organization and validation was presented.

The existing curriculum was described as a cultural product of Euro-American origin with three dimensions: explicit (written in curriculum guides or appearing in textbooks), implicit (subliminal transmission of values, practices, and perceptions), and null (inferential transmission of values, practices, and perceptions by omission or selective inclusion).

A curriculum that might better serve culturally diverse populations was described as having two aspects, particularistic and inclusive. The particularistic aspect of the curriculum extends and validates the learner's culture and the learning already in progress. The inclusive aspect of the curriculum addresses the common needs of all students.

The approach to organizing the curriculum for equitable access to learning presented in this chapter included two domains (descriptive and expressive), three strands (psychological, sociological, and health and environmental), and a strategy for integrating the curriculum across disciplines.

The approach to curriculum validation in this chapter presented questions related to the particularistic and inclusive aspects of the curriculum, balanced polarity of the two curriculum domains, the inclusion of the three curriculum strands, and the integration of the curriculum across disciplines.

Suggested Learning Experiences

1. Examine a teaching unit to determine the extent to which it incorporates the suggestions included in this chapter for reframing the curriculum for culturally diverse populations.
2. Try to locate a prototype that meets the criteria established in this chapter for a curriculum for culturally diverse populations. Use the curriculum validation questions in this chapter to establish the validity of the prototype you have identified.
3. Examine a regularly used public school curriculum guide or textbook to determine the goals of the implicit curriculum.
4. Review examples of teaching units and curriculum guides to determine the definition of culture employed. To what extent is the definition of culture employed in these materials consistent with the one you have constructed at this point?

Critical Reading

Anyon, J. (1980). Social class and the hidden curriculum of work. *Journal of Education*, 162(1), 67–92.
This article reports a study describing the hidden curriculum of schools at four different social class levels.

Banks, J. A. (1995). Multicultural education and curriculum transformation. *Journal of Negro Education*, 64(4), 390–400.
The author describes five dimensions of multicultural education.

Bennett, C. (2001). Genres of research in multicultural education. *Review of Educational Research*, 71(2), 171–217.
The author presents a framework that organized research in multicultural education into four clusters.

Cornbleth, C. (1998). An American curriculum? *Teachers College Record*, 99(4), 622–646.
The author describes three perspectives of America presented in teaching history in the classrooms where she conducted observations.

Freebody, P., and Baker, C. D. (1985). Children's first schoolbooks: Introduction to the culture of literacy. *Harvard Educational Review*, 55(4), 381–398.
This article presents an analysis of the hidden curriculum contained in reading textbooks in the elementary school.

CHAPTER 6

Redesigning Instruction

Focus Questions

1. What factors contribute to meaningful school learning for students from specific cultural and ethnic backgrounds?
2. How can a teacher provide appropriate instruction for every student in a multicultural classroom setting?
3. How much responsibility can students assume for their own learning and under what conditions?

Introduction

This chapter builds on the content from previous chapters to identify learning experiences for underserved populations of students that are more meaningful and productive than those found in traditional classrooms. The high rate of academic failure experienced by students from specific ethnic groups when compared to others suggests that school practices do not make learning equally accessible, meaningful, or productive for all ethnic groups. Disparities in the effects of school practices are evident in the discrepancies among ethnic groups in high school dropout rates, performance on standardized tests, and variations in grade point averages. For example, the National Center for Educational Statistics (*Mini-Digest of Educational Statistics,* 1994) reported the percent of high school dropouts among persons of 16 to 24 years of age to include 27.5 percent Hispanic origin, 13.6 percent Black (non-Hispanic), and 7.9

percent White (non-Hispanic). A 1995 report from the same agency reveals that Black, Hispanics, and American Indian students exhibited lower average achievement test scores in science and mathematics than White and Asian students. Certainly, there is variation within ethnic groups on all measures of school performance. This within-group variance may be viewed as individual differences; however, it is difficult to apply this explanation to patterns of variation between ethnic groups.

Explanations for poor academic performance have influenced changes in school practices for identified populations of students. The discussion in this chapter examines the relationship among explanations for group variance in school performance, the rationale provided, and the interventions recommended. The discussion in this chapter also examines essential practices in designing meaningful and productive learning experiences for students from different cultural and ethnic backgrounds, particularly those presently underserved.

Explaining School Failure

Four broad categories of perspectives are used to explain differences found in academic and intellectual performance among students from various ethnic and cultural backgrounds: genetic inferiority, cultural deficit, cultural mismatch, and contextual interaction. There is a significant relationship between explanations given for school failure and particular interventions proposed.

The Genetic Inferiority Perspective

The perspective offering the least hope is that of genetic inferiority or biological determinism. Proponents of this point of view believe that some races are innately inferior to others (Jensen and Johnson, 1994; Lichten, 2004; Lynn, 1999; Rushton and Rushton, 2003). Much of this work is based on the claim that there is a relationship between brain size and intelligence. These scholars believe that intelligence is a biologically determined and irreversible condition of birth that cannot be altered by schooling. Thus, the logical response for schools is to continue the usual practice of providing the best academic preparation for the most able students, usually from the White race, and appropriate training for those who are less capable, the majority of whom are people of color.

The Cultural Deficit Perspective

Cultural deficit is a second perspective on school failure. Proponents of this perspective believe that the values and practices children from some ethnic groups learn at home are deficient. These deficiencies may be inherent in the culture itself or a response to prejudice and racism within the larger society. A recent proponent of the deficit perspective is Dr. Ruby Payne who claims that the middle class has "hidden rules" or "mental models" not available to the poor. Payne (1996, 2001, 2003, 2005) contends that the lives of children living in poverty are characterized by values, behavior, and an orientation to life and work that is dysfunctional. She believes that poor children do not learn to value work, do not have a sense of self-discipline, and live in situations characterized by conflict, disorder, and violence. Many of the scenarios in Payne's publications are stereotypical life situations of people of color. She argues that it is unlikely that poor children will succeed in school and in life without mentors and sponsors who will lead the way out of poverty by providing access to the "hidden rules" of the middle class and access to appropriate role models.

Historically, African Americans have been singled out as especially culturally deficient due to the consequences of slavery and racism. The two primary aspects of African American culture believed to be deficient are family relationships and language usage. Research studies such as those conducted by Frazier (1932, 1937), Liebow (1966), Rainwater (1965), and Bernard (1966) found African American families pathological or dysfunctional when compared with Euro-American families. An underlying assumption of these studies is that African Americans have been assimilated, and no traces of African culture have been retained. In these so-called dysfunctional families, children are believed to be deprived of the guidance, nurturing, and support necessary to become well-balanced and intellectually capable individuals. A basic problem with using Euro-American families as a standard is the assumption that there is one universally correct way for families to exist. Using this aspect of Euro-American cultural practices as a standard for evaluation can lead to the conclusion that African American culture is inferior.

The proponents of the cultural deficit perspective find language to be as deficient as family structure. Bereiter and Engelmann's (1966) position that African American English is inferior and illogical is based on research conducted by British sociolinguist Bernstein (1961), who found that members of the lower classes in England use a "restricted" language code that hampers abstract and complex thinking and expression of ideas. Members of the upper class use an "elaborated" code that permits abstract and complex thinking and expression of ideas. Bereiter and Engelmann pointed out similarities between language use of the British lower class and African American children. They concluded that African American children use a lower-class language not suited for abstract and complex thinking and expression. Bereiter and Engelmann believe this deficit can be overcome by teaching African American children standard English.

The misunderstanding of African American language usage and its relationship to learning in school was evident in the controversy that resulted from the 1996 decision by the Oakland Unified School District in California. The district decided to use the children's home language as a basis for teaching standard or academic English and to introduce basic concepts in other areas of the curriculum to facilitate learning. The use of the child's native language, home-culture, and prior knowledge as a basis for school learning has been well established in educational theory and research beginning with the work of John Dewey (1938) and Lev Vygotsky (1978). Yet, those operating from a deficit perspective, and those influenced by this perspective who lack accurate information, opposed making such basic connections between the home-culture and school learning for African American children.

The general approach advocated by proponents of the cultural deficit perspective for improving school performance is to "improve" the home-life conditions of the children and to provide more structured learning to remediate the "deficiencies." What is meant by improving the home-life conditions is teaching parents of "culturally deficient" students Euro-American practices of childrearing. The underlying principle is changing the children to fit the school program rather than altering the school program to make better linkages between the home-culture and school practices. Head Start, Project Follow Through, and Title I are good examples of the application of this perspective. These programs were part of President Lyndon Johnson's war on poverty that began during the 1960s. According to Kagan (2002) the intent of the public policy supporting Head Start was to "make poor and minority women better mothers or somehow compensate for their poor parenting" (p. 526). This policy governed all of the compensatory education programs initiated during this time period. The intent and orientation of these programs have not changed. Initially, Head Start served children from three to five years of age with the intent of preparing them for learning in school. Project Follow Through was instituted to provide a continuation of the goals of Head Start for older children. Title I is intended to provide remediation for children from culturally deprived and low-income backgrounds who have poor academic performance in reading and mathematics.

The Cultural Mismatch Perspective

A third perspective on differences in academic performance among various ethnic and cultural groups is that of cultural mismatch or cultural congruence. Proponents of the cultural mismatch perspective believe that the disproportionate rate of school failure among certain ethnic groups is largely attributable to the fact that schooling practices are derived from

Euro-American culture. Thus, children from Euro-American culture have an apparent advantage over children from other ethnic groups. Presently, schooling practices require children from ethnic minority groups to learn through cultural practices and perceptions other than their own. The extent to which this is true for any given individual member of a particular ethnic group is influenced by the degree of acculturation experienced outside of school.

The proponents of this perspective contend that improving the academic performance of students from those ethnic groups not performing well in school requires the following:

1. Legitimizing the knowledge the children bring to school.
2. Making meaningful connections between school learning and cultural knowledge or knowledge acquired outside of school.
3. Creating a hybrid culture in school that is congruent with many of the values and practices children bring from the home and peer culture.
4. Creating a community of learners where collaboration is the norm rather than competition.
5. Balancing the rights of students and teachers.
6. Providing curriculum content and pedagogical practices that support a consistent and coherent core of identity and intergenerational continuity with the past.

Seminal research studies support this perspective, including those related to Native Hawaiian students reported by Au (1992), and Au and Mason (1981); Native American students reported by McCarty, Lynch, Wallace, and Benally (1991), and McCarty (2002); Mexican American students reported by Moll (1986, 1988), and Moll, Saez, and Dworin (2001); and African American students reported by Michaels (1981), and Lee (1995).

The Contextual Interaction Perspective

A fourth perspective on differences in academic performance among various ethnic and cultural groups is that of contextual interaction (Cortes, 1986). Those supporting this view postulate that academic achievement is a function of the dynamic interaction between the societal context (the family and the community) and the school context; and, within the school, between educational input factors (e.g. theories, assumptions, administrative and pedagogical knowledge, human and material resources, school policies, and staff attributes), instructional elements (e.g. curriculum design, instructional methodology, and materials and resources available), and student qualities (e.g. academic skills and knowledge, language proficiency, self-image, life goals, motivation, and sociocultural attributes).

Cortes summarized the contextual interaction model as follows:

> The examination of a wide variety of societal and school factors, including their interaction both at one point in time and dynamically over time, provides the essence of the Contextual Interaction Model. This model rejects single cause explanations and instead seeks to incorporate a multiplicity of factors that may influence educational achievement. It rejects static correlations and instead substitutes the consideration of observable dynamic interactions over time in an attempt to assess causation. It rejects the examination of societal and school factors outside of a specific context and instead examines the dynamic operation of these multiple factors within specific contexts. Finally, it provides a basis for the comparison of contexts in order to identify different ways in which sociocultural factors interact with and influence educational experience, including educational achievement. (p. 23)

The proponents of the contextual interaction model do not propose a particular intervention, but rather suggest that a combination of actions are more likely to have an effect. In some cases the entire schooling process needs to be reformed along with specific aspects of the home-community.

Meaningful Learning in Elementary Schools

An examination of research on different approaches to school learning for ethnic groups presently underserved by the nation's elementary schools reveals three essential practices: (a) empowering students to direct their own learning, (b) facilitating meaningful parent and community participation in decision making, and (c) linking learning experiences with cultural values and practices. The following examples illustrate the application of each of these practices. Each of these practices is present in all of the examples to varying degrees; however, each example is used to exemplify only one practice.

Empowering Students

For many ethnic minority children who speak a nonstandard dialect of English or who speak English as a second language, literacy acquisition is illusive and the failure rate is high. Recently, I undertook a case study implementing an approach to initiating literacy that had been successful in a limited number of individual cases under the direction of one teacher. This case study involved fifteen elementary school teachers in a small inner-city school that is approximately 96 percent African American. 13 of the 15 teachers agreed to try this new approach with at least one child in each classroom; however, they could involve more than one child or the entire class if they chose.

The directions to the teachers were simple: Select and assign a passage for each child to prepare to read aloud to a small group or the entire class. The teachers were told that they could assign individual passages from a story to be read aloud in small groups or each student could have an independently assigned passage such as a poem. There was discussion of the use of poetry to help children who speak a nonstandard dialect or English as a second language become familiar with English syntax. Each child was to be given adequate time to prepare to read the assigned passage. Children would be called on to read only when they indicated a feeling of being prepared. Children were not to be constrained or directed in the approaches used to prepare for reading the passage. The assignment could be given at the end of the day and preparation could take place at home, or class time could be used. Children could use in-class preparation time to work together freely in soliciting and providing assistance and support for each other.

The teachers met in grade-level clusters to discuss the new approach. The directions were flexible enough for teachers to choose three different approaches. Ultimately, each teacher's preference for a particular approach was based on personal experience and perception of what was most likely to prove effective. Four teachers chose to assign all of their students the same poem. These children paid little attention to the assignment, lost their papers, and gave various reasons why they did not have time to prepare. In each of the four classrooms, one or two children who were not good readers took the assignment seriously and actually returned able to read the passage fluently. These teachers felt the approach they had chosen was appropriate, and continued it even when their colleagues reported higher rates of success using a different approach.

Two teachers assigned individual unrelated passages. These teachers also tended to listen to the children read individually. The children showed significant progress in their reading. The teachers reported the children attending to expression and its relationship to meaning when reading quotations. This certainly had not been the case using other methods of reading instruction.

Seven teachers assigned each child an individual passage from a story that was to be read aloud in small groups. The assignments were given overnight or over the weekend. Thus, the children were expected to prepare at home. These teachers also allowed a few minutes in class for additional preparation before the reading experience was to begin. The students in these teachers' classrooms showed the most dramatic improvement in reading fluency. The teachers reported that the stories were read smoothly. One teacher commented that she suspected that the children were "just reading words and not comprehending meaning." She was surprised, however, when the children were able to respond appropriately to her comprehension questions at the conclusion of the story. One sixth-grade teacher reported with some amazement that he had half-heartedly given the assignment on Friday, not believing it would make a difference in the children's performance or attentiveness. He was pleasantly surprised on Monday when all but one child read the assigned passage fluently. This particular child was limited English-speaking and in the early stages of second-language acquisition. This teacher was so impressed by the progress of students in the class who had a history of poor reading performance that he decided to work with this one student individually using the method of repeated reading. After hearing the teacher read the passage aloud several times, the student was able to read it fluently. The entire class read the story again to allow this one student to participate. The teacher reported that subsequently even this limited English-speaking student continued to make dramatic progress.

The seven teachers who assigned individual passages from the same story reported that within two to three weeks, the children's reading improved so dramatically that they were able to read unfamiliar passages fluently with only a few minutes of preparation. In this situation, the children felt comfortable and confident in their own ability to perform. They showed increased patience and were enthusiastic about helping their peers acquire confidence like their own. They became so enthusiastic about reading that it was difficult to get them to do other work or take recess.

The key aspects of this strategy for supporting the acquisition of reading skills are (a) giving an assignment that allows for private practice time, (b) allowing the children to choose their own approach to learning, and (c) allowing children to perform individually when they feel competent to do so. The first two aspects of this reading strategy are consistent with recommendations by Au and Mason (1981) in the "balance of rights hypothesis" where the teacher decides what is to be learned and the students choose the approach to learning. One advantage of the balance of rights hypothesis is that students may benefit from using practices from their experiential background that are unfamiliar to the teacher and may not be made available. Allowing the children to perform individually takes advantage of the public performance aspect of African American cultural practices. Incorporating this practice into reading instruction fosters pride in demonstrating academic competence for peer approval.

Parent–Community Participation

Torres-Guzman *et al.* (1994) described an ethnographic study in a Latino community revealing the presence of funds of knowledge within individual households linked together in a network that increases the resources available to all community members in meeting their daily needs. For example, within a particular household there might be knowledge about electricity or carpentry, and in another there might be knowledge about masonry or architecture. Through the informal networks established within the community, these households might share their expertise in constructing homes. These researchers found that established social networks can provide support for academic learning in school.

One teacher developed a language arts module employing community funds of knowledge as academic content. Parents, students' relatives, and other community members were invited into the classroom to share their expertise with the students. They described their work, the tools they used, the procedures they employed, and explained how they acquired the skills. The students asked questions, took notes, and wrote papers documenting the knowledge shared with the class or with individual students. The fact that many of the community members had limited formal schooling did not prove to be a negative factor. The students were hesitant at first because they were not accustomed to viewing their parents and relatives as academic resources; however, they soon became enthusiastic and highly motivated. Learning for these students was highly contextualized in the sense that they were acquiring literacy through working with people from their local community who had shared values and perceptions, used a familiar discourse style, and the content was part of their daily lives.

Linkages with Cultural Practices and Values

In traditional classrooms organized around a teacher-directed question–response–evaluation approach, Native American students have appeared nonresponsive. In many cases, the questions in this type of sequence require "right" answers taken directly from the textbook. This type of teacher–student interaction and the content presented in textbooks exemplify the absence of linkages between traditional school practices and the values and practices of Native American culture. McCarty and colleagues (1991) found that by changing the approach to an inquiry-based curriculum focused on socially and culturally relevant content and where the students are encouraged to work together, the students responded enthusiastically to classroom questioning. The inquiry-based curriculum allowed the students to investigate, observe, and analyze personal experiences and phenomena from the past and present in their own community.

In the study reported by McCarty and colleagues (1991), a teacher-demonstrator at the Rough Rock Demonstration School conducted a demonstration lesson in which the students were shown a group of photographic posters depicting local scenes and were asked to identify those things needed in their community. The students responded enthusiastically by identifying things encountered in their daily lives such as houses, sheep, and community members with different roles and responsibilities. The students were then asked to work in small groups to sort the items into two groups and explain their categorizations. The students engaged in lively debate that resulted in categorizing the items into "wants" and "needs." Through this process the students arrived at an important concept forming the basis for a generalization about how people in the community work together to solve mutual problems that would be further developed later.

In analyzing the responses of the Native American students to the inquiry-based curriculum, McCarty and her colleagues contended that " 'the answer' requires a more complex analysis of the relationship between pedagogy, learner characteristics, and classroom interaction than is afforded by conventional categorizations of learning 'styles' according to analytic versus holistic, or verbal versus nonverbal performances" (p. 50).

Critical analysis reveals that the instruction in the inquiry-based curriculum connects with Native American students in three ways. First, the content reflects, validates, and extends what students have learned and value from socialization within their own culture. Second, the learning experiences in class are consistent with the way students have been socialized to learn outside of school. This includes an "interactive learning process—one in which children build increasingly sophisticated and realistic understandings incrementally, by ordering and extending their own observations" (p. 51). Third, this approach to learning is consistent with the Navajo cultural philosophy about learning, fundamental to which is the idea that "knowledge is meant to be used, learners cannot approach higher levels without the supportive knowledge and understanding that enable application of higher knowledge" (p. 51). An essential part of this philosophy is "individual action and responsibility in learning" (p. 51). Thus, the teacher in this situation behaves in a way that empowers students to actively pursue learning.

The factors that make school learning meaningful and productive for Navajo children are important for those from other cultural and ethnic groups. Teachers can design meaningful learning experiences for specific groups of youngsters by employing culturally appropriate communicative patterns, social interaction patterns, information-processing strategies, and culturally valued knowledge and skills in curriculum content.

Although each cultural group has developed ways of learning and processing information and essential values and practices, the study of several different cultures will reveal clusters of overlapping and criss-crossing patterns among the groups. Recognizing this phenomenon is important for those teaching in multicultural school settings because it makes instructional planning more manageable. A more complete discussion of the relationship between culture and school learning is provided in Chapter 7.

Meaningful Learning in Secondary Schools

Four Essential Elements

In discussing meaningful learning in elementary schools three essential practices were identified: (a) empowering students to direct their own learning, (b) facilitating meaningful parent and community participation in decision making, and (c) linking learning experiences with cultural values and practices. These practices are also important at the secondary level. However, youngsters at the secondary level are more concerned with finding a place for themselves in the adult community than they were at the elementary level. Thus, a fourth essential practice at the secondary level is that of directly linking learning experiences to real-life situations such as those found in the workplace and identifiable role-specific practices.

Several well-known programs utilize instructional approaches that incorporate these four essential elements of learning for underserved populations of students, including the Algebra Project founded by Moses, Foxfire founded by Wigginton, and the Community Writing Project founded by Moll. The published descriptions of these projects provide insights into the roles of teachers and students, and how the instructional approaches and content are directly related to the local community in which the students reside.

The Algebra Project

The Algebra Project, founded by Moses—a parent, activist, and mathematician—is a math–science project in the inner city of Cambridge, Massachusetts, in which the local community is organized to make algebra available to all seventh- and eighth-grade students regardless of their level of skill development or academic achievement. The directors of the project used techniques from the Civil Rights Movement to organize the community to challenge the ability model for making algebra available to students. Moses, Kamii, Swap, and Howard (1989) transformed issues of mathematics education into broader political questions such as:

What is algebra for? Why do we want children to study it? What do we need to include in the mathematics education of every middle school student, to provide each and everyone of them with access to the college preparatory mathematics curriculum in high school? Why is it important to gain such access? (p. 428)

Transforming mathematics education into a political issue addresses the second element of meaningful learning for a specific population by facilitating community participation in decision making. This serves to increase students' motivation and empowers parents to actively protect their children's best interests, rather than leaving all educational decisions to school personnel who have their own ideas about who should have access to which aspects of the curriculum. Placing students in certain curriculum tracks based on ability and prior performance is an example of limiting access.

In the Algebra Project, instruction is based on motivation rather than ability as a prerequisite for intellectual development and achievement. According to Moses and his colleagues (1989), "when learning is perceived as a function of effective effort, one seeks factors inhibiting children when they are having difficulty learning or understanding a concept, rather than 'disabilities' that disallow learning" (p. 437). That is, in most current teaching practices ability is viewed as an inherently inalterable phenomenon that limits intellectual functioning and academic achievement. In the Algebra Project instruction is viewed as an enabling factor that can support students in overcoming knowledge and skill barriers that inhibit learning specific content or in specific situations. Thus, the teacher used pedagogical knowledge and knowledge of the students, much as a detective would, to locate and correct those aspects of prerequisite knowledge and skills that served as barriers to subsequent learning.

Instruction in the Algebra Project employs the third dimension of meaningful learning for a specific population by building upon the students' learning preferences and strengths derived from their cultural and experiential background to extend their knowledge and skills. That is, the students use the familiar to extend their knowledge and understandings. The instruction begins in the expressive domain (see Chapter 5) with the students gathering informal knowledge in familiar places, developing questions, identifying relationships, and moving to the descriptive domain to construct formal knowledge that is procedural and empirical–analytical. This is most evident in the five-step teaching and learning procedure for supporting sixth graders in their transition from arithmetic to algebra. The five-step approach includes the following:

1. Physical event.

2. Picture or model of this event.
3. Intuitive (idiomatic) language description of this event.
4. A description of this event in regimented or academic English.
5. Symbolic representation of the event.

Students in the Algebra Project begin with the fourth element of meaningful learning for a specific population, that of employing learning experiences that simulate real-life situations and identifiable role-specific practices. For example, sixth-grade students are introduced to algebra through a trip on the Red Line of Boston's subway system, which serves as a concrete physical event that forms a common frame of reference from which the students and their teachers can formulate questions and solve mathematical problems related to the concept of equivalence.

> Students then use this process to explore the concept of equivalence, in the broad cultural context of every day events such as cooking, coaching, teaching, painting, and repairing. They explore any concept in which an object A is substituted for another object B to achieve a certain goal. They conclude the discussion of equivalence in subway travel with open-ended construction of equivalent trips, leading to an introduction of displacements as "trips that have the same number of stops and go in the same direction."
>
> (Moses *et al.*, 1989, p. 434)

The first element of meaningful learning for diverse students at the secondary level, empowering students to direct their own learning, is also present in the Algebra Project. The students assume more responsibility for their own learning by setting personal goals and using their teachers, peers, and textbooks as resources. Instruction is teacher-intensive rather than teacher-centered or directed. The teacher acts as coach and detective using scaffolding techniques to extend students' knowledge and skills while searching out barriers and alleviating them through pedagogical knowledge and knowledge of the students. Within this learning community, the teachers study curriculum content as well as their own teaching practices. Parents have the option of attending Saturday classes that use the same approaches provided for the students. Thus, the school as a learning community provides a social context for learning that is comfortable, supportive, and engaging.

The Foxfire Approach

A second example of an effective program incorporating the four elements of meaningful learning for students from underserved populations is Foxfire. This program started as a language arts program for Appalachian high school students in which language arts skills were developed through documenting "the remains of what once was a totally self-sufficient Appalachian culture" (Wigginton, 1977, p. 51). Foxfire then expanded to include a county television network, a music company that produces records and sponsors concerts, an environmental division for studying ecological problems, a photography division that produces photography shows for schools, a drama division that produced a play about Appalachia, and a building construction division (Wigginton, 1990). Foxfire has grown to include a museum; a framework for developing active, collaborative, learner-centered environments; and teacher learning experiences (www.foxfire.org/).

The Foxfire approach differs from the Algebra Project in facilitating meaningful parent and community participation in decision making. Wigginton, an English teacher, used the community as the text for extending the students' knowledge and skills, rather than organizing the community around a political issue involving school policies and practices. The adults in the community who were valued by the students became resources for their learning. The students took photographs and conducted interviews that were tape recorded, transcribed, and ultimately transformed into articles or chapters in Foxfire publications. These publications were highly valued by the adults within the community as well as outside.

Like the Algebra Project, motivation rather than ability was viewed as essential for academic development in Wigginton's class. He believed that making linkages with the community and the "addition of an identifiable end product . . . made a genuine motivational difference" (Wiggington, 1977, p. 51). Many students came to him with limited skills in language arts. The students were empowered to direct their own learning and to use personal learning preferences as they conducted their interviews. Again, the expressive domain described in Chapter 5 was employed as a vehicle for developing the descriptive domain.

Most instruction in the Foxfire approach employs learning experiences that simulate real-life situations and identifiable role-specific practices. Wigginton (1977) contended that

> what most students desire more than nearly anything else is the self-confidence and self-esteem and dignity that come from knowing that what they are doing is important. That it is making a difference. That it is not just busy work and meaningless exercise, but it matters. In some cases, it is work that might not get done at all were they not involved. (p. 51)

These students acted as historians and journalists in documenting Appalachian culture. In the Foxfire Project, by making linkages with the community and developing a collaborative work environment for the students, the teacher provided a social context for learning that was comfortable, supportive, and engaging.

The Community Writing Project

A third example of a strategy incorporating the four elements of meaningful learning for underserved populations of students emerged from an ethnographic study of a project for teaching writing to limited English-speaking students (Moll, 1986). In a study of the local community in which the students lived it was found that most of the writing was functional and practical, involving activities such as making grocery lists and taking telephone messages. Most other literacy events in the home focused on the students' homework. Interviews with the parents revealed a high value placed on writing and other literacy skills. The parents also had broader concerns about social issues within their community, such as English proficiency, employment, and immigration. Moll (1986) stated that "as the project proceeded, we began to view the teaching of writing in the context of the community, and to organize writing instruction responsive to the concrete circumstances encountered" (p. 105). For example, in one module the theme was the importance of bilingualism. The students conducted a survey of public opinion in their local community. These data were transcribed and organized into a report that was distributed in the community. Initially, the teacher guided the students through the steps of organizing for the survey. However, when the students began to write their papers they relied more on each other to make decisions about the organization and presentation of information.

Other Common Factors

There are several important common factors among the three examples given. First, each of the program organizers had a well thought-out approach for initiating the project and involving the local community, although each played a different role in relationship to the school and used a different approach in initiating contact. Moses was a parent and former teacher who began his involvement by working with his own children, then worked together with teachers to design meaningful learning experiences in algebra for all seventh- and eighth-grade students. He used a political approach that built on his experience in the Civil Rights Movement to involve the local community. Wigginton was an English teacher and member of the local community. He began by rethinking his own approach to teaching the curriculum content. Thus, the approach he chose was to make the community the text for his own classroom instruction. His enthusiasm as well as that of his students spread and other teachers became involved. Moll is a researcher who, along with his colleagues, developed several "writing-as-communication" modules employing data gathered in their ethnographic study. Parents and other community members became resources for classroom learning.

Second, the program organizers had in-depth knowledge of the students' home-culture. They understood the cultural values, practices, and perceptions of the larger community either from their own personal experiences or from ethnographic data gathering. Moses had been directly involved in the Civil Rights Movement and used that understanding to mobilize the African American community around the issue of access to higher-level mathematics. Wigginton was part of the local community. He had grown up in the area and had firsthand knowledge of the people, their values, practices, and perceptions. Moll conducted an ethnographic study to gather information about the students' community. The approach Moll used is consistent with the RIQ approach recommended in Chapter 4. Third, each organizer had a single goal: to improve the academic performance of a particular targeted population. Each challenged the belief that ability is a prerequisite condition for intellectual or academic development. Rather, each believed instead that motivation is the key factor, and demonstrated that motivation is tied to the meaningfulness of the curriculum content and instructional approach.

Creating a Supportive Context for Learning

A harmonious learning community characterized by mutually supportive relationships among teachers and students is evident in each program exemplifying the essential elements of meaningful learning in elementary and secondary schools. The discussion in the remainder of this chapter addresses how teachers can promote positive relationships that create a supportive context for school learning. Four particularly important factors in creating a supportive context for learning are (a) the role of the teacher, (b) the participation structure, (c) peer culture, and (d) relationships between teachers and students.

The Role of the Teacher

Teachers need to be actively involved in the learning community; learning with and from their students as much as their students learn from them. In their role as active members of a learning community, teachers can use their advanced competence as able learners to model learning strategies, assist students in their learning, and collaborate with students in constructing a mutually supportive context for learning. Using the techniques described in Chapter 4, teachers can learn from their students the nature of the subject matter that is of greatest interest to them and the approaches to learning that have been the most productive. Interacting with students can provide insights into appropriate relationships among members of the learning community including balances of power, rights, responsibilities, and leadership.

Part of the teacher's role is like that of a coach or orchestrator who strives to build harmony, support, and teamwork among the players. Each player in an orchestra or on a baseball team brings certain talents and skills that are well developed and others that are not so well developed. Some players have practiced in isolation and will need to become team players, whereas some have well-developed team skills but need to strengthen other skills. Teachers, acting as coaches and mentors, work to create a learning community where collaboration is an essential factor in promoting academic and personal growth by using the strengths and skills of all community members.

Participation Structure

Interactions and relationships among students are important aspects of learning. In a traditional classroom, the teacher directs all talk and action. Au and Kawakami (1991) contended that

> the teacher must have the vision of working collaboratively with students to shape the class into a community of learners. In this community context, the teacher has the opportunity to support the children's learning, and the children have the opportunity to support one another's learning. The teacher leads the community of learners and has the greatest responsibility for its shaping, at least in the beginning. (p. 282)

In describing the context of this community of learners, Au and Kawakami pointed out that "emphasis is on cooperation, collaboration and what the class as a whole can accomplish, not competition and individual achievement at the expense of others" (p. 282).

The collaborative learning environment described here should not be confused with the cooperative learning described by Slavin (1983) as "classroom techniques in which students work on learning activities in small groups and receive rewards or recognition based on their group's performance" (p. 315). In the collaborative learning community, relationships and collaboration among the students are naturally occurring and purposefully focused on learning while minimizing individual and group competition. In contrast, cooperative learning relationships are structured, manipulated, and controlled by the teacher with group competition replacing individual competition in many cases.

Researchers who have conducted major studies involving specific ethnic groups of students have concluded that natural collaboration in learning communities is more consistent with practices in many students' home-culture and is more productive than traditional teacher-directed structures. This is what was found, for example, in studies involving the Warm Springs Indian students (Philips, 1972), Native Hawaiian students (Au and Mason, 1981), Odawa Indian students (Erickson and Mohatt, 1982), Mexican American students (Moll, 1986), African American students (MacLeod, 1991; Moses et al., 1989), and Appalachian students (Wigginton, 1977, 1991).

Creating a collaborative learning community supports the improvement of academic performance. For example, Au and Mason (1981) documented the time lost from learning in a classroom where the teacher tried to get Native Hawaiian children to conform to traditional classroom rules of turn-taking. In a comparable situation another teacher who was more focused on learning outcomes and allowed the children more freedom of choice in participation style had increased academic productivity.

Peer Culture

As youngsters progress through school they build relationships among themselves that constitute rule-governed communities separate from the adult world that are referred to as *peer culture*. Schools are structured such that students spend more time with their peer groups than in personal contact with adults. Over time, the bonds and relationships among peers become more important and powerful than those between students and their teachers. That is, it is more important to be an accepted member of the peer group than to please teachers. At this point, the peer group becomes a powerful entity to be reckoned with by teachers and students. For many students, alienation from the peer group is more painful than school failure. Thus, many students, particularly those from oppressed groups, unconsciously choose the peer group over conforming to school practices and increasing their potential for academic success.

The power of peer culture is most evident in school when it conflicts with teachers' expectations for students' behavior and responses in the classroom. Problems begin for many youngsters when the school culture and the home-culture conflict on basic factors or when the demands and expectations of the school are inconsistent with the real-life experiences of the students. When the conflict escalates and the school and teachers are unrelenting in their determination to force students to conform to school practices, student resistance can result. An example might be where English is spoken as a second language and youngsters are not allowed to speak their native language when socializing with their peers outside the classroom.

School resistance is found at both the elementary and secondary levels (D'Amato, 1988; Macleod, 1991, 1995; Solomon, 1992). Resistance in schools and classrooms is maintained by the reciprocal behavior of teachers and students; however, neither group seems fully aware of the presence of the conflict, how it developed, or how best to resolve it. School resistance may take several different forms, the most obvious of which are: (a) refusing to follow school rules and not conforming to the expected behavior, (b) deliberately and overtly displaying different values, (c) overtly defying the authority of school personnel, (d) strongly displaying ethnic group pride, and (e) clearly establishing ethnic group boundaries for its members. These behaviors are a predictable psychological response to being in a situation that is personally invalidating and culturally incongruous. The psychological need to feel like a worthwhile human being is violated by the often unfriendly persistence of school personnel in forcing students to conform to unfamiliar and unacceptable practices that conflict with their sense of the way things should be done and the relationships that should exist between people. Students' resistance can be viewed as a form of unconscious psychological self-protection. The unrelenting persistence on the part of school personnel can be viewed as uninformed, counterproductive, and potentially catastrophic (Noguera, 1995).

How can teachers prevent school resistance? Using the techniques of RIQ discussed in Chapter 4 to acquire and apply knowledge of students' home-culture and school experiences in planning instruction and promoting positive relationships within the classroom can help prevent school resistance. This means using knowledge about what students value and how they learn best to frame the curriculum and design productive learning experiences. Approaches to linking students' experiential background and learning preferences to curriculum structure are discussed in Chapter 5. It is also important to apply knowledge of social interaction practices among students and within the home-culture in creating a supportive context for school learning.

How can teachers recognize and deal with resistance? First, it is important to recognize patterns of behavior that signal conflict. For example, the most readily observable pattern is when a small group of students from the same ethnic group, social class, or academic performance level act in concert to resist school work, pressure their peers to resist school work, or disrupt a class (Anyon, 1980; D'Amato, 1988; Gilmore, 1985; Kohl, 1994). More effort is required to recognize a pattern of resistance when a teacher or several teachers have one or two students in a class who refuse to cooperate. Identifying a particular pattern may require examining student behavior across the entire school. An easy way to make a quick assessment of resistance across an entire school is to examine referral, detention, and suspension records; parental contact records; and the high school dropout rate. These records often reveal patterns based on group membership.

Second, it is important to identify ways to adjust classroom practices to accommodate students' experiential backgrounds, values, and perceptions while the teacher assumes responsibility for determining the learning objectives (Au and Mason, 1981; Cummins, 1986). Learning experiences can be adjusted to accommodate students' needs without a loss of curriculum content or quality. For example, Au and Mason (1981), as a result of their research with Native Hawaiian children, proposed a balance-of-rights hypothesis in which the students' influence over social interaction and approaches to learning in the classroom is increased while the teacher retains primary influence over the content and goals of instruction. In this case, allowing the students to interact more naturally and to use communication strategies common to their home-culture created a type of collaboration that supported academic growth. The teacher did not change instructional objectives, but rather, made learning accessible and meaningful.

It should be kept in mind that students in the elementary and secondary schools are not usually engaging in deliberate conflict with teachers and many are confused by teachers' responses to their behavior. Both students and teachers frequently act unconsciously out of cultural norms that have been part of their early socialization. It should also be kept in mind that factors other than peer-group association contribute to school failure. Part of the reason for school resistance in the first place is that the way instruction is delivered makes it inaccessible to some students. For example, Michaels (1981) described a situation in which a teacher based pre-literacy skills instruction on the unconscious premise that all children are familiar with the linear "topic-centered" narrative style common to the Euro-American culture. This is not true for children from the African American culture where a holistic "topic-associated" narrative style is employed. Instruction was inaccessible to these children. Consequently, it is possible for these children to spend six or more years in the elementary school without acquiring basic literacy skills, although they have put forth an inordinate amount of effort and are deemed to be of at least "average" intelligence. Repeated failure of this type can cause even the most conscientious students to abandon a task.

In summary, learning about students' experiential backgrounds, perceptions, home-culture, and peer relationships are important factors in creating a supportive learning community. Employing knowledge about students and their experiential background to create mutually supportive relationships, to make learning more accessible and meaningful, and to reframe curriculum content to incorporate students' values and perceptions is more likely to prevent or minimize resistance to school practices and to foster positive interactions between adults and peer culture.

Relationships Between Teachers and Students

The social context of the classroom is mutually constructed by teachers and students whether that is the intention or not. Both teachers and students bring their own cultural values, practices and perceptions into the classroom. Where a common culture is shared among teachers and students, harmony is more likely to naturally exist than in situations where this is not the case. In classroom settings where a common culture is not shared, careful attention must be given to differences in values, practices, and perceptions in order to foster harmony and prevent conflict.

Making Links With the Home-Culture – Teachers can build harmonious and mutually supportive relationships with students by being knowledgeable about socially acceptable relations among people in different situations. Such knowledge can be acquired through the RIQ approach described in Chapter 4 or by being a member of a particular cultural group. Teachers can learn how to promote positive relationships with students from different cultural and experiential backgrounds by observing *positive* interactions among peers, between students and adults from the same cultural group, and in classrooms where teachers and students share a common culture. For example, in a classic article, McDermott (1977) described how Amish culture is linked to the way Amish teachers and students relate to each other:

> Socialization patterns among the Amish are quite different from those found elsewhere in America. Indeed, many aspects of Amish identity in America have been forged in opposition to and in defense against other ways of being human in a modern technological society. Such a defensive strategy, common among minority cultures, is marked by the merging of individual identities into a group life that is organized around unifying symbols transmitted by a small number of authoritarian leaders (Siegel, 1970). The Amish educational system fits this model nicely. Its symbols are religious and are used to establish trusting relations. The teacher is in total control of the children's development, telling them what to do and when and how to do it. In terms of learning to read and enhancing an Amish identity, this system is highly successful. Children and their teachers live in a closed community with highly specific routines, where everyone is accountable to everyone else. Amish community members use

a specific code to achieve common sense and mutual trust. In this context, instructions are not blind commands but, rather, sensible suggestions about what to do next to further common goals. There is a warm relational fabric that underlies the instructions and transforms them from orders into sensible ways of organizing everyday life. What appears to many to be an authoritarian and oppressive system for organizing a classroom may in fact make great sense to the children. Outsiders simply miss the cues which ground teacher–student activities in trust and accountability. (p. 205)

Another example of the link between students' home-culture and relationships within the classroom is found in Au and Mason's (1981) description of the performance of low-income Hawaiian children under the direction of two different teaching approaches. The first teacher, referred to as low contact (LC), used a traditional approach to instruction where the teacher controlled all action and interaction within the classroom. The children were required to raise their hands when the teacher addressed a question to the group and to respond when he or she was called on. Children who spoke out without first being acknowledged by the teacher were reprimanded. In this classroom, the teacher and the children were in constant conflict with the teacher trying to maintain traditional classroom conduct while the students were trying to introduce those ways of behaving common to their culture. Neither the teacher nor the children were fully aware of what was causing the conflict. A great deal of learning time was lost in this struggle.

In describing a classroom conducted by a high contact (HC) teacher, whose cultural background was similar to the students', Au and Mason stated the following:

In contrast, the children readily followed rules of the open turn structure set by Teacher HC; instruction was initiated quickly and proceeded smoothly. In the open turn structure, she did not nominate any one child to speak; rather, the children were allowed to negotiate for turns of speaking among themselves, without waiting for the teacher to decide who should answer. Teacher HC was not bothered when several children shared a turn of speaking, even when their speech overlapped her own. It is not surprising that the children felt at ease in the open turn structure, because its rules resemble those of Hawaiian talk story. The fact that this structure was only present in the lessons of Teacher HC, and that it produced one of the highest rates of academic engagement, suggest that an interactional structure that is culturally congruent for young students is an important characteristic of well-managed classrooms. (p. 143)

How would a teacher form relationships with students in a classroom where there is more than one culture? Facilitating collaboration and allowing students to choose their own groups or partners is one way to accommodate differences. When the curriculum content and learning experiences are meaningful, students are likely to choose partners and group members with whom they share common interests and compatible approaches to learning. Over time and with positive experiences in the classroom, the frequency with which students choose partners outside of their particular cultural group may increase.

Some teachers worry about ethnic or racial segregation and, consequently, give more attention to this phenomenon than to the actual learning that should take place in the classroom or to building positive relationships with students. Where this occurs, some students are not allowed to take advantage of culturally derived preferences for social interaction and learning strategies that support academic growth. When students are deprived in this way they suffer academically and socially. The relationship between these students and their teacher is likely to be negative.

Showing Respect, Concern, and Interest – A second important aspect of building positive relationships with students is for teachers to show respect, concern, and interest in their students regardless of their cultural background. Teachers can show respect for students by being polite and avoiding statements or actions that publicly humiliate, embarrass, or reprimand. Acknowledging unique qualities, accomplishments, and concerns of individual students supports the development of a trusting relationship and in some cases has a bonding effect. Such acts should be honest and sincere. This should not be merely an attempt to make a student feel good. For some cultural groups public praise is unacceptable, while for others it is highly desirable. Again, the teacher must be knowledgeable about the students' home-culture and must be a keen observer in attending to how students respond in different situations.

Chapter Summary

In this chapter, the discussion of redesigning instruction addressed explanations for failure, essential practices for meaningful learning in elementary and secondary schools, and ways to create a supportive context for learning.

Explanations for school failure represent four different perspectives including genetic inferiority, cultural deficit, cultural mismatch, and contextual interaction. The proponents of each perspective make recommendations for interventions except those subscribing to the genetic inferiority position. The proponents of the cultural deficit perspective recommend early intervention in the form of remediation and training parents in Euro-American childrearing practices. Those supporting the cultural mismatch perspective recommend making instruction more compatible with the students' home-culture. Proponents of the contextual interaction perspective recommend altering a combination of factors that influence school performance.

The essential elements of meaningful learning in elementary school include (a) empowering students to direct their own learning, (b) facilitating meaningful parent and community participation in decision making, and (c) linkages with cultural values and practices. One additional essential element included for secondary schools is directly linking learning experiences to real-life situations and role-specific practices.

Finally, a supportive context for learning addresses the role of the teacher, the participation structure within the classroom, peer culture, and relationships between teachers and students. Each of these factors is considered in relationship to building a collaborative learning community.

Suggested Learning Experiences

The first two learning experiences listed here require making arrangements with a local school and explaining to the principal and the classroom teacher exactly what will be done and what will be gained from conducting the interviews and observations. In your contact with school personnel it should be emphasized that this is not an effort to evaluate the teacher or to draw conclusions about school effectiveness. The purpose is simply to gain a better understanding of students' perceptions.

1. Interview several students from different ethnic groups at the grade level or in the subject area you plan to teach. Ask such questions as: How would you describe your most exciting learning experience? Was there something specific about this learning experience that helped you learn more? What was the most difficult learning experience you have had in this class? Why was the experience difficult? If you could redesign this class or course, what would it be like?

2. Follow up the interview with a classroom observation. Try to determine the discrepancy between what the student believes would be an ideal classroom experience and what actually exists. Develop your own hypothesis about the relationship among students' needs, their expectations, and teachers' classroom practices.

3. Re-examine your working definition of culture. Make revisions based on the new insights you have gained so far.

Critical Reading

Anyon, J. (1981). Social class and school knowledge. *Curriculum Inquiry*, 11(1), 3–42.

The author reports a case study of five elementary schools in contrasting social class settings in two school districts in New Jersey. She points out the similarities and differences in the curriculum provided.

Cummins, J. (1986). Empowering minority students: A framework for intervention. *Harvard Educational Review*, 56(1), 18–36.

The author makes recommendations for altering the relationship between educators and ethnic minority students and schools and ethnic minority communities.

Lee, C. D. (1995). A culturally based cognitive apprenticeship: Teaching African American high school students skills in literacy interpretation. *Reading Research Quarterly*, 30(4), 608–630.

The author uses aspects of African American informal language usage as a scaffold for teaching African American students to interpret complex literary text.

Michaels, S. (1981). "Sharing time": Children's narrative styles and differential access to literacy. *Language in Society*, 10, 423–442.

The author analyzes "sharing time" in an ethnically mixed classroom. She describes teacher behavior that facilitates acquisition of a literate discourse style where the teacher and children share an informal discourse style as compared to the conflicting and non-productive efforts with children who do not share the teacher's informal discourse style.

Noguera, P. A. (1995). Preventing and producing violence: A critical analysis of responses to school violence. *Harvard Educational Review*, 65(2), 189–212.

The author discusses the negative impact of the underlying philosophical orientation to social control and disciplinary practices in schools on students, teachers, and the school community.

CHAPTER 7

A Framework for Understanding Cultural Diversity in the Classroom

Focus Questions

1. What is the relationship among students' cultural and experiential backgrounds, instructional approaches employed by the teacher, and academic performance?
2. What is the relationship between culturally appropriate social discourse and socially constructed learning experiences in the classroom?
3. What is the relationship among culturally mediated cognition, culturally valued curriculum content, and culturally appropriate social discourse?

Introduction

The discussion in the previous chapter focused on meaningful learning in elementary and secondary schools. Central to this discussion was the relationship between culture and school learning. In an earlier discussion in Chapter 1, a typology was presented with three positions and six indicators. Teachers' perception of culture and ideology are the framing indicators in this typology. Teachers' ideological stance and their understanding of culture frame how they view curriculum, learning, pedagogy, and the social context for learning in school. In sum, their understanding of culture influences the extent to which teachers provide meaningful and productive learning experiences for their students. This chapter presents a framework for understanding cultural diversity in the classroom and for learning to teach traditionally underserved students from diverse cultural and experiential backgrounds. The first part of this chapter presents a study reported by Hollins (2006) where an approach identified as structured dialogue served as a tool to facilitate transforming the culture of practice in a low-performing school, whereby teachers learned to teach traditionally underserved urban students. What these teachers learned is made explicit in the second part of this chapter in the form of a framework aimed at revealing the deep meaning of culture in school learning. Key components of this framework are culturally mediated cognition and culturally mediated instruction.

The Culture of Practice in a Low-Performing School

Darling-Hammond (2000), in a study of teacher quality and student achievement as addressed in state policy, found that "quantitative analyses indicate that measures of teacher preparation and certification are by far the strongest correlates of student achievement in reading and mathematics, both before and after controlling for student poverty and language status" (p. 1). She further pointed out that

> students who are assigned to several ineffective teachers in a row have significantly lower achievement and gains in achievement than those assigned to several highly effective teachers in sequence . . . Teacher effects appear to be additive and cumulative, and generally not compensatory. (p. 2)

This suggests, for example, that if a student is assigned an ineffective teacher in first, second, and third grade, that student is likely to develop reading problems that will continue throughout his or her school experience. This cumulative effect of teacher quality is evident in low-performing urban schools.

The purpose of this discussion is to make you aware of the culture of practice in low-performing urban schools. This awareness will enable you to monitor your own development as a classroom teacher and to avoid being unconsciously inducted into the existing culture of practice. Hollins (2006) reported a three-year study of two low-performing urban schools where structured dialogue was used as an intervention to help change teaching practices. Structured dialogue is an approach where teachers come together in a study group format for the purpose of discussing their classroom practices. In their discussions teachers described the successes and challenges they faced in their classrooms and provided evidence for each. Teachers learned from each other how to improve classroom practices and student learning outcomes.

In this study, Hollins (2006) identified a developmental trajectory for changes in the culture of practice at low-performing urban schools. This trajectory consisted of three positions and three markers. The positions were described as a natal or initial culture found in the low-performing schools at the beginning of the study, a transitional position where teachers replaced some of their old practices and values with new ones, and a transformational culture where teachers fully embraced new values, practices, and perceptions. The three markers for change in the teachers' culture of practice were related to teachers' perceptions of students, teachers' perceptions of instruction, and the relationship among teachers. Each of the three positions was characterized with a particular perception of students and instruction, and a particular way of relating among colleagues. (See Table 7.1.)

Table 7.1 Developmental Trajectory

Natal Culture	Cultural Transition	Cultural Transformation
• Teacher talk is about what students don't know and can't do and how students and parents don't care about learning.	• Teacher talk changes to what students need to support their learning.	• Teachers assume full responsibility for student learning outcomes and take great pride in students' accomplishments.
• Good teaching practice is generic. Learning outcomes are based on effort and intelligence.	• Teachers make connections between teaching practices and learning outcomes, but not student characteristics.	• Teachers make connections among teaching practices, student characteristics, and learning outcomes.
• Teaching practices are private. Induction into the professional community is automatic and without planning or intent.	• Trust develops within the professional community.	• Teachers talk openly about their practice and take responsibility for professional development within the professional community.

In the natal position, the teachers as a group at the low-performing schools tended to hold a deficit perspective of their students where the focus was on students' lack of knowledge and skill, a negative view of students' life conditions, and the view that parents were not interested or supportive of their children's education. The teachers viewed good instruction as generic and considered that it should foster similar outcomes for all students. Differences in learning outcomes were attributed to student effort, intelligence, and family social-class status. In this position, teachers seldom visited each other's classrooms or talked with each other about their instructional practices. Classroom instruction was a private matter.

New teachers were automatically socialized into this natal culture when hired at these low-performing schools with little thought or planning on the part of the experienced teachers.

During the second year of the study teachers entered the transitional position where their talk about students was less negative. Teachers began to notice that not all instructional approaches yielded the same outcomes for their students. This led to discussions about the relationship between instructional approaches and learning outcomes. Talk about teaching practices was more personal, although teachers were cautious about taking responsibility for learning outcomes. Teachers began to give attention to the induction of new teachers by developing informal mentoring relationships where guidance and suggestions about classroom practices were provided.

The transformational position emerged during the third year of the study. Teacher talk about students was very positive. Teachers talked about what students know, what they need to know, and what instructional approaches work best. Teachers discussed the relationship among teaching approaches, student attributes, and learning outcomes. Teachers took responsibility for students' learning outcomes. They talked openly about their own strengths and weaknesses. Teaching practices were made public. Teachers solicited assistance from their colleagues. They visited each other's classrooms and assumed responsibility for their own learning and for that of their colleagues. Experienced teachers took responsibility for planning for the induction of new teachers.

The developmental trajectory presented in Hollins (2006) and the typology in Chapter 1 of this book are related. The trajectory and the typology each present three positions with related categories of perceptual response indicators for conceptualizing teaching practices. Embedded in the positions and indicators in each of these constructs is a way of conceptualizing teaching practices that addresses perceptions of students and instruction, which in turn influences the extent to which teachers take responsibility for student learning outcomes. When comparing the positions and indicators in the typology described in the first chapter of this book with the developmental trajectory described in Hollins (2006), apparent similarities exist between the indicators across positions in the typology and the trajectory. For example, the Type I teachers in the typology are very similar to the teachers in the natal culture position in the trajectory on indicators for teachers' perception of students and instruction.

Indicators in the transformational position on the developmental trajectory and in Type III in the typology point to the application of teachers' knowledge and understanding of the relationship among student attributes and experiences, instructional practices, and learning outcomes as support for productive teaching. Hollins (2006) presented structured dialogue as a tool for facilitating the transformation of a community of practice, as well as the practice of individual teachers. You may be able to use this approach to improve your own practice as a beginning teacher.

The trajectory and the typology are useful to teachers in different ways. The typology is intended to describe the perceptual position and response of individual teachers employed in K–12 schools. The typology is useful as a tool for deep introspection and planning for personal growth. The developmental trajectory describes the transformation of the culture of practice in a low-performing school to a learning community focused on improving student learning outcomes. Recognizing the different indicators of positions in a culture of practice at a school is helpful in understanding how to interact with colleagues, and how to monitor your own professional growth and participation in a community of practice.

The typology presented in the first chapter of this book identified characteristics of teacher perception and practices in three positions, but does not provide a framework for understanding the relationship between culture and school practices. The purpose of the remainder of this chapter is to provide a framework for understanding the relationship among learners' cultural and experiential backgrounds, classroom practices, and learning outcomes.

Understanding Cultural Diversity in the Classroom

Rationale for a Framework

This framework is intended to provide a theoretical construct for synthesizing knowledge from previous chapters and explicating the underlying structure to facilitate application to practice. The concepts in this framework provide deeper insight into the purpose for locating self within a culturally diverse society, for inquiring into students' cultural and experiential backgrounds, and for deconstructing the elements of meaningful learning for diverse students in elementary and secondary schools. This framework makes explicit the relationship among culture, cognition, pedagogical practices, and learning outcomes.

This framework for understanding cultural diversity in the classroom has two major components, *culturally mediated cognition* and *culturally mediated instruction*. Culturally mediated cognition refers to the way in which memory structures and intellectual processes are developed and supported within a cultural context. Culturally mediated instruction incorporates culturally mediated cognition, culturally valued knowledge in curriculum content, and culturally appropriate social situations for learning. Explicating the components of this framework provides important insights into the relationship among culture, cognition, pedagogical practices, and learning outcomes for underserved students. (see Table 7.2.)

The framework for understanding cultural diversity in the classroom is theoretically grounded in the work of Piaget and Vygotsky and draws on information processing theory to explicate the structural connections among culture, cognition, pedagogical practices, and learning for students from culturally diverse backgrounds. It is important to note that the structural connections supporting student learning are found among individuals and groups located in different school settings; and that, while culture is dynamic and constantly changing, individuals engage in particular cognitive apprenticeships and acquire particular experiences that influence learning. Bransford, Brown, and Cocking (1999) pointed out that, "all learning involves transfer from previous experiences" (p. 56).

Culturally Mediated Cognition

Culturally mediated cognition refers to the mutuality of the relationship between cognitive development (including the formation of memory structures and mental operations for information processing and knowledge construction) and the cultural context in which it is embedded. Cognition and culture are mutually constructed in the child. The child's enculturation depends on the development of intellectual capacity that, in turn, depends on the enculturation process for actualization. For example, verbal memory structures and language acquisition are mutually constructed. The development of verbal memory structures depends on language acquisition that, in turn, depends on verbal memory structures. The biological capacity for both language and verbal memory must exist. This is not a question of nature versus nurture; but rather, recognition of the interdependence, integration, and mutuality of biological, psychological, and sociological processes.

Table 7.2 Framework for Understanding Culture in School Learning

Culturally Mediated Cognition	Culturally Mediated Instruction	Learning Outcomes
• Memory structures • Intellectual processes	• Culturally valued subject matter	• Analyze, interpret, and construct knowledge
	• Culturally appropriate social discourse	• Active and responsible social participation
	• Culturally based pedagogy	• Sensitive and responsive human interaction

Early Perspectives

The works of Jean Piaget (1896–1980), a Swiss developmental psychologist, and Lev Vygotsky (1896–1934), a Russian developmental psychologist, continue to have a major influence on investigations of the relationship between culture and cognition. Piaget's studies focused on the developmental stages of children as related to their acquisition of knowledge. He described the mental development of children as consisting of three stages: sensorimotor (birth to 18 months), where the child lacks any symbolic function; symbolic or preconcrete-operational (18 months to 7 years), where the child develops abilities to represent things with symbols; and concrete-operational (9 to 12 years), where the child develops the ability to complete mental operations without the assistance of physical objects or actions. Formal operations, the ability to examine thoughts and ideas, develops during preadolescence and adolescence. The processes supporting the child's development are *assimilation* (the meshing of new and existing knowledge) and *accommodation* (the reconstructing of existing knowledge to accommodate new information). Piaget favored psychobiological factors over cultural factors in explaining human behavior and cognitive development; however, neo-Piagetian psychologists have modified his theory to include the role of culture and language in intellectual development (Case, 1987).

In contrast, Vygotsky favored cultural factors in explaining cognitive development. His work focused on the social origins and cultural roots of individual development. Central to Vygotsky's (1978) theory is the concept of the zone of proximal development, which he defined as "the distance between the actual developmental level as determined by independent problem solving and the level of potential development as determined through problem solving under adult guidance or collaboration with more capable peers" (p. 86). According to Moll (1993), the zone of proximal development

> embodies or integrates key elements of the theory: the emphasis on social activity and cultural practice as sources of thinking, the importance of mediation in human psychological functioning, the centrality of pedagogy in development, and the inseparability of the individual from the social. (p. 15)

These key elements of the zone of proximal development are central to contemporary perspectives on learning.

Contemporary Perspectives

Contemporary thinking about how learning takes place continues to build on the work of Vygotsky and Piaget. One example is Rogoff's (1990) description of children as apprentices in thinking where learning occurs through observing and participating with peers and more able members of the same culture. She used the term *guided participation* to refer to the idea that both guidance and participation in culturally valued activities are essential aspects of children's apprenticeship in thinking. Lave and Wenger (1991) built on Vygotsky's notion of the zone of proximal development to construct a concept of learning independent of "the context of pedagogical structuring" referred to as "legitimate peripheral participation" (p. 49). Legitimate peripheral participation is a theory of social practice that engages newcomers in learning from mature members of a community of practice. Newcomers assume responsibility for legitimate aspects of practice to the extent that they have acquired the appropriate behaviors, knowledge, and skills. Lave and Wenger emphasized the value of practice over instruction as a source for learning.

The concepts of apprenticeship in thinking and legitimate peripheral participation hold significant potential for application in identifying ways to improve school learning for presently underserved populations of students. These concepts are incorporated in the discussion on cultural mediation in instruction presented later in this chapter.

Linking Culture and Information Processing

Vygotsky theorized that mental processes reflect the specific organizational properties of social life (Rogoff and Wertsch, 1984). According to Rogoff and Wertsch:

> Vygotsky's formulation claims . . . that the very structure of individual functioning derives from and reflects the structure of social functioning. Thus, his claim is much stronger than simply that individuals' mental processes develop in a social milieu. That is, Vygotsky views individuals' mental processes as having specific organizational properties that reflect those of the social life from which they derive. The composition, structure, and means of action are internalized from their social origins. This means that variation in the organization of social functioning can be expected to lead to variation in the organization of individual psychological functioning. (p. 2)

Vygotsky's theory points to strong linkages among cognition, culture, and memory.

Information-processing theories (by focusing on attention, perception, encoding, storage, and retrieval of information from memory) provide schemata for examining linkages among cognition, culture, and memory (see Figure 7.1). This can be accomplished by analyzing the relationship'

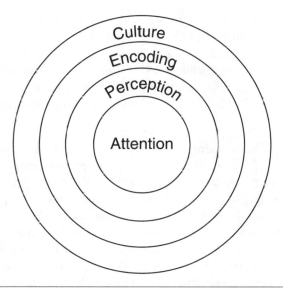

Figure 7.1 Culture and Information Processing. Culture frames information processing by selectively focusing attention, influencing meaning, and influencing schemata for encoding.

between cultural practices and the development of memory structures and mental operations.

Primary Components of Information Input

Attention – The extent of processing that a particular unit or frame of information receives in the short-term memory is referred to as *attention*. Information receiving substantial attention involving meaningful rehearsal or practice through application, experience, and elaboration passes through short-term memory for storage in long-term memory. Information receiving superficial attention may enter short-term memory or be immediately discarded.

Attention may be influenced by cultural practices or environmental circumstances. For example, a child socialized in an environment with people who have very similar eye and hair color will learn to give attention to other physical features when describing or identifying individuals. Conversely, a child socialized among people who vary with regard to eye and hair color will give attention to these physical features in describing or identifying individuals. A child from the latter environment may have difficulty recalling physical features of individuals that are not associated with eye and hair color.

Encoding – The means by which incoming information is processed for storage in long-term memory is referred to as *encoding*. How encoding occurs is influenced by organization, the way material is systematically connected; elaboration, the linking of unfamiliar information with what is familiar; and schemata, the structure systematically organizing large chunks of information (Schunk, 1991). Regardless of cultural influences, information is more easily encoded if it is meaningful, logically organized, connected to what the learner already knows, and supported by a meaningful structure.

Perception – The meaning attached to sensory input (auditory, visual, kinesthetic) is referred to as *perception*. When sensory input is received it is held in a sensory register and compared with knowledge in long-term memory. Perception is based on the identification of patterns and relationships and is influenced by the characteristics of a particular phenomenon, prior experience, and expectations. Pattern recognition may involve "bottom-up" or "top-down" processing. An example of bottom-up processing is the use of phonics in the acquisition of initial reading skills. Whole-language instruction where children learn to read through meaningful experiences with language (listening, speaking, reading, and writing) is an example of top-down processing.

Whether one prefers top-down or bottom-up processing may be influenced by cultural practices. For example, Hall (1989) described different ways of knowing and understanding found among high-context and low-context cultures. High-context cultures are characterized by a holistic (top-down) approach to information processing in which meaning is "extracted" from the environment and the situation. Low-context cultures use a linear, sequential building-block (bottom-up) approach to information processing in which meaning is "constructed."

Memory Structures

Memory structures are described as episodic (e.g. actions, events, and locations), semantic (e.g. ideas, concepts, and skills), verbal (e.g. songs and speeches), visual (e.g. charts, maps, and photographs), long-term (permanent storage), and short-term (temporary storage). Registers for receiving information associated with each memory structure include hearing, touch, taste, and smell (see Figure 7.2).

Memory is more efficient when information is organized into meaningful units. A schema is a macrostructure that organizes large chunks of information into meaningful units. A schema represents a standard pattern associated with a concept, principle, skill, or event. For example, a schema for riding a city bus might consist of having exact change, waiting at a designated bus stop, boarding the appropriate bus for the intended destination, paying the driver, being seated, recognizing when the bus is

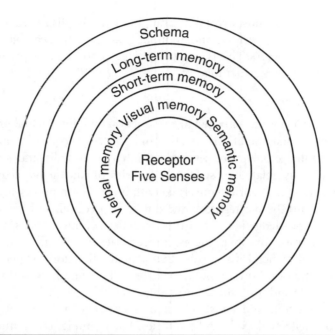

Figure 7.2 Memory Structures. Incoming information receiving sufficient attention from sensory receptors is temporarily stored in short-term memory in semantic, verbal, or visual structures. Information receiving sufficient rehearsal is transferred to long-term memory where it may be organized into schemata for efficient retrieval.

approaching the intended destination, signaling the driver, and getting off the bus. Schemata serve the primary functions of supporting predictability associated with learned or expected patterns and providing structure for the integration of new information.

Cultural Practices and Memory Structures

Cole (1974) indicated that most researchers have found that conducting a valid and reliable study of cognitive development and memory structures in cross-cultural situations requires the use of familiar cultural content that is presented through usual social practices found within the particular culture of which the subjects are members. An example of the influence of cultural practices on recall is a study reported by Lennenberg and Roberts (1956) as described by Cole (1974). In this study, monolingual Zuni Indians, bilingual English-speaking Zuni Indians, and monolingual English speakers were compared on their ability to recall colors in the yellow–orange section of the color spectrum. The Zuni language does not differentiate colors in this range, thus it is not a part of the social practice among the Zuni Indians. As would be expected, monolingual Zuni speakers made the most errors in recall, bilingual English-speaking Zuni Indians made fewer errors, and monolingual English-speaking subjects made the fewest errors. This is also an example of how culture provides the content for memory structures.

Mental Operations

Memory structures are activated in conjunction with intellectual processes to perform mental operations resulting in knowledge acquisition and construction. Intellectual processes involve intellectual skills and strategies that are directly related to specific categories of knowledge acquisition and construction. Theories concerned with information processing divide knowledge into three categories: declarative, procedural, and conditional. Declarative knowledge includes attitudes, beliefs, opinions, facts, generalizations, theories, and hypotheses. Procedural knowledge includes the application of principles and rules that provide direction for performing cognitive activities. Conditional knowledge is knowing how and when to use declarative and procedural knowledge (Schunk, 1991).

The acquisition and construction of knowledge in each category is linked to intellectual skills and strategies. For example, intellectual skills link to procedural knowledge and consist of rules and principles that guide actions such as thinking, remembering, and perceiving. Intellectual strategies combine knowing what (declarative knowledge) and knowing how (procedural knowledge) in determining when, or the condition under which, certain actions should occur. Intellectual strategies include observation, abstraction, inferential reasoning (analogical and metaphorical reasoning), categorization, and problem solving (including bottom-up, top-down, linear, and holistic).

Cultural Practices and Mental Operations

It has already been pointed out that Vygotsky believed that mental processes reflect the specific organizational properties of social life. This idea is consistent with contemporary research findings that point to specific cultural practices as influencing the development of intellectual processes. Research on inferential reasoning provides one example of the relationship between cultural practices and the development of intellectual processes. Ortony, Turner, and Larson-Shapiro (1985) conducted a study of figurative language comprehension among a group of inner-city African American students in Grades 4, 5, and 6, in which the students were found to have a more sophisticated level of comprehension than would have been anticipated using Piaget's developmental theory to predict cognitive development. These researchers attributed this advanced performance in comprehending figurative language to its prevalence in African American communicative practices such as sermons, verbal games, folktales, proverbs, and folk sayings. Aspects of figurative language used in these genres include hyperbole, irony, metaphor, and simile.

Many studies have been done on the relationship between cultural schemata and reading comprehension. In one such study conducted by Reynolds, Taylor, Steffensen, Shirley, and Anderson (1982), African American and Euro-American eighth graders were given a passage to read that dealt with verbal games of ritual insult called "sounding" and "playing the dozens" that are common to the African American culture. African American students tended to interpret the passage in a culturally appropriate way. Euro-American students tended to interpret the verbal play as physically aggressive behavior. These researchers found a close relationship between the subjects' cultural background and their ability to make appropriate inferences from the material read.

Linking Culture, Information Processing, and Instruction

The preceding discussion of the relationship between culture and information processing pointed to an important link between culture and classroom instruction. The link between culture and classroom instruction is derived from evidence that cultural practices shape the development of memory structures and mental operations, both of which are tools for learning within and outside of school. This evidence has led me to postulate that the effectiveness of classroom instruction is influenced by the extent to which it incorporates critical aspects of the home-culture. This postulate forms the basic premise for my formulation of the principle referred to as cultural mediation in instruction. This principle is supported by two postulates that are based on the centrality of the students' home-culture in framing memory structures and mental operations. First, teaching and learning are more meaningful and productive when curriculum content and instructional processes include culturally mediated cognition, culturally appropriate social situations for learning, and culturally valued knowledge. Second, the authenticity of schooling is validated for students by the interactions and relationships between adult members of their community and school personnel.

Examination of the relationship between school practices and the home-culture of students who are traditionally underserved reveals approaches to instruction that can be divided into three categories: culturally mediated instruction, cultural accommodation, and cultural immersion. A basic characteristic of each category is the extent to which critical aspects of the students' home-culture are central to the instructional process. Briefly defined, *culturally mediated instruction* is characterized by the use of culturally mediated cognition, culturally appropriate social situations for learning, and culturally valued knowledge in curriculum content. *Cultural accommodation* is characterized by the use of teaching strategies that challenge universalistic theories of learning and instruction by relying on specific cultural constructs to facilitate learning. *Cultural immersion* is a process whereby the students' home-culture is overshadowed by the use of "generic" teaching strategies based on universalistic theories of cognition, learning, and instruction. Detailed descriptions of these approaches are presented later in this chapter.

It is important to point out that students from underserved populations attending public schools are frequently subjected to cultural immersion, whereas many Euro-American students experience culturally mediated instruction. This fact may account for some of the discrepancies in academic performance for students from underserved populations when compared to Euro-American students.

The argument that students from underserved populations need to adjust to the way schools work in order to prepare for participation in the larger society is somewhat naive. Most students in the elementary and secondary schools have not acquired the academic maturity or intellectual skill necessary to bridge the gap between their own cultural knowledge and that of another culture during the early stages of learning new content or skills. Many of these students are totally dependent on their teachers and the methods of instruction they employ. When teachers insist on employing nonproductive methods their students are denied access to the academic preparation necessary for productive participation in the society.

Culturally Mediated Instruction

Culturally mediated instruction is characterized by the use of *culturally mediated cognition, culturally appropriate social situations for learning,* and *culturally valued knowledge in curriculum content.* Culturally mediated cognition in instruction refers to approaches using the ways of knowing, understanding, representing, and expressing typically employed in a particular culture. For example, Hall (1989) described different ways of knowing and understanding found among high-context and low-context cultures. High-context cultures are characterized by a holistic approach to information processing in which meaning is "extracted" from the environment and the situation. Low-context cultures use a linear, sequential building-block approach to information processing in which meaning is "constructed." Culturally mediated cognition requires knowing and using these differences in classroom instruction.

Culturally appropriate social situations for learning refers to relationships among students and between teachers and students during classroom instruction that are consistent with cultural values and practices. For example, McCarty *et al.* (1991) found that when instruction is consistent with "natural learning–teaching interactions outside the classroom," and articulates a "Navajo philosophy of knowledge," Navajo students traditionally described as nonanalytical and nonverbal engage in verbal interaction and inductive/analytical reasoning with an inquiry-based curriculum. Thus, social arrangements are important aspects of productive instruction.

Culturally valued knowledge in curriculum content refers to the inclusion of knowledge valued within the students' home-culture. Wigginton (1977) made use of culturally valued knowledge in the Foxfire Project where the students documented the oral history of their own community for publication. Another example is Rison's (1990) application of cultural content such as that included in rap music and other cultural elements to raise the achievement levels of African American students in mathematics in several school districts in Texas.

Cultural mediation can be divided into two subcategories: authentic cultural mediation and intermittent cultural mediation.

Authentic Cultural Mediation – In authentic cultural mediation schooling practices are an extension of the enculturation process found in the child's home and local community (see Figure 7.3). It involves the use of culturally mediated cognition, culturally valued curriculum content, and learning experiences presented in socially constructed learning situations that are consistent with practices found in the student's home-culture. The practice of authentic cultural mediation in instruction requires the type of

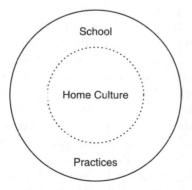

Figure 7.3 Cultural Mediation. Ideally, the home-culture is at the core of school learning. School practices build on and extend the learning and socialization initiated and supported in the home–culture.

extensive knowledge of the student's home-culture that may be best acquired through the cultural apprenticeship available to members. Thus, culturally mediated instruction is most likely to occur where the teacher and students share a common culture and experiential background.

Where teachers and students share a common culture, they are likely to share ways of knowing, understanding, representing, and expressing ideas. This supports naturally occurring and routine links between classroom learning and culturally based memory structures and mental operations. During classroom instruction, new knowledge is routinely connected to what already exists in the student's memory structure using familiar intellectual processes. This is illustrated in Lipka's (1991) study of a Yup'ik Indian teacher teaching Yup'ik Indian children described later in this chapter.

In authentic cultural mediation, school practices are an extension of cultural knowledge associated with customs, traditions, and values from the students' home-culture. The curriculum content is based on knowledge valued by the local community and reflects the history and culture of its people. Accomplishments of adult members of the students' home-culture are acknowledged and valued.

The extent of the linkage between school practices and the student's home-culture found in authentic cultural mediation is more likely to consistently support the acquisition of all types of knowledge than cultural accommodation or cultural immersion. However, in public schools as they presently exist, authentic cultural mediation in instruction is available for some groups of Euro-American students, but rarely for students from underserved populations.

Lipka (1991) presented a case study of a Yup'ik Eskimo teacher that demonstrates authentic cultural mediation in instruction. In this case, the teacher and students share the same culture and the teacher is a member of the local community. The teacher's native language is Yup'ik. Although the language of instruction is English, the children speak to each other and to the teacher in Yup'ik, making only occasional use of English phrases. The teacher uses English when speaking to the children, making only occasional use of Yup'ik phrases.

In Lipka's study the lesson takes place at the end of the day before the annual beaver round-up festival. The teacher begins the lesson by telling the children they will need a pencil. Then the children are asked if they remember the story read the day before. The story was about beaver trapping. The boys are very animated in their description of the process of beaver trapping. The teacher asks the children if they have ever seen anyone make a beaver blanket. The teacher tells the children that they can make a beaver blanket on the floor. The children are invited to join the teacher on the floor. Some children do and some do not. The teacher demonstrates and models the process as children take turns observing the teacher and each other. When the teacher and the children have completed their beaver blankets and have written on them, the teacher tells a story of how his family survived a near tragedy on the river when he was a little boy.

What some outsiders might view as a preholiday filler art activity turns out to be a lesson about an important Yup'ik tradition and important cultural values emphasizing subsistence and survival. The lesson acknowledges the importance of the work done by the adults in the local community. The social relationships in the classroom incorporate Yup'ik values of individual autonomy and group harmony and solidarity. The teacher decides what is to be learned and models an approach. Teacher talk is limited and is carried out intermittently as the teacher works on his own art project while the students take turns observing the teacher and each other. The children have the autonomy to decide whether to follow the teacher's approach and directives, to act independently, or to observe other children when completing the task. The children are allowed to talk among themselves without interruption from the teacher as they work on the task.

In comparing Yup'ik teachers' and non-Yup'ik teachers' approach in introducing a lesson, Lipka pointed out the following:

> The non-Yup'ik teacher states in a linear manner, first this and then this, prior to doing anything. The verbal messages are decontextualized from the content and the action in which the students are to engage. This procedure of introducing the lesson to students is common educational procedure (Good and Brophy, 1987) and is considered good pedagogy. These differences in ordering of introductory statements between Anglo and Yup'ik teachers are not mere happenstance; they are culturally grounded in Yup'ik and mainstream American culture. (p. 213)

In contrast, the Yup'ik teacher's activities

> begin without the customary lengthy verbal introduction Anglos expect. This suggests differences in cognitive ordering and structuring. The students seem quite comfortable following the modeled behavior. The teacher's instructional style also includes modeling (doing his "own work"), joining in with the students (seated on the floor with the students as he blends into the class), and reinforcing peer-group solidarity and deep respect for individuals. (p. 213)

The Anglo teacher engaged the Yup'ik children in cultural immersion rather than culturally mediated instruction.

Intermittent Cultural Mediation – In intermittent cultural mediation, the teachers and their students share a common culture, but find themselves in a situation where the constraints of the schooling process prevent routine use of culturally appropriate social situations for learning and knowledge valued by their cultural group. Also, the history and culture of these teachers and their students are not well represented in the curriculum content. In intermittent cultural mediation, teachers share a full repertoire of cultural understandings with their students and, consequently, the use of culturally shaped memory structures and intellectual processes is likely to routinely occur.

In intermittent cultural mediation, the teacher may deliberately employ constructs from the students' culture and experiential background to facilitate learning. This may include the use of culturally mediated cognition, culturally sanctioned social interaction practices and protocols, and/or culturally valued knowledge in curriculum content. At any given point in intermittent cultural mediation, the teacher may choose to use any one of these factors or none at all. The teacher's decisions are based on the perceived needs of the students. For example, the teacher may speak the students' language when introducing new concepts, but routinely speak the official language of the society at large. Like authentic cultural mediation, intermittent cultural mediation is more likely to support all types of learning than cultural accommodation or cultural immersion.

Intermittent cultural mediation in instruction requires the type of extensive knowledge of the students' home-culture that may be best acquired through cultural apprenticeship. Some individuals who are members of a particular ethnic group by birth may be acculturated through direct or indirect contact with the majority culture to the extent that they are unable to engage in cultural mediation in instruction for students from their own ethnic group. These individuals may acquire the insight necessary for intermittent cultural mediation in instruction through an external apprenticeship the same as any other outsider. Although an outsider is unlikely to acquire all of the nuances of cultural meaning shared by insiders, an appreciable level of proficiency in intermittent cultural mediation may be acquired through a fully executed external apprenticeship with an expert practitioner.

A cultural apprenticeship usually occurs with membership and socialization in a particular culture from childhood; however, an external apprenticeship for non-members may occur through extensive intimate contact extended to those accepted as members of the culture who favor the adopted culture over their original culture, or trusted individuals with legitimate reasons for acquiring such intimate knowledge. The basic attributes of a quality external apprenticeship include mutual trust and respect between the apprentice and the expert practitioner; a mutual willingness to listen to each other and share feelings, perceptions, and reactions to events, situations, and students; and a mutual concern for improving practice within the profession.

An example of intermittent cultural mediation in instruction is the Algebra Project (Moses *et al.*, 1989). In this case, Moses shared a common culture with the majority of the students in the project and is a member of the local community. He was active in the Civil Rights Movement of the 1960s. The goal of the Algebra Project was to provide equal access to college preparatory algebra for all students in a situation where African American and other students from particular ethnic groups were systematically placed in low-track mathematics classes. In this African American community, algebra was not considered culturally valued knowledge. Moses used the culturally valued concept of equal access to increase the value of algebra in the community and for the students. The traditions of organizing the community during the Civil Rights Movement were applied to get parents and the community involved with the Algebra Project.

Intermittent cultural mediation is evident in approaches used in the Algebra Project in the form of culturally shaped memory structures and intellectual processes. The linkages made between students' existing mental schema and new knowledge is evident in the five-step teaching procedure employed in the project:

1. Introduction of a familiar physical event.
2. Presentation of a picture or model of this event.
3. Description of the event using the students' language.
4. Description of the event using academic English.
5. Representation of the event symbolically. (Moses *et al.*, 1989)

The instruction extended the students' cognitive schema to include algebraic concepts.

Intermittent cultural mediation was evident in the Algebra Project in social interaction practices and protocols such as communalism or shared responsibility and early autonomy for preadolescents and adolescents. The students were allowed to set their own goals and monitor their own progress. Adults were available for assistance or support as needed.

A second example of intermittent cultural mediation in instruction is Wigginton's Foxfire Project. Wigginton and the students shared a common culture. Wigginton grew up in the same area as the school where he implemented the Foxfire Project and returned to the community as a teacher. In the Foxfire Project, teachers used cultural journalism as a vehicle for teaching academic skills. Olmstead (1988) defined cultural journalism as "featuring, highlighting, and documenting aspects of the traditions, customs, and values of a culturally distinct group of people through some format—newspapers, magazines, radio, slide-tape—which can be done by anybody, by amateurs." When doing cultural journalism the students

> go out into their community with tape recorders and cameras to interview older residents about their own personal histories, local history, skills, and traditions. Back in the classroom, they transcribe their taped interviews, develop film and print photos, write introductions, and arrange the material into layouts that will become the pages of Foxfire magazine. (p. 33)

Each of these examples of cultural mediation in instruction engages the students' memory structures and intellectual processes in different ways by using a different text for learning. In the first example, authentic cultural mediation, Lipka reported on a teacher who builds on a cultural tradition by reading a related story, engaging the students in storytelling, participating in an art project, and relating a personal experience story. In the second example, intermittent cultural mediation, Moses employed a political strategy to link traditional school content with community values, used a familiar physical event as a common reference point, and traditional algebra textbooks were available as resources. In the third example, intermittent cultural mediation, Wigginton used the community as the curriculum content and the text supporting the development of intellectual skills and strategies related to literacy.

Cultural Accommodation

Cultural accommodation in instruction involves the use of isolated aspects of culture in contrived situations to facilitate learning (see Figure 7.4).

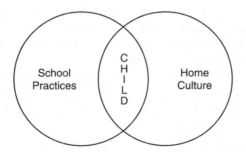

Figure 7.4 Cultural Accommodation. Linkage between the home-culture and school practices improves access to learning for students from traditionally underserved populations.

The most commonly used aspects of culture include socially constructed learning situations consistent with practices found in the students' home-culture and culturally valued knowledge in curriculum content. Easily observed patterns of social interaction and communication are aspects of students' cultural and experiential background that are chosen most often for inclusion in classroom instruction. Culturally mediated cognition is not consistently employed in cultural accommodation.

The primary goal of cultural accommodation is to facilitate teaching and learning in situations where teachers and students do not share the same culture and there is a standard curriculum. Teachers practicing cultural accommodation need to be knowledgeable about the students' cultural background; however, the extensive knowledge necessary for authentic cultural mediation is not required.

The practices in cultural accommodation can be selected to support culturally based memory structures and intellectual processes, although this is less likely to occur than in authentic or intermittent cultural mediation where teachers and students share a common culture. The degree of success the students will achieve is relative to the consistency of application and the salience of those aspects of cultural practices and values selected for incorporation into instruction. Applying Au and Mason's (1981) balance-of-rights hypothesis, where the teacher retains responsibility for the content of instruction while the students participate in deciding how they go about learning, increases opportunities for students to make important linkages between the content of instruction and their culturally based memory structures and intellectual processes.

Au and Kawakami (1985) presented an example of cultural accommodation employing students' culturally based intellectual processes, while engaging in a culturally appropriate social situation for learning. Au and Kawakami described a study conducted at the Kamehameha Elementary Education Program (KEEP) in Honolulu. In this situation, the salient aspect of culture is a particular speech event referred to as *talk story*. Talk story involves a type of participatory storytelling. As a speaker tells a story the listener demonstrates understanding by extending the story. Thus, several individuals may speak simultaneously for short intervals. The authors found that

> making two departures from conventional school practices greatly improved the children's learning to read. The first departure is to focus reading instruction on comprehension or understanding of the text, rather than solely on word identification, even when children are in kindergarten or first grade. The second is to conduct lessons using a culturally compatible, rather than incompatible, style of interaction. (p. 406)

Additionally, talk story involves intellectual processes associated with inferential reasoning that supports the development of reading comprehension.

A second example of cultural accommodation is a study reported by Dillon (1989). This author reported on an ethnographic study in one rural secondary, low-track English-reading classroom consisting primarily of low socioeconomic, predominantly African American students and a Euro-American male teacher. The teacher actively sought information about the students by engaging in conversations with them, their parents, and other members of the community. The knowledge the teacher gained about his students allowed him to develop strong personal relationships with them. The teacher and the students mutually constructed the social organization in the classroom that was informal, collaborative, and supportive. The teacher interacted with the students informally in ways that acknowledged their lives outside of school. The teacher helped the students with their assignments as needed. The informal quality of this teacher's classroom and close supportive relationships that developed were similar to those the students experienced outside of school.

Dillon interpreted the results from her study to indicate that the teacher's success with these students was

> defined by his ability to do the following: (a) create a culturally congruent social organization in his classroom that accounted for the cultural backgrounds of his students, and (b) vary his teaching style to allow him to effectively communicate with his students during lesson interactions resulting in increased opportunities for student learning and improved student attitudes toward learning and school in general. (p. 227)

In this teacher's classroom there is evidence of culturally appropriate social situations for learning and opportunities for students to make use of culturally based memory structures and intellectual processes through collaboration.

Cultural Immersion

The practice of cultural immersion involves repeated exposure to curriculum content, instructional approaches, and socially constructed learning situations that are based on cultural practices other than those of the students' being taught (see Figure 7.5). Teachers may practice cultural immersion because they believe in universalistic notions of teaching and learning, have limited knowledge of their students' cultural background, or believe that acculturation is as important as the acquisition of academic knowledge and skill.

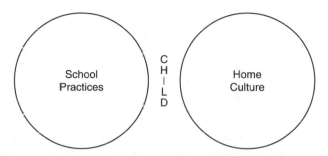

Figure 7.5 Cultural Immersion. School practices are not related to those in the home-culture. Students may learn by chance to make connections between learning within and outside school.

In cultural immersion, instructional time may be used for resocializing students who have different cultural practices and values than those preferred in the school setting. An example is students who speak a non-standard dialect of English. Some teachers feel compelled to change how students speak at the expense of other learning. Value-based efforts to change students' language from a nonstandard dialect to a standard dialect are seldom successful. Also, many beginning teachers who are limited by their preparation and experience may not be aware of other options or the consequences of their actions.

Cultural immersion can take two different forms—implicit and explicit. Implicit forms of cultural immersion occur in classrooms where instruction is focused on remediation or acceleration in the acquisition of basic skills using traditional methodology and materials, paying close attention to pacing and monitoring instruction, precisely sequenced objectives, employing carefully delineated steps, and with little or no attention to cultural mediation in cognition or culturally appropriate social arrangements for learning. Remediation may be perceived as the need for increased intensity in instruction through smaller and more precise steps, additional tutoring, and increased time on task. Parents may be involved as tutors or in other ways support youngsters' academic learning. The hidden curriculum of schooling for those referred to as culturally deprived or disadvantaged includes "elevating" them to mainstream status. The Chicago Mastery Learning Program and Curriculum Alignment described by Levine and Stark (1982) are examples of implicit cultural immersion. These practices do not incorporate any aspects of the cultural or experiential background of students outside of school.

The Chicago Mastery Learning Program presents a "generic" instructional process that includes a system of pretesting, teaching, post-testing, and reteaching when necessary. The goal is to insure that content is mastered before allowing a student to move to the next sequence.

Curriculum Alignment is a process for matching district curriculum objectives and instructional practices with the objectives of standardized tests in order to improve test scores.

Explicit cultural immersion represents overt rather than covert attempts to resocialize youngsters viewed as outside the mainstream and to inculcate in them mainstream perceptions and behaviors: that is, to assist students in conforming to existing social norms while simultaneously focusing on the acquisition of basic skills. In such programs, youngsters are encouraged to abandon their own cultural values and practices in favor of those of the majority culture. In this category, program developers acknowledge the role of social and cultural influences in the schooling process and believe in the importance of "elevating" children from underserved populations to Euro-American ways. The solution to the problem is perceived as increased intensity in instruction the same as in implicit cultural immersion, augmented with concentrated efforts in the area of child development and mental health. Parents are directly involved in the resocialization process, acting as tutors and in other ways supporting their youngsters' academic learning. An organized program reflecting these practices is the Social Skills Curriculum for Inner-City Children in the New Haven school system (Comer, 1987).

Cultural immersion practices for underserved populations of students do not usually involve culturally mediated cognition, culturally appropriate social situations for learning, or culturally valued knowledge. These practices do not engage culturally based memory structures or intellectual processes. Instead, cultural immersion largely relies on drill-and-practice or rote learning, rather than developing meaning and understanding for underserved students. Students studying complex concepts in this way usually have difficulty with application and transfer. Cultural immersion works best in cases requiring the recall of limited amounts of knowledge for short periods of time, and situations that involve information practiced to the point of automaticity and used regularly in everyday life.

Examples of positive outcomes employing cultural immersion techniques include the method of repeated reading described by Samuels (1979) and the rote learning of arithmetic facts. The method of repeated reading is used in the primary grades to teach beginning reading to children experiencing difficulty. The method consists of rereading a short, meaningful passage several times until an adequate level of fluency is reached. The main purpose of this approach is to bypass decoding to build fluency and speed in word recognition. One explanation for the success found in these cases is that in both instances practice can be done frequently enough to achieve a level of automaticity that does not require understanding the underlying concepts and principles. Both operations are used daily. In cases where practice is not so regular and levels of automaticity are not reached, success is less likely.

Chapter Summary

The transformation of the culture of practice in a low-performing school was presented at the beginning of this chapter as evidence that teachers can learn to teach traditionally underserved students. Through structured dialogue, documenting their own practices, and observing their students' responses to instruction, these teachers were able to reveal for themselves the relationship among culture, cognition, and classroom instruction. The relationship among culture, cognition, and classroom instruction is the basis for the framework for understanding cultural diversity in the classroom presented in this chapter. The rationale for presenting such a framework is the evidence that it has potential for providing a basis for designing more productive school experiences for presently underserved populations in the nation's public schools. The development of this framework is based on the early work of Piaget and Vygotsky, as well as that of contemporary followers of these theorists, and theories of information processing.

The influence of cultural practices on memory structures and intellectual processes is directly related to classroom instruction. The basic premise of the framework for understanding cultural diversity in the classroom is that teaching and learning are more meaningful and productive when curriculum content and instructional processes include culturally mediated cognition, culturally appropriate social situations for learning, and culturally valued knowledge.

Approaches to instruction are placed in one of three categories based on the relationship to the students' home-culture. The first, culturally mediated instruction, incorporates culturally mediated cognition, culturally appropriate social situations for learning, and culturally valued knowledge in curriculum content. The second, cultural accommodation, is characterized by the use of teaching strategies that challenge universalistic theories of learning and instruction by relying on specific cultural constructs to facilitate learning. The third, cultural immersion, is a process whereby the student's home-culture is overshadowed by the use of "generic" teaching strategies based on a universalistic perspective on cognition, learning, and instruction.

Suggested Learning Experiences

1. Try to identify a productive instructional program in which there is no discrepancy in the academic performance of majority-group

children and those from traditionally underserved populations. Explain how this program supports or contradicts the principle of cultural mediation in instruction.

2. Formulate your own theory for teaching in a culturally diverse setting. Determine a means for validation.

3. Interview several teachers who teach in a culturally diverse setting. Ask the following questions:
   A. What patterns of strength in intellectual skills and strategies have you observed?
   B. What approaches to instruction work best in your particular classroom? How do you explain this?

4. Collaborate with a peer in observing instruction in a culturally diverse setting or in a school where an underserved group is in the majority. Try to categorize the instruction according to the framework presented in this chapter. Compare your findings with those of your colleague.

5. Review and rewrite, if necessary, your working definition of culture.

Critical Reading

Au, K. H., and Kawakami, A. J. (1985). Research currents: Talk story and learning to read. *Language Arts*, 62(4), 406–411.

The authors describe a speech event that, when employed in teaching reading to Native Hawaiian children, shows a significant positive effect. In this chapter it is used as an example of cultural accommodation in classroom instruction.

Comer, J. P. (1987). New Haven's school-community connection. *Educational Leadership*, 44(6), 13–16.

The author describes a program aimed at improving the academic performance of inner-city African American children. The program has a strong focus on social skills development. In this chapter, it is used as an example of cultural immersion in classroom instruction.

Lipka, J. (1991). Toward a culturally based pedagogy: A case study of one Yup'ik Eskimo teacher. *Anthropology and Education Quarterly*, 22, 203–223.

The author reports a case study that is presented in this chapter as an example of authentic cultural mediation in instruction.

CHAPTER 8

Transforming Professional Practice

Focus Questions

1. What approaches to professional growth are most likely to benefit a novice teacher in becoming an expert?
2. As a member of the profession, to what extent can an individual classroom teacher participate in transforming the community of professional practice?

Introduction

The central purpose of this book so far has been to assist the reader in becoming more adept at understanding and applying productive practice in teaching a culturally diverse population of students. However, gaining confidence in applying what has been presented in this book so far and continuing to progress toward becoming an expert teacher requires special attention to planning for professional growth.

The purpose of this final chapter is to identify options and approaches for professional growth that build on what has been presented in previous chapters. You can use the content of this chapter to develop a personal approach to professional development, to assess the quality of involvement in professional development experiences, and, to the extent possible, contribute to improving the community of professional practice at the school where you are employed.

In the discussion that follows, transforming professional practice means gaining confidence in improving your own practice and sharing personal insights within the professional community. This requires taking advantage of opportunities to collaborate with colleagues locally and nationally, when possible, and carefully selecting the professional development experiences that will be the most beneficial and that will use time efficiently.

Approaches to Transforming Professional Practice

Transforming professional practice involves improving your own practice and contributing to professional growth among colleagues within the community of practice. Improving your own practice is a thoughtful and deliberate process that involves documenting and reflecting on your practice, engaging in meaningful collaboration with colleagues, seeking planned learning opportunities such as conferences and seminars, and engaging in study of the professional literature. Contributing to the community of practice requires active engagement in problem solving and sharing successes and seeking assistance with some of the challenges you experience when engaged in daily classroom practice.

Participating in a Community of Practice

The teachers at a particular school are participants in a professional community of practice. This community of practice functions much like a culture and is often referred to as a culture of practice because teachers working together in a particular school over time come to share beliefs, practices, and values. The culture of practice influences learning outcomes for students at the school. For example, two classic studies, Anyon (1980) and Page (1987), provide comparisons of teaching practices in schools serving students from different social class backgrounds. Anyon (1980) categorized the elementary schools in her study as working class, middle class, affluent professional, and executive elite. In each of these schools learning was very different. In the working-class school, learning was rote and mechanical where students learned to follow procedures and engaged in very little decision making. In contrast, in the executive elite school, students were required to develop their analytic and intellectual abilities, to conceptualize and apply principles and rules in problem solving, and to develop skills in decision making.

Similarly, Page (1987) reported a study of two high schools in the same school district where teachers perceived the students at one school as working class and students at the other school were perceived as coming from professional-class families. Working-class students received a skills-based curriculum and their teachers held low expectations for their academic performance and for their future accomplishments as adults. In contrast, students from middle-class professional families received a curriculum that stressed academic and intellectual achievement and that prepared them for more advanced study at the college level. Based on the results of this study, Page (1987) concluded that:

> In short, the culture of a school both shapes teachers' understanding of their mode of operation and of the students and is grounded in faculty members' shared definitions. It is linked to the larger social order by staff members' shared perceptions of the social class of the school's typical student and of the educational demands of the community. At the same time, the culture is reflected and re-created in classrooms as teachers provide the school's version of a curriculum appropriate for students of a particular social class. (p. 90)

First year beginning teachers who have not yet established routines of classroom practice or have not conditionalized their pedagogical content knowledge to support their students' learning are potentially receptive to subconscious enculturation into the beliefs, values, and practices of the established community of practice at their school sites. Beginning teachers from the best teacher education programs can be unaware of their susceptibility to this enculturation. One reason for this is that new teachers and many experienced teachers tend to intuitively trust the perceptions of their more experienced colleagues without attention to the quality of their practice, even in the context of low-performing schools. It is important for teachers to be aware of the culture of practice at the schools where they are employed; to learn to contextualize their own pedagogical content knowledge to support their students' learning; and to develop strategies for studying and improving their own practice and for contributing to the professional growth of their colleagues.

In a longitudinal study of low-performing elementary schools reported by Hollins (2006), discussed in Chapter 7, it was found that new teachers were automatically inducted into a culture of practice with shared beliefs, practices, and values. The teachers at these schools believed that generic teaching strategies should work equally well for all students. They believed that variations in learning outcomes resulted from differences in individual students' efforts, intellectual ability, social class, and the extent of parental support. These teachers rarely discussed the relationship among instructional strategies, students' experiential backgrounds, and learning outcomes. This led the teachers to conclude that they used appropriate strategies; it was the quality of the students they taught that caused the school to be low-performing.

The community of practice in the low-performing schools Hollins (2006) studied was transformed to a learning community through the use of structured dialogue in a study group format. Structured dialogue is a tool that enabled teachers to share and examine the successes and challenges they experienced in their classrooms. This collaborative process enabled teachers to contextualize their pedagogical practices to better support their students' learning. Ultimately, the teachers came to better understand the relationship among instruction, student characteristics, and learning outcomes; to believe their students could learn; to accept responsibility for student learning outcomes; and to significantly improve learning outcomes for their students.

Schools have for many years relied on teacher collaboration to improve the curriculum and instructional approaches in the classroom. At many elementary schools teachers have engaged in unit or grade-level meetings where they discussed issues concerning their students and worked on different projects. Teachers in both high schools and elementary schools participated in various curriculum development activities. Administrators and teacher educators believed teacher "buy-in" to be important in the successful implementation of new approaches introduced in various settings. Teacher "buy-in" is an overused term without a clearly understood definition or a well-developed theoretical basis. When teachers did not buy in to a particular approach their behavior was labeled as resistance. This buy-in resistance paradigm was derived from an individualistic behaviorist perspective where the essential approaches used for professional development were grounded in a transmission model employing workshops that included lectures, demonstrations, and modeling with occasional follow-up and coaching. The improvements in classroom practices sought through these workshops were based more on informal administrative assessments than on teacher input. The concerns teachers faced in their daily classroom practice were seldom addressed in district-sponsored professional development, although the content was useful in many ways. The often tedious task of translating information presented at workshops into practice was left to the individual classroom teacher, usually with little support and collaboration among teachers.

Over the past two decades new perspectives on teacher learning based on constructivist and sociocultural perspectives have become more salient. According to Richardson (2003) the constructivist perspective on learning has two approaches, social constructivism and psychological constructivism. Richardson states that:

> In both approaches, there is an assumption that meaning or knowledge is actively constructed in the human mind. However social

constructivism focuses on how the development of that formal knowledge has been created or determined within power, economic, social and political forces. This includes both its structure and the epistemological frameworks in which it is embedded. The psychological approach focuses on the ways in which meaning is created within the individual mind and, more recently, how shared meaning is developed within a group process. (p. 1625)

The sociocultural perspective is based on the work of Lev Vygotsky. According to John-Steiner and Mahn (1996), "Vygotsky conceptualized development as the transformation of socially shared activities into internalized processes" (p. 192). The sociocultural perspective emphasizes the interdependence between individual and social processes in the construction of knowledge. In this sense the professional growth and development of individual teachers is dependent on the construction of knowledge within the group, and the construction of knowledge within the group depends on individual growth and contributions to the group. In this way knowledge distributed among individuals within the group benefits the group as a whole and further extends the knowledge of individuals through the sharing process.

Teacher professional development based on sociocultural and social constructivist perspectives is situated within a community of professional practice; engages the individual and the group in an interdependent and reciprocal professional growth process; emanates from the concerns, experiences, and daily routines of classroom practice; and engages teachers in constructing their own contextualized pedagogical knowledge as they study their own practices individually and collectively. Sociocultural and social constructivist perspectives are the theoretical frameworks for approaches to professional development involving teacher collaboration such as that found in study groups, lesson study, and teacher networks.

Teacher Study Groups – The basic purpose of a study group is to draw upon the knowledge distributed within a professional community or among the members of a group of teachers to improve practices and outcomes in a particular context, for a particular group of students, or in a particular area of the school curriculum. Teachers in a productive study group take an inquiry stance in which members are willing to work towards a common goal. In an attempt to achieve this goal teachers share insights acquired through their own practice, through professional education, from the professional literature, and from dialogue with other colleagues; present personal challenges and dilemmas confronted during classroom practice for examination and feedback from colleagues in the group; and contribute to and benefit from the collective knowledge and experience of the group. In this way study groups promote professional growth for individual teachers and for the professional community formed by the group. This reciprocal learning process brings about changes in the beliefs, values, and practices within the professional community and has the potential for a positive impact on student learning outcomes as teachers learn to more effectively contextualize their practice. Study groups are particularly powerful when positioned within a school where teachers share students from similar backgrounds, face similar challenges, and share similar curricular goals.

Lesson Study – An approach to professional development called lesson study that engages a group of teachers in collaboratively planning, observing, analyzing, and writing a reflection on a lesson for the purpose of improving a particular aspect of classroom practice originated in Japan. In Japan, the Ministry of Education, Culture, Sports, Science and Technology funds designated research schools where curricular innovations under consideration are examined through repeated cycles of lesson study. According to a description of the approach by Lewis, Perry, and Murata (2006):

> Teachers at the designated research schools study existing curricula and materials (often including approaches from abroad), adapt or develop approaches they think will work in their own settings, and study students' responses to the new types of instruction. After cycles of internal lesson study, teachers conduct public research lessons that bring to life the local vision of the innovation, enabling visiting educators to observe the instructional approach and the students' learning and development, and providing a public forum for lively discussion of the local theory of the innovation. (p. 6)

These authors view the lesson study approach as similar to the National Writing Project in the United States in that both approaches involved university-based researchers and both are promoted as a professional practice by teachers engaged in shared observations and examination of students' work.

Teacher Networks – When teachers engage in collaborative professional communities that extend beyond their school to include teachers from across a district, a state or nationally, they form what is called teacher networks. These networks serve as a source of sustained professional development by providing opportunities for teachers to enhance their content knowledge and pedagogical content knowledge (McDonald and Klein, 2003). Teachers are provided access to a wide range of experiences, perspectives, and insights from colleagues in settings that are similar to and different from their own. In the network approach, teacher expertise is highly valued and teachers are provided opportunities for leadership in this regard. However, through these networks teachers also have access to experts who provide new information, support, and counsel in a variety of areas. In school district networks, teachers tend to have regularly scheduled face-to-face meetings. Larger networks often rely on the internet for communication among teachers supported by workshops and seminars.

Examples of national networks include the National Writing Project (www.writingproject.org) that provides many professional development opportunities for teachers and maintains an online discussion on issues of concern in the teaching of writing. Teachers lead many of the professional development sessions where they share their work and examine related student work. In the Bread Loaf Rural Teacher Network (www.strom.clemson.edu/teams/literacy/RTN.html) teachers receive full fellowships for graduate study at Middlebury College, return to their school communities, and engage in collaborative projects with other teachers in the network across the nation. These teaching projects are related to writing, literature, and theater arts.

In the American Social History Project (ASHP) (www.ashp.cuny.edu) teachers from several middle and high schools in New York City and faculty from the City University of New York work collaboratively in seminars at the Graduate Center in hands-on experiences with the teacher resources provided as a part of the project. The purpose of the project is to support teachers in using the latest scholarship, technology, and active learning methods available for their classrooms. Additionally, opportunities are provided for teachers across the nation to participate in workshops and seminars and to purchase and use the resources provided by the Graduate Center at the City University of New York.

In transforming professional practice, teachers reflect on their own practice, observe the practice of expert teachers, and participate in professional learning communities to formulate and test hypotheses about teaching students from different experiential backgrounds. Other avenues used as information sources for improving professional practice include school district-sponsored staff development, professional conferences, university courses and seminars, and personal scholarship.

Studying One's Own Practice

The documentation and study of your own practice requires careful examination of students' responses to learning experiences, curriculum content, and the social context within the classroom. The study of your own practice should reveal the extent to which the intended knowledge and skills are acquired as well as the extent to which the classroom is comfortable and supportive for the students. Careful attention should be given to linkages among cognition, culture, and instruction. Examples of such linkages are presented in Chapter 7. You will need to remember that memory structures and intellectual processes are culturally shaped and are essential factors in the acquisition of new knowledge.

In cases where there is a disproportionately high rate of failure for a total class or for a particular group of students with similar cultural and background experiences, or other shared characteristics, there is reason to investigate the possibility of a problem with the learning experiences, how the content is framed, or the social context within the classroom. The investigation of such situations can require extensive study on your part. A careful study of teaching practices should help to determine whether instruction is biased in favor of or against groups of students with certain attributes or experiences in common. For example, if students from middle-income backgrounds always perform better than students from low-income backgrounds this might suggest that instruction is biased in favor of middle-income students. In this case, you need to study more thoroughly the needs of low-income students. The goal for professional development in this case is not to decrease the academic achievement of middle-income students, but rather, to develop more effective instruction for low-income students that will provide equitable learning outcomes.

When students show a lack of interest in a particular content or learning experience you can try to reframe the content or develop more meaningful and interesting learning experiences. Students tend to show more interest when curriculum content is tied to what they know and value. This might mean connecting the curriculum content more directly with the students' experiences or with specific adult or professional/occupational roles.

Studying Expert Practice

Observing other teachers in public school settings is not common practice. Typically, each teacher has a group of students for whom he or she is responsible and an instructional aide is likely to be the only other adult in the classroom. The tradition of teaching in isolation prevents access to expert teachers who can serve as mentors and models of good practice. Unless you are teaching at a school that has identified mentor teachers, you may have to work at identifying an expert teacher and gaining access to his or her classroom. This means talking with individual teachers about the challenges (rather than problems) faced in the classroom and seeking advice for meeting these challenges. This means describing situations and students as challenging rather than problematic and soliciting options rather than commiserating.

The purpose for observing expert teachers is threefold. First, it provides a non-threatening situation for analyzing and discussing classroom instruction with an expert teacher and other colleagues. Second, it provides opportunities for reflecting on your own practice in relationship to that of an expert teacher in a similar situation. Finally, it helps you to identify ways to improve your own practice. In this instance, observation is equivalent to modeling and practice. The expert teacher models productive instruction while other teachers observe and analyze in an attempt to understand what the expert does, how it is done, and whether it can be applied to situations in their own classrooms. The observer returns to his or her classroom and tries to practice what has been observed.

An expert teacher may be described as one employing productive practices. These teachers have the ability to create learning experiences that link with what students already know and value, and they develop a supportive social context for learning. The quality of productive learning in their classrooms is validated in samples of their students' work, performance on standardized and criterion reference tests, and students' perception of the learning environment.

Observing and comprehending the work of an expert teacher takes time and planning. Ideally, observation is an apprenticeship-type situation continued over an extended period of time. In such instances, the apprentice is able to observe and dialogue with the expert teacher and receive guidance in applying what has been gleaned from the interaction. Where such an ideal situation is not possible the amount of time designated for observation must be sufficient for developing and testing hypotheses concerning processes and interactions in the classroom. The observation should be long enough for the observer to begin to predict the actions and responses of the expert teacher. This could require making several observations in sequence or at different intervals depending on the nature of the situation or process being observed.

Where expert teachers are not readily available, videotapes can be used for observations. Videotapes provide a great deal of flexibility in scheduling, reviewing, and controlling action for discussion and analysis in small groups and by individual teachers. Using videotapes allows for immediate comparisons between different approaches and teaching strategies. When teachers have had sufficient experience in observing and discussing videotapes or expert teachers, they may be ready to begin working together as partners observing in each other's classrooms and providing constructive feedback to improve classroom practices. Working together as partners is more comfortable where there is mutual support and each teacher is confident that the other will not evaluate or judge his or her performance.

Monitoring Personal Professional Growth

Actively participating in a community of practice requires attention to personal professional growth. This means monitoring and enhancing your own content and pedagogical content knowledge, self-knowledge, knowledge of students' home-culture and experiential backgrounds, how you interact with students, and how you frame the curriculum to make learning meaningful for your students.

Content and Pedagogical Content Knowledge

Research has revealed that deep understanding of subject matter is associated with student learning outcomes (Wenglinsky, 2000). In an analysis of data from the 1996 National Assessment of Educational Progress (NAEP), Wenglinsky (2000) found that "students whose teachers majored or minored in the subject they are teaching outperform their peers by about 40 percent of a grade level in both math and science" (p. 7). Taking courses, seminars, and participating in professional development and teacher networks focused on new knowledge in particular subject-matter areas can be helpful in improving effectiveness in teaching.

Your preservice teacher preparation program includes a great deal of propositional and procedural knowledge usually supported by guided field experience. Typically, teacher educators try to find the best field placements with the best models of good teaching to provide opportunities for candidates to observe and apply pedagogical content knowledge. However, when you are hired for your first position you may have a different student population for whom you will need to contextualize your pedagogical content knowledge. This means that the approaches to instruction you use will need to be adapted to take into consideration your students' prior knowledge, experiential backgrounds, and learning propensities. Learning to contextualize your instructional practices means carefully observing how your students respond, taking this into consideration in planning, and sharing your observations with colleagues for feedback.

Self-Knowledge

Locke (1988) pointed out that,

> each teacher brings to the classroom a great deal of "cultural baggage." This baggage may cause the teacher to take certain things for granted and to behave in ways and manners of which he/she may

not be aware. The teacher must explore his/her values, opinions, attitudes, and beliefs in terms of their cultural origin. (p. 132)

When teachers examine their own cultural origins, it enhances understanding the significance of culture in the classroom. The heuristics presented in Chapter 3 can be used to frame reflection on personal experiences and perceptions as you progress from being a novice teacher toward becoming an expert.

Knowledge of Students' Home-Culture

The importance of students' background experiences has been stressed throughout this book. A systematic approach to acquiring relevant information, RIQ, is presented in Chapter 4. Learning about students' experiences should be a continuous process and should be included as part of professional development. It is important, if you teach in a culturally diverse setting, to increase your knowledge of the home-culture of your students in order to identify cultural practices and values that can be utilized to improve academic performance and empower students to actively engage in learning.

Interacting with Students

The relationship you develop with your students is a critical aspect of productive teaching that involves social interaction and communication. Different cultural groups have different social interaction practices and protocols with which you need to become familiar. The students themselves are good resources for information about preferred modes of social interaction and communication as well as about their experiences and concerns. Listening to students' voices is often an overlooked factor in teacher preparation and professional development. The importance of listening to students' voices is clearly presented in studies reported by Lewis (2003) and Fine (1989). In each of these studies, the authors pointed out how the voices or life experiences of the students can be used to enrich and increase the meaning of school learning. Fine described silencing in the inner-city school she studied in the following way:

> Some conversations within schools were closed; others were dichotomized. Yet a few conversations, indeed those most relevant to inequitable social arrangements, remained psychologized: managed as personal problems inside the offices of school psychologists or counselors. The lived experiences of all adolescents, and particularly those surviving city life in poverty, place their physical and mental well-being as well as that of their kin in constant jeopardy. And yet conversations about these very conditions of life, about alcoholism,

drug abuse, domestic violence, environmental hazards, gentrifica-
tion, and poor health—to the extent that they happened at all—
remained confined to individual sessions with counselors. (p. 165)

Fine suggested that the realities of students' lives can be woven into the
school curriculum and thus engage students in more meaningful learning.
Listening to the voices of students from different cultural and ethnic
groups is an important aspect of professional development.

Lewis (2003) provided a very candid account of how teachers and other
school personnel ignore race and racism in the everyday interactions
among students in classrooms and schoolyards, and the pain and humiliation many students suffer as a consequence. She explains how teachers
contribute to and, in some cases, participate in acts of racism. Lewis
pointed out that "racial categorizations are used to decide who is similar
and different; opportunities and resources are then distributed along racial
lines as people are included in or excluded from a range of institutions,
activities, or opportunities because of their categorization" (p. 152). The
inclusion, exclusion, and distribution of opportunities and resources to
which Lewis refers are, as she documents, evident across school districts, in
classrooms, and in the schoolyard. Teachers need to actively participate
in correcting school situations that make students uncomfortable and
interfere with learning.

Rethinking the School Curriculum

Rethinking the curriculum is more challenging in the present era of
accountability based on testing, sanctions, rewards, public school choice,
and the general and specific impact of No Child Left Behind (NCLB).
According to Fusarelli (2004):

NCLB establishes a comprehensive framework of standards, testing,
and accountability absent in previous federal legislation, and in the
process, it removes some discretion from local education authorities
in determining what the goals and outcomes of education should
be. In effect, "national report cards" will be issued to each school and
district in the United States. School districts will be given rewards
for demonstrated success (in the form of greater federal dollars),
whereas failing schools and districts will be punished through with-
drawal of federal funds, pressure for privatization, and public school
choice. (p. 72)

An important goal of NCLB is to narrow the achievement gap between
white middle-class students and low-income students of color. The
strategy for closing the achievement gap is by providing highly qualified
teachers, a public education system with high academic standards, and

school and district accountability for adequate yearly progress (AYP). One positive aspect of the NCLB accountability system is that the performance of subgroups on standardized tests is disaggregated such that schools and school districts are required to address discrepancies among the groups at each school. However, some critics argue that the focus on testing narrows the curriculum and further limits what students learn in school and takes away much of the flexibility teachers need to adapt instruction to students' learning needs (Fusarelli, 2004).

Most state departments of education and school districts have adopted policies and programs that are believed to support the goals of NCLB. Federal regulations under the NCLB legislation mandate the use of "scientifically based" approaches to classroom instruction. McDermott and Jensen (2005) argue that this is a concern because of the political influences on the linkage between research and policy. These authors pointed out that "the phonics-based reading programs regarded by DOE [the United States Department of Education] as scientifically based, for example, have been a conservative cause since the early 1990s" (p. 46). Meyer (2002) argues that scripted reading programs such as Open Court hold students and teachers as curriculum hostages where teachers are not allowed to adapt the curriculum to meet the needs of their students. It should be kept in mind that the use of scripted programs in the elementary schools is not new. Scripted programs have been around for several decades and have been used at teacher discretion as part of a much larger program with additional resources for meeting individual student needs. The present approach to the use of scripted programs may be more a response to the NCLB mandates than the nature of these programs.

The mandates for NCLB do not change the fact that individual teachers are responsible for student learning outcomes and for making the curriculum meaningful for particular groups of students. Teachers in culturally diverse settings should seek out professional development experiences that include redesigning the school curriculum (content and pedagogy) in ways that make use of the experiences and competencies youngsters bring to school. Chapter 5 presents approaches to reframing school curricula in this way.

Curriculum content in general should be meaningful and relevant for all youngsters. The curriculum should be explicitly related to the daily lives of the students and they should understand how it relates to their future adult lives. The curriculum should help youngsters maintain a sense of identity and personal worth and a feeling of connectedness to people like themselves as well as those who are different. Youngsters should find a positive representation of their cultural heritage within the curriculum.

Working with a Mentor

Many school districts have implemented one of a variety of forms of a new or beginning teacher induction program. In many of these programs first-year beginning teachers are assigned a mentor. In the ideal situation the mentor teacher is a competent and effective teacher with several years of productive teaching experience; teaches the same or a related subject or grade level in your building; has interest in supporting the professional development of new teachers; has excellent interpersonal and communication skills; and has time during the school day to work with a mentee. In formal mentoring programs like the Beginning Teacher Support and Assessment (BTSA) program in California, mentor teachers are encouraged to use predetermined standards to guide their work with mentees.

According to Carver and Katz (2004), mentors in the BTSA program use professional teaching standards developed in 1997 by the California Commission on Teacher Credentialing to "prompt reflection about student learning and teaching practice, formulate professional goals for improving teaching practice, and guide the progress of teacher's developing practice toward his or her goals" (p. 451). In the California BTSA program, the role of the mentor teacher is to support the beginning teacher in acquiring the skills and competencies included in the professional teaching standards for the state and conduct a formative assessment of the mentee's progress as a way to guide the work of the mentee and as part of the school district's teacher evaluation process.

Not all mentoring programs are as formal as that in California. However, getting the best benefit and support from your mentor requires thoughtful planning and preparation. Four tools that will be helpful in preparation for working with your mentor are: (a) curriculum or content standards mandated by your school district or state for your grade level and/or subject area, (b) teacher manuals for the instructional programs you are using, (c) teacher competency standards or standards for teacher evaluation provided by your district or state, and (d) a journal for documenting your teaching practices and your students' responses. As soon as possible after you are hired, you should read through the first three documents noting any questions or concerns you might want to raise with your mentor at a meeting early in the school year. Keeping a journal documenting your classroom practices and your students' responses will be particularly helpful in framing your discussions with your mentor about teaching practices and student learning. In preparation for each meeting with your mentor you need to review the notes you have made related to your teaching practices and your students' responses and those concerning teaching materials and professional standards. When you have prioritized your questions you have created your agenda for your meeting with your mentor. When planning meetings with your mentor you should keep in mind that research reveals that beginning teachers who met with a mentor a few times a year showed improvements in their instructional skills; however, those who met with their mentor weekly showed significantly great improvement (Kilburg and Hancock, 2006). Being prepared will enable you to more effectively use the time with your mentor.

Informal Teacher Support Groups

If you are hired into a position where you work in isolation, you are not part of a professional community of practice, you do not have access to a mentor, and you are teaching a population with which you are not familiar or students who have had repeatedly negative school experiences, it can be beneficial to join or start a teacher support group made up of teachers in a similar situation. The purpose of a teacher support group is collaboration on identifying alternatives and options for increasing meaningful and productive learning experiences for students in specific situations or under specific conditions. The purpose is not to share "war stories." At best, sharing war stories is a waste of valuable time that could be used to plan alternatives and options for improving the situation. It can also contribute to burnout and disenchantment.

Participating in a teacher support group requires preparation. In order for a support group to be productive the participants need to (a) list and develop written descriptions of the challenges and issues to be addressed, (b) prioritize the list, (c) select two or three top priorities and develop questions that need to be answered in order to identify alternatives and options, and (d) solicit assistance from colleagues in gathering data to answer questions and in identifying alternatives and options for addressing challenges and issues.

School District Staff Development

School district-sponsored staff development can be a vehicle for addressing specific challenges and issues such as those identified by participating in teacher support groups. You can significantly influence staff development programs in school districts by volunteering for planning committees or by contacting the appropriate district-level department to make recommendations. A productive planning process includes the four steps identified for participating in teacher support groups. The resource persons identified and the process employed in staff development should be specifically designed to assist teachers in acquiring the information needed to address highly salient challenges and issues they have identified.

Different types of resources for planning school district staff development programs include (a) expert teachers within the local school district;
(b) parents, other community members, and local community service
agencies; (c) faculty from nearby colleges or universities; (d) nationally
recognized experts; and (e) consultants with prepackaged programs.
Each of these resources can serve as an avenue for addressing challenges
and issues identified by local classroom teachers. Factors influencing the
selection of resources should include appropriateness for meeting the
needs of local teachers, accessibility for follow-up, and expense to teachers
and the school district. Caution should be exercised in relying on consultants with prepackaged programs. Transporting programs that have
been successful in one location may not produce the same results in
another and may not be appropriate for the specific challenges and issues
teachers need to address.

Professional Conferences

Annual conferences such as those sponsored by the International Reading
Association, the National Council for Social Studies, and other national
associations can be excellent resources for professional development.
These conferences usually offer a wide range of sessions including workshops, seminars, and reports presented by classroom teachers, university
professors, researchers, authors, and special consultants. In order to make
the best use of the time and resources invested, sessions should be selected
well in advance and based on previously identified needs.

University Courses and Seminars

Local colleges and universities usually offer a wide variety of regular and
special courses, seminars, and programs that can meet your needs as a
classroom teacher. University course offerings can be located in semester
and quarter schedules, catalogues, bulletins, and continuing or extended
education announcements. University catalogues contain descriptions
of courses that are offered regularly. Contact local professors who
teach individual courses to be certain that specific challenges, issues, and
questions are addressed.

Teachers as Scholars

An important part of professional development is active scholarship.
Being a member of a professional community of practice includes actively
consuming and creating new knowledge as well as sharing with and
learning from colleagues and students. This means that each teacher needs
a professional development plan that includes reading books and journal
articles related to the area and level of instruction in his or her classroom,

meaningful collaboration with colleagues on issues of mutual interest and concern, ongoing study of your own practice, and engaging in community activities that provide opportunities for becoming better acquainted with students and the communities in which they live.

You can participate in seminars as an active scholar in search of new knowledge and engage in generating new understandings concerning the students you teach. Seminars can provide opportunities to meet with colleagues from both the school and the university to discuss research findings, explore theory in practice, build theory from practice, develop collaborative research projects, and report on and hear reports of action research.

Seminars may consist of long- or short-term study groups. These groups may be formal or informal. A study group may be made up of a small cluster of teachers working within the same age-grade level (i.e. primary, intermediate, middle school) and university faculty members with knowledge of approaches to teaching specific content to certain groups of students and who are also interested in collaborating with classroom teachers.

In addition to professional growth, you may receive other benefits from your professional development plan such as university credit, inservice credit, financial compensation for the time involved, release time during the school year, and awards for study or research grants. These benefits need to be sought out and directly requested from the appropriate individuals and agencies.

Chapter Summary

In this chapter, the focus is on issues of professional development related to craft knowledge and approaches to transforming professional practice for a culturally diverse population of students. Important aspects of craft knowledge include self-knowledge, knowledge of students' home-culture and community life, interacting with students, and rethinking the school curriculum and instructional practices. Approaches to transforming professional practice include studying one's own practice, studying expert practice, participating in teacher support groups, school district-organized professional development, professional conferences, university courses and seminars, and personal scholarship.

Suggested Learning Experiences

1. Begin studying your own practice by examining the attributes of students who perform well in comparison to those who perform

poorly. Use this analysis as a basis for understanding biases in your practice. Retain those aspects of your practice that support students who are performing well. Based on what you have read in this book, gather information and experiment with ways to provide more productive learning experiences for those students who are performing poorly.

2. Initiate a study group by inviting a small group of teachers from the same school or who teach the same content or grade level to meet and discuss common challenges you face in your classroom.

3. Identify particular issues or challenges related to teaching students from specific cultural or ethnic backgrounds that are of interest to you. Check with the local teachers' association to get a list of state or national conferences scheduled for the local area or nearby. Request a conference program. Check the listings for sessions that address the specific issues you have identified.

4. Contact the local county office of education to get a listing of professional development activities offered for classroom teachers. Check the list for topics related to the issues that are of interest to you.

Critical Reading

Showers, B. (1985). Teachers coaching teachers. *Educational Leadership*, 42(7), 43–48.

   The author describes the purpose and process of coaching in building a "community of teachers who continuously engage in the study of their craft."

Shulman, J. H. (1991). Classroom casebooks. *Educational Leadership*, 49(3), 28–31.

   The author presents a brief description of classroom casebooks, including their usefulness and a sample entry by a teacher.

Shulman, J. H., and Mesa-Bains, A. (eds) (1990). *Teaching diverse students: cases and commentaries.* Hillsdale, NJ: Lawrence Erlbaum Associates.

   These authors present a compilation of teacher narratives described as "cases" with commentaries by educators representing different points of view. These narratives provide unusual insights into situations, feelings, reactions, teacher reflection, and other educators' analysis.

References

Acker, S. (1987). Feminist theory and the study of gender and education. *International Review of Education*, 33, 419–435.

Adams, B. S., Pardo, W. E., and Schniedewind, N. (1991). Changing "The way things are done around here." *Educational Leadership*, 49(4), 37–42.

Adams, D. (1988). Fundamental considerations: The deep meaning of Native American schooling, 1800–1900. *Harvard Educational Review*, 58(1), 1–28.

Alba, R. (1990). *Ethnic Identity: The transformation of White America.* New Haven: Yale University Press.

Alvarez, A. N. (2002). Racial identity and Asian Americans: Supports and challenges. *New Directions for Student Services*, 97, 33–43.

Anderson, L. W., and Pellicer, L. O. (1990). Synthesis of research on compensatory and remedial education. *Educational Leadership*, 48(1), 10–16.

Anyon, J. (1980). Social class and the hidden curriculum of work. *Journal of Education*, 162(1), 67–92.

Applegate, J. S. (1990). Theory, culture, and behavior: Object relations in context. *Child and Adolescent Social Work*, 7(2), 85–105.

Aronowitz, S., and Giroux, H. (1988). Schooling, culture, and literacy in the age of broken dreams: A review of Bloom and Hirsch. *Harvard Educational Review*, 58(2), 172–194.

Asher, N. (2002). Class acts: Indian American high school students negotiate professional and ethnic identities. *Urban Education*, 37(2), 267–295.

Au, K. H. (1980). Participation structures in a reading lesson with Hawaiian children: Analysis of a culturally appropriate instructional event. *Anthropology and Education*, 11(2), 91–115.

Au, K. H. (1992). Constructing the theme of a story. *Language Arts*, 69, 106–111.

Au, K. H. (1993). *Literacy Instruction in Multicultural Settings.* Fort Worth, TX: Harcourt Brace Javanovich College Publishers.

Au, K. H., and Kawakami, A. J. (1985). Research currents: Talk story and learning to read. *Language Arts*, 62(4), 406–411.

Au, K. H., and Kawakami, A. J. (1991). Culture and ownership: Schooling of minority students. *Childhood Education*, 67(5), 280–284.

Au, K. H., and Mason, J. M. (1981). Social organizational factors in learning to read: The balance of rights hypothesis. *Reading Research Quarterly*, 17(1), 115–151.

Ayers, W. (1988). Young children and the problem of the color line. *Democracy and Education*, 3(1), 20–26.

Bachtold, L. M. (1984). Antecedents of caregiver attitudes and social behavior of Hupa Indian and Anglo-American preschoolers in California. *Child Study Journal*, 13(4), 217–233.

Banks, J. A. (1988a). Ethnicity, class, cognitive, and motivational styles: Research and teaching implications. *Journal of Negro Education*, 57(4), 452–466.

Banks, J. A. (1988b). *Multiethnic Education: Theory and practice*. Boston: Allyn and Bacon.

Banks, J. A. (1989). Integrating the curriculum with ethnic content: Approaches and guidelines. In J. A. Banks and C. A. McGee Banks (eds), *Multicultural Education: Issues and perspectives*, pp. 167–188. Boston: Allyn and Bacon.

Banks, J. A (1991). *Teaching Strategies for Ethnic Studies*. Boston: Allyn and Bacon.

Banks, J. A. (1991/1992). Multicultural education: For freedom's sake. *Educational Leadership*, 49(4), 32–36.

Banks, J. A. (1995). Multicultural education and curriculum transformation. *Journal of Negro Education*, 64(4), 390–400.

Baptiste, H. P., Jr. (1986). Multicultural education and urban schools from a sociohistorical perspective: Internalizing multiculturalism. *Journal of Educational Equity and Leadership*, 6(4), 295–312.

Barrett, R. A. (1984). *Culture and Conduct: An excursion in anthropology*. Belmont, CA: Wadsworth.

Baugh, J. (1988). Why what works hasn't worked for nontraditional students. *Journal of Negro Education*, 57, 417–431.

Bellah, R. N., Madsen, R., Sullivan, W. M., Swindler, A., and Tipton, S. M. (1985). *Habits of the Heart*. New York: Harper and Row.

Bennett, C. I. (1986). *Comprehensive Multicultural Education: Theory and practice*. Boston: Allyn and Bacon.

Bennett, C. I. (2001). Genres of research in multicultural education. *Review of Educational Research*, 71(2), 171–217.

Bennett, L., Jr. (1993). *Before the Mayflower* (6th ed.). New York: Penguin Books.

Bereiter, C., and Engelman, S. (1966). *Teaching Disadvantaged Children in the Preschool*. Englewood Cliffs, NJ: Prentice-Hall.

Berger, J. (1991, June 21). Arguing about America. *New York Times*, p. A10, Column 3.

Berliner, D. (1986). Does culture affect reading comprehension? *Instructor*, 96(3), 28–29.

Bernard, J. (1966). *Marriage and Family among Negroes*. Englewood Cliffs, NJ: Prentice-Hall.

Bernstein, B. (1961). Aspects of language and learning in the genesis of the social process. *Journal of Child Psychology and Psychiatry*, I, 313–324.

Blum, L. (1999). What is "racism" in antiracist education? *Teachers College Record*, 100(4), 860–880.

Bond, H. M. (1939). *Negro Education in Alabama: A study in cotton and steel*. Washington, DC: The Associated Publishers.

Boykin, A W., and Allen, B. (1988). Rhythmic-movement facilitated learning in working class Afro-American children. *Journal of Genetic Psychology*, 149, 335–347.

Bransford, J. D., Brown, A. L., and Cocking, R. R. (eds) (1999). *How People Learn: Brain, mind, experience, and school*. Washington, DC: National Academy Press.

Bureau of the Census (1991, February). *Statistical Brief*. Washington, DC: U.S. Government Printing Office.

Carter, R. T. (2000). Reimagining race in education: A new paradigm from psychology. *Teachers College Record*, 102(5), 864–897.

Carter, T. P., and Chatfield, M. L. (1986). Effective bilingual schools: Implications for policy and practice. *American Journal of Education*, 95(1), 200–234.

Carver, C. L., and Katz, D. S. (2004). Teaching at the boundary of acceptable practice: What is a new teacher mentor to do? *Journal of Teacher Education*, 55(5), 449–462.

Case, R. (1987). Neo-Piagetian theory: Retrospect and prospect. *International Journal of Psychology*, 22, 773–791.

Cecil, N. L. (1988). Black dialect and academic success: A study of teacher expectations. *Reading Improvement*, 25(1), 34–38.

Children's Defense Fund. Poverty increases for the fourth year in a row in 2004. Online at www.childrensdefense.org/site/News2?page=NewsArticle (accessed September 18, 2006).

Close, E. (1993). *The Rage of a Privileged Class*. New York: HarperCollins.

Cockrell, K. S., Placier, P. L., Cockrell, D. H., and Middleton, J. N. (1999). Coming to terms with "diversity" and "multiculturalism" in teacher education: Learning about our students, changing our practice. *Teaching and Teacher Education*, 15, 251–366.

Cole, M. (1974). *Culture and Thought: A psychological introduction*. New York: Wiley.

Cole, M. (1988). Cross-cultural research in the socio-historical tradition. *Human Development*, 31, 137–157.

Collins, J. (1988). Language and class in minority education. *Anthropology and Education Quarterly*, 19, 299–326.

Comer, J. P. (1987). New Haven's school-community connection. *Educational Leadership*, 44(6), 13–16.

Cornbleth, C. (1998). An American curriculum? *Teachers College Record*, 99(4), 622–646.

Cortes, C. E. (1986). The education of language minority students: A contextual interaction model. In C. E. Cortes, *Beyond Language: Social and cultural factors in schooling language minority students*, pp. 3–34. Sacramento: Bilingual Education Office, California State Department of Education.

Cottrol, R. J. (1994/1995). America the multicultural. In *Annual Editions: Multicultural Education*. New York: Dushkin, pp. 25–28.

Cummins, J. (1986). Empowering minority students: A framework for intervention. *Harvard Educational Research*, 56(1), 18–36.

D'Amato, J. (1988). "Acting": Hawaiian children's resistance to teachers. *The Elementary School Journal*, 88(5), 529–544.

Darling-Hammond, L. (2000). Teacher quality and student achievement: A review of state policy evidence. *Education Policy Analysis Archives*, 8(1). Online at http://epaa.asu.edu/epaa/vol8.html (retrieved October 26, 2007).

Dewey, J. (1938). *Experience and Education*. New York: Collier Books.

Dillon, D. R. (1989). Showing them that I want them to learn and that I care about who they are: A microethnography of the social organization of a secondary low-track English-reading classroom. *American Educational Research Journal*, 26(2), 227–259.

Dreeben, R., and Gamoran, A. (1986). Race, instruction, and learning. *American Sociological Review*, 51, 660–669.

DuBois, W. E. B. (1973). *The Philadelphia Negro: A social study*. Millwood, NY: Kraus-Thomson. (Original work published 1889.)

DuBois, W. E. B. (1973). *The Suppression of the African Slave Trade to the United States of America, 1638–1870*. Millwood, NY: Kraus-Thomson. (Original work published 1896.)

Edelman, M. W. (1987). *Families in Peril: An agenda for social change*. Cambridge, MA: Harvard University Press.

Edelman, M. W. (1990). Why America may go to hell. *America*, 162(12), 310–314.

Erickson, F. (1987). Transformation and school success: The politics and culture of educational achievement. *Anthropology and Education Quarterly*, 18, 335–356.

Erickson, F., and Mohatt, G. (1982). Cultural organization of participation structures in two classrooms of Indian students. In G. B. Spindler (ed.), *Doing the Ethnography of Schooling: Educational anthropology in action*, pp. 132–174. New York: Holt, Rinehart and Winston.

Escovar, P. L., and Lazarus, P. J. (1982). Cross-cultural childrearing practices: Implications for school psychologists. *School Psychology International*, 3, 143–148.

Feather, N. T. (1975). *Values in Education and Society*. New York: The Free Press.

Fine, M. (1989). Silencing and nurturing voice in an improbable context: Urban adolescents in public school. In H. Giroux and R. Simon (eds), *Critical Pedagogy, the State and Cultural Struggle*, pp. 152–173. Albany: State University of New York Press.

Foley, D. E. (1991). Reconsidering anthropological explanations of ethnic school failure. *Anthropology and Education Quarterly*, 22, 60–94.

Frazier, E. F. (1932). *The Negro Family in Chicago*. Chicago: University of Chicago Press.

Frazier, E. F. (1937). Negro Harlem: An ecological study. *American Journal of Sociology*, 43, 72–88.

Freebody, P., and Baker, C. D. (1985). Children's first schoolbooks: Introduction to the culture of literacy. *Harvard Educational Review*, 55(4), 381–398.

French, S. E., Seidman, E., Allen, L., and Aber, J. L. (2006). The development of ethnic identity during adolescence. *Developmental Psychology*, 42(1), 1–10.

Fusarelli, L. D. (2004). The potential impact of the No Child Left Behind Act on equity and diversity in American Education. *Education Policy*, 18(1), 71–94.

Gagne, R. M., and White, R. T. (1978). Memory structures and learning outcomes. *Review of Educational Research*, 48(2), 187–222.

Garibaldi, A. (1992). Educating and motivating African American males to succeed. *Journal of Negro Education*, 61, 4–11.

Gay, G. (1983). Multiethnic education: Historical developments and future prospects. *Phi Delta Kappan*, 64(8), 560–563.

Geographic Profile of Employment and Unemployment (1991, June). Washington, DC: U.S. Department of Labor Bureau of Labor Statistics, Bulletin 2381.

Gibson, M. A. (1984). Approaches to multicultural education in the United States: Some concepts and assumptions. *Anthropology and Education Quarterly*, 15, 94–119.

Gilmore, P. (1985). "Gimme room": School resistance, attitude, and access to literacy. *Journal of Education*, 167(1), 111–128.

Goldberg, D. T. (1990). *The Anatomy of Racism*. Minneapolis: University of Minneapolis Press.

Good, H. G., and Teller, J. D. (1973). *A History of American education* (3rd ed.). New York: Macmillan.

Good, T. L., and Brophy, I. (1987). *Looking in Classrooms*. London: Harper and Row.

Goodlad, J. I., and Oakes, J. (1988). We must offer equal access to knowledge. *Educational Leadership*, 45(5), 16–22.

Grant, C. A., and Sleeter, C. E. (1989). *Turning on Learning: Five approaches for multicultural teaching plans for race, class, gender, and disability*. Columbus, OH: Merrill.

Gray, E., and Cosgrove, J. (1985). Ethnocentric perception of childrearing practices in protective services. *Child Abuse and Neglect*, 9, 389–396.

Hakuta, K., and Gould, L. J. (1987). Synthesis of research in bilingual education. *Educational Leadership*, 44(6), 39–45.

Hall, E. T. (1977). *Beyond Culture*. Garden City, NY: Anchor Books.

Hall, E. T. (1989). Unstated features of the cultural context of learning. *The Educational Forum*, 54(1), 21–34.

Helms, J. E. (1990). *Black and White Racial Identity: Theory, research, and practice*. New York: Greenwood Press.

Helms, J. E. (1995). An update of Helms's White and people of color racial identity models. In J. G. Ponterotto, J. M. Casas, L. A. Susuki, and C. M. Alexander (eds), *Handbook of Multicultural Counseling*, pp. 181–198. Thousand Oaks, CA: Sage.

Hill, R. B. (1972). *The Strengths of Black Families*. New York: Emerson Hall.

Hill, S. (2001). Class, race, and gender: Dimensions of child rearing in African American families. *Journal of Black Studies*, 31(4), 494–508.

Hilliard, A. G., III (1991). Why we must pluralize the curriculum. *Educational Leadership*, 49(4), 12–15.

Hodge, J. L. (1990). Equality: Beyond dualism and oppression. In D. T. Goldberg (ed.), *Anatomy of Racism*. Minneapolis: University of Minnesota Press.

Hodgkinson, H. (1988). The right schools for the right kids. *Educational Leadership*, 45(5), 10–14.

Hodgkinson, H. (1991). Reform versus reality. *Phi Delta Kappan*, 73(1), 8–16.

Hollins, E. R. (1982). The Marva Collins story revisited. *Journal of Teacher Education*, 32(1), 37–40.

Hollins, E. R. (1990). Debunking the myth of a monolithic white American culture; or, moving toward cultural inclusion. *American Behavioral Scientist*, 34(2), 201–209.

Hollins, E. R. (2006). Transforming practice in urban schools. *Educational Leadership*, 63(6), 48–52.

Hollins, E. R., and Spencer, K. (1990). Restructuring schools for cultural inclusion: Changing the schooling process for African American youngsters. *Journal of Education*, 172(2), 89–100.

Jensen, A. R. (1969). How much can we boost IQ and scholastic achievement? *Harvard Educational Review*, 39, 1–123.

Jensen, A. R., and Johnson, F. W. (1994). Race and sex differences in head size and IQ. *Intelligence*, 18(3), 309–333.

John-Steiner, V., and Mahn, H. (1996). Sociocultural approaches to learning and development: A Vygotskian framework. *Educational Psychologist*, 31(3/4), 191–206.

Kagan, J. (2002). Empowerment and education: Civil rights, expert-advocates, and parent politics in Head Start, 1964–1980. *Teachers College Record*, 104(3), 516–562.

Katz, S. R. (2000). Promoting bilingualism in the era of Unz: Making sense of the gap between research, policy, and practice in teacher education. *Multicultural Education*, 8(1), 2–7.

Kennedy, M. M. (1991). Some surprising findings on how teachers learn to teach. *Educational Leadership*, 49(3), 14–17.

Kilburg, G. M., and Hancock, T. (2006). Addressing sources of collateral damage in four mentoring programs. *Teachers College Record*, 108(7), 1321–1338.

Kirp, D. L. (1990, October 7). No angels, no demons. *San Francisco Examiner: Image*, pp. 23–29.

Kohl, H. R. (1994). *I Won't Learn from You: And other thoughts on creative maladjustment.* New York: New Press, distributed by W. W. Norton.

Krall, F. R. (1988). From the inside out. Personal history as educational research. *Educational Theory*, 38(4), 467–479.

Ladson-Billings, G. (1990). Culturally relevant teaching: Effective instruction for black students. *The College Board Review*, 155, 20–25.

Lasch, C. (1979). *The Culture of Narcissism: American life in an age of diminishing expectations.* New York: Norton.

Lave, J., and Wenger, E. (1991). *Situated Learning: Legitimate peripheral participation.* New York: Cambridge University Press.

Lee, C. D. (1991). Big picture talkers/words walking without masters: The instructional implications of ethnic voices for an expanded literacy. *Journal of Negro Education*, 60(3), 291–304.

Lee, C. D. (1995). A culturally based cognitive apprenticeship: Teaching African American high school students skills in literacy interpretation. *Reading Research Quarterly*, 30(4), 608–630.

Lee, S. J. (2001). More than "model minorities" or "delinquents": A look at Hmong American high school students. *Harvard Educational Review*, 71(3), 505–528.

Lesser, G. S., Fifer, G., and Clark, D. H. (1965). Mental abilities of children from different social-class and cultural groups. *Monographs of the Society for Research in Child Development*, 30(4).

Lester, J. (1993, July 30). "Warlords" and white lies. *San Francisco Chronicle*, p. A-23.

Levine, D. U., and Stark, J. (1982). Instructional and organizational arrangements that improve achievement in inner-city schools. *Educational Leadership*, 40(3), 41–46.

LeVine, R. A. (1988). Human parental care: Universal goals, cultural strategies, individual behavior. *New Directions for Child Development*, 40, 3–11.

Lewis, A. E. (2003). *Race in the Schoolyard: Negotiating the color line in classrooms and communities*. New Brunswick, NJ: Rutgers University Press.

Lewis, C., Perry, R., and Murata, A. (2006). How should research contribute to instructional improvement? The case of lesson study. *Educational Researcher*, 35(3), 3–14.

Lichten, W. (2004). On the law of intelligence. *Developmental Review*, 24(3), 252–288.

Liebow, E. (1966). *Tally's Corner*. Boston: Little, Brown.

Lipka, J. (1991). Toward a culturally based pedagogy: A case study of one Yup'ik Eskimo teacher. *Anthropology and Education Quarterly*, 22, 203–223.

Locke, D. C. (1988). Teaching culturally different students: Growing pine trees or bonsai trees. *Contemporary Education*, 59(3), 130–133.

Loehlin, J. C., Lindzey, G., and Spuhler, J. N. (1975). *Race Differences in Intelligence*. San Francisco: Freeman.

Lucas, T., Henze, R., and Donato, R. (1990). Promoting the success of Latino language-minority students: An exploratory study of six high schools. *Harvard Educational Review*, 60, 315–328.

Lynn, R. (1999). Sex differences in intelligence and brain size: A developmental theory. *Intelligence*, 27(1), 1–12.

McAdoo, H. (1978). Factors related to stability in upwardly mobile black families. *Journal of Marriage and the Family*, 40, 762–778.

McCarty, T. (2002). *A Place to be Navajo: Rough Rock and the struggle for self-determination in indigenous schooling*. Mahwah, NJ: Lawrence Erlbaum Associates Publishers.

McCarty, T. L., Lynch, R. H., Wallace, S., and Benally, A. (1991). Classroom inquiry and Navajo learning styles: A call for reassessment. *Anthropology and Education Quarterly*, 22, 42–59.

McDermott, K. A., and Jensen, L. S. (2005). Dubious sovereignty: Federal conditions of aid and the No Child Left Behind Act. *Peabody Journal of Education*, 90(2), 39–56.

McDermott, R. P. (1977). Social relations as contexts for learning in school. *Harvard Educational Review*, 47(2), 198–213.

McDonald, J. P., and Klein, E. J. (2003). Networking for teacher learning: Toward a theory of effective design. *Teachers College Record*, 105(8), 1606–1621.

MacLeod, J. (1991). Bridging street and school. *Journal of Negro Education*, 60(3), 260–275.

MacLeod, J. (1995). *Ain't No Makin' It*. Boulder, CO: Westview Press.

McPhail, I. P. (1987). Literacy as a liberating experience. *English Quarterly*, 20(1), 9–15.

Marable, M. (1990, August–September). The rhetoric of racial harmony: Finding substance in culture and ethnicity. *Sojourners*, 14–18.

Maume, D. J., Jr. (1999). Glass ceilings and glass escalators: Occupational segregation and race and sex differences in managerial promotions. *Work and Occupations*, 26(4), 483–509.

Menacker, J. (1990). Equal educational opportunity: Is it an issue of race or socioeconomic status? *Urban Education*, 25(3), 317–325.

Meyer, R. J. (2002). Captives of the script: Killing us softly with phonics. *Language Arts*, 79(6), 452–461.

Michaels, S. (1981). "Sharing time": Children's narrative styles and differential access to literacy. *Language in Society*, 10, 423–442.

Mini-Digest of Educational Statistics (1994). Washington, DC: U.S. Office of Education, National Center for Educational Statistics.

Moll, L. C. (1986). Writing as communication: Creating strategic learning environments for students. *Theory into Practice*, 25(2), 102–108.

Moll, L. C. (1988). Some key issues in teaching Latino students. *Language Arts*, 65(5), 465–472.

Moll, L. C. (1993). *Vygotsky and Education*. New York: Cambridge University Press.

Moll, L. C., Saez, R., and Dworin, J. (2001). *Elementary School Journal*, 101(4), 435–449.

Moses, R. P., Kamii, M., Swap, S. M., and Howard, J. (1989). The Algebra Project: Organizing in the spirit of Ella. *Harvard Educational Review*, 59(4), 423–443.

Nicholson-Crotty, S., and Meier, K. J. (2003). Crime and punishment: The politics of federal criminal justice sanctions. *Political Research Quarterly*, 56(2), 119–126.

Nieto, S. (1992). *Affirming Diversity: The sociopolitical context of multicultural education*. New York: Longman.

Noguera, P. A. (1995). Preventing and producing violence: A critical analysis of responses to school violence. *Harvard Educational Review*, 65(2), 189–212.

Ogbu, J. (1981). Origins of human competence: A cultural–ecological perspective. *Child Development*, 52, 413–429.

Ogbu, J. (1983). Minority status and schooling in plural societies. *Comparative Education Review*, 27(2), 168–190.

Ogbu, J. (1985). Research currents: Cultural–ecological influences on minority school learning. *Language Arts*, 62(8), 860–869.

Ogbu, J. (1987). Variability in minority school performance: A problem in search of an explanation. *Anthropology and Education Quarterly*, 18, 312–334.

Ogbu, J. (1988). Cultural diversity and human development. *New Directions for Child Development*, 42, 11–25.

Olmstead, K. J. (1988). Expanding cultural awareness: Wigginton on cultural journalism. *English Journal*, 77, 31–38.

Ornstein, A. C., and Levine, D. U. (1989). Social class, race, and school achievement: Problems and prospects. *Journal of Teacher Education*, 40, 17–23.

Ortony, A., Turner, T. J., and Larson-Shapiro, N. (1985). Cultural and instructional influences on figurative language comprehension by inner city children. *Research in the Teaching of English*, 19(1), 25–36.

Page, R. (1987). Teachers' perceptions of students: A link between classrooms, school cultures, and the social order. *Anthropology and Education Quarterly*, 18, 77–99.

Pai, Y. (1990). *Cultural Foundations of Education*. Columbus, OH: Merrill.

Payne, R. K. (1996). *A Framework for Understanding Poverty: Modules 1–7 Workbook*. Highlands, TX: aha! Process.

Payne, R. K. (2001). *A Framework for Understanding Poverty* (2nd revised ed.). Highlands, TX: aha! Process.

Payne, R. K. (2003). No child left behind: What's really behind it all? Part I. *Instructional Leader*, (16)2, 1–3.

Payne, R. K. (2005). *A Framework for Understanding Poverty* (4th revised ed.). Highlands, TX: aha! Process.

Philips, S. U. (1972). Participant structures and communicative competence: Warm Springs children in community and classroom. In C. B. Cazden (ed.), *Functions of Language in the Classroom*, pp. 270–394. New York: Teachers College Press.

Philips, S. U. (1983). *The Invisible Culture: Communication in classroom and community on the Warm Springs Indian Reservation*. New York: Longman.

Pratte, R. (1979). *Pluralism in Education: Conflict, clarity, and commitment*. Springfield, IL: Thomas Publishers.

Pratte, R. (1990). *Cultural Foundations of Education*. Columbus, OH: Merrill.

Proweller, A. (1999). Shifting identities in private education: Reconstructing race at/in the cultural center. *Teachers College Record*, 100(4), 776–808.

Quarles, B. (1987). *The Negro in the Making of America*. New York: Collier.

Rainwater, L. (1965). *Family Design*. Chicago: Aldine.

Ramirez, B. A. (1988). Culturally and linguistically diverse children. *Teaching Exceptional Children*, 20(4), 45–51.

Ratner, R. (1984). Horace M. Kallen and cultural pluralism. *Modern Judaism*, 4(2), 185–200.

Ravitch, D. (1990). Multiculturalism: E Pluribus Plures. *The American Scholar*, 59, 337–354.

Ravitch, D. (1991/1992). A culture in common. *Educational Leadership*, 49(4), 8–11.

Reed, S., and Sautter, R. C. (1990). Children of poverty: The status of 12 million young Americans. *Phi Delta Kappan*, 71(10), KI–KI2.

Reynolds, R. E., Taylor, M. A., Steffensen, M. S., Shirley, L. L., and Anderson, R. C. (1982).

Cultural schemata and reading comprehension. *Reading Research Quarterly*, 17(3), 353–366.

Richardson, V. (2003). Constructivist pedagogy. *Teachers College Record*, 105(9), 1623–1640.

Rison, A. (1990). *How to Teach Black Children*. Austin, TX: Sunbelt Theatre Production.

Roe v. Wade (1973). *United States Supreme Court Reports*, 410, 113.

Rogoff, B. (1990). *Apprenticeship in Thinking*. New York: Oxford University Press.

Rogoff, B., and Wertsch, J. V. (1984). *Children's Learning in the "Zone of Proximal Development."* San Francisco: Jossey-Bass.

Rokeach, M. (1973). *The Nature of Human Values*. New York: The Free Press.

Rosenshine, B. V. (1986). Synthesis of research on explicit teaching. *Educational Leadership*, 43(7), 60–69.

Roth, R. (1984). Schooling, literacy acquisition and cultural transmission. *Journal of Education*, 166(3), 291–308.

Rushton, J. P., and Rushton, E. W. (2003). Brain size, IQ, and racial-group differences: Evidence from musculoskeletal traits. *Intelligence*, 31(2), 139–155.

Salmon, P. B. (1983). Strengthening America through stronger education. *American Education*, 19(3), 27–29.

Samuels, S. J. (1979). The method of repeated readings. *The Reading Teacher*, 32(4), 403–408.

Samuels, W. J. (1991). Dynamics of cultural change. *Society*, 29(1), 23–26.

Saravia-Shore, M., and Arvizu, S. F. (1992). *Cross-cultural Literacy: Ethnographies of communication in multiethnic classrooms*. New York: Garland.

Schorr, L. B. (1989). *Within Our Reach: Breaking the cycle of disadvantage*. New York: Doubleday Books.

Schunk, D. H. (1991). *Learning Theories: An educational perspective*. New York: Macmillan.

Shaul, R. (1970). Foreword. In P. Freire, *Pedagogy of the Oppressed*. New York: Herder and Herder.

Shulman, L. S. (1987). Knowledge and teaching: Foundations of the new reform. *Harvard Educational Review*, 57(1), 1–8.

Siegel, B. (1970). Defensive structuring and environmental stress. *American Journal of Sociology*, 76, 11–32.

Slavin, R. E. (1983). *Cooperative Learning*. New York: Longman.

Slavin, R. E. (1987). Making Chapter I make a difference. *Phi Delta Kappan*, 69(2), 110–119.

Sleeter, C. E. (1989). Multicultural education as a form of resistance to oppression. *Journal of Education*, 171(3), 51–71.

Sleeter, C. E., and Grant, C. A. (1987). An analysis of multicultural education in the United States. *Harvard Educational Review*, 57(4), 421–444.

Smith, W. I., and Drumming, S. T. (1989). On the strategies blacks employ in deductive reasoning. *Journal of Black Psychology*, 16, 1–22.

Smolicz, J. (1996). Multiculturalism and an overarching framework of values: Some educational responses for ethnically plural societies. In E. R. Hollins (ed.), *Transforming Curriculum for a Culturally Diverse Society*, pp. 59–74. Mahwah, NJ: Lawrence Erlbaum Associates.

Solomon, R. P. (1992). *Black Resistance in High School*. Albany: State University of New York Press.

Sowell, T. (1991). A world view of cultural diversity. *Society*, 29(1), 37–44.

Spencer, M. (1982). Preschool children's social cognition and cultural cognition: A cognitive developmental interpretation of race dissonance findings. *Journal of Psychology*, 112, 275–286.

Stalker, J. C. (1988). Official English or English only. *English Journal*, 77(3), 18–23.

Staples, R., and Mirande, A. (1980). Racial and cultural variations among American families: A decennial review of the literature on minority families. *Journal of Marriage and the Family*, 42(4), 887–903.

Stephens, S. (2000). *Handbook for Culturally Responsive Science Curriculum*. Fairbanks, AK: Alaska Native Knowledge Network.

Suarez-Orozco, M. M. (2001). Globalization, immigration, and education: The research agenda. *Harvard Educational Review*, 71(3), 345–365.

Sue, S., and Padilla, A. (1986). Ethnic minority issues in the United States: Challenges for the educational system. In *Beyond Language: Social and cultural factors in schooling language minority students*, pp. 35–72. Sacramento: Bilingual Education Office, California State Department of Education.

Taba, H. (1955). *School Culture.* Washington, DC: American Council on Education.

Torres-Guzman, M. E., Mercado, C. I., Quintero, A. H., and Viera, D. R. (1994). Teaching and learning in Puerto Rican/Latino collaboratives: Implications for teacher education. In E. R. Hollins, J. E. King, and W. C. Hayman (eds), *Teaching Culturally Diverse Populations: Formulating a knowledge base*. New York: State University of New York Press.

Trueba, H. T. (1988). Culturally based explanations of minority students' academic achievement. *Anthropology and Education Quarterly*, 19, 270–287.

U.S. Bureau of the Census (1987). *Current Population Reports* (ser. P-60, no. 157).

U.S. Department of Education, Office of Educational Research and Improvement (1995). *Understanding Racial–Ethnic Differences in Secondary School Science and Mathematics Achievement.* Washington, DC: U.S. Department of Education, Office of Educational Research and Improvement.

U.S. Department of Labor, Bureau of Labor Statistics. *Earnings by Educational Attainment and Sex, 1979 and 2002.* Online at http://www.bls.gov/cps/cpsatabs.htm (retrieved October 26, 2007).

U.S. Department of Labor, Bureau of Labor Statistics. *Unemployment Rate by Race, Age, and Sex, 2001–2003.* Online at http://www.bls.gov/cps/cpsatabs.htm (retrieved October 26, 2007).

U.S. Department of Labor, Bureau of Vital Statistics. (1991, June). *Geographic Profile of Employment and Unemployment, 1990* (Bulletin 2381). Washington, DC: U.S. Government Printing Office.

Vygotsky, L. S. (1978). *Thought and Language.* Cambridge, MA: MIT Press.

Vygotsky, L. S. (1978). *Mind and Society: The development of higher mental processes.* Cambridge, MA: Harvard University Press.

Wacker, R. F. (1979). Assimilation and cultural pluralism in American social thought. *Phylon*, 40(4), 325–333.

Webster v. Reproductive Health Services. (1989). *United States Supreme Court Reports*, 490, 106.

Wenglinsky, H. (2000). *How Teaching Matters: Bringing the classroom back into discussions of teacher quality.* Princeton, NJ: Education Testing Service. Online at www.ets.org/research/pic.

Wertsch, J. V. (1979). From social interaction to higher psychological processes: A clarification and application of Vygotsky's theory. *Human Development*, 22, 1–22.

Wesley, C. H. (1969). *Richard Allen: Apostle of freedom.* Washington, DC: Associated Publishers. (Original work published 1935.)

Whitaker, M. (1993, November 15). White and Black lies. *Newsweek*, pp. 52–3.

Wigginton, E. (1977). The Foxfire approach: It can work for you. *Media and Methods*, 14(3), 48–51.

Wigginton, E. (1990). Will the curriculum be broken? *Appalachian Journal*, 17(4), 396–403.

Wigginton, E. (1991). Culture begins at home. *Educational Leadership*, 49(4), 60–94.

Williams, G. W. (1989). *History of the Negro Race in America from 1619 to 1880: Negroes as slaves, as soldiers, and as citizens* (2 vols). Salem, NH: Ayers. (Original works published 1882 and 1883.)

Williams, H. B., and Williams, E. (1979). Some aspects of childrearing practices in three minority subcultures in the United States. *Journal of Negro Education*, 63(3), 408–418.

Wong, J. (1990, September 19). Conservative scholars see "multiculturalism" as a plague. *Chronicle of Higher Education*, p. A41.

Woodson, C. G. (1921). *The History of the Negro Church.* Washington, DC: Associated Publishers.

Woodson, C. G. (1933). *Mis-education of the Negro.* Washington, DC: Associated Publishers.

Woodson, C. G. (1968). *The Education of the Negro prior to 1861.* Washington, DC: Associated Publishers. (Original work published 1919.)

Zeichner, K. M., and Liston, D. P. (1990). Traditions of reform in U.S. teacher education. *Journal of Teacher Education,* 41(2), 3–20.

Author Index

Subject Index

Note: page numbers in italics denote tables or figures separate from the textual reference